YEADON'S REGISTER

of

L N E R

LOCOMOTIVES

Volume Eight

GRESLEY K3 & K4 CLASSES

ACKNOWLEDGEMENTS

Once again, my wife must have the primary tribute. Without her patience and forbearance, regular feeding and housecare, it would be quite impossible for me to continue transferring my hand-written registers into printed form for you. Hopefully, she must still consider the effort to be worthwhile, because I am given every encouragement to put my records so that fellow enthusiasts, particularly modellers, can benefit from them.

The thousands of figures contained in each one would inevitably destroy interest in them were they not leavened so lavishly with illustrations..For these, I am indebted to countless photographers, most of them of my own generation, and now - sadly - no longer alive. Thus many of them can see no direct credit for their help, and also a large proportion of my collection show no indication whatever of who took the picture, or even when, and where. It is now 62 years since I began to put the LNER collection together, and I simply cannot recall the source from which many of the 30,000 were purchased, a lot of them indirectly from other collectors. So, if you see an illustration included which you are sure is a photo that you took, I would welcome you giving me the date and location via the publishers.

First published in the United Kingdom by
CHALLENGER PUBLICATIONS
15 Lovers Lane, Grasscroft, Oldham, OL4 4DP
Printed by Amadeus Press, Huddersfield

INTRODUCTION

Dating from 1920, the first ten were pure G N R production, and they classed them H4. They were designed for working main line express goods trains, and were the first development of Gresley power, stemming from the introduction of 3 cylinders with derived valve gear for the middle one, on 2-8-0 mineral engine no.461 in 1918. Ample steam was needed to serve their capability for high power, hence the boiler diameter of no less than 6 feet. But innovation stopped at the rear end of the firebox, because they were still fitted with cab, and tender, of the type that Gresley inherited from Ivatt.

By quite unforeseen chance, the long drawn out coal strike of 1921 threw a spotlight on their haulage ability, because they proved invaluable for substituting for the Atlantics on main line passenger trains. The shortage of coal caused many couples of the normal 8 to 10 coach trains to be combined into single ones of anything in the range of 16, and even up to 20 coaches. The new 2-6-0's were drafted in to work them, and their ability to do so successfully without having to be piloted, earned them a reputation which became legendary.

With Gresley being appointed Chief Mechanical Engineer of the L N E R, it is no surprise that this design was adopted as the Group Standard for mixed traffic operation. From 1924 to early 1937 a further 183 were built, and it then formed the basis for the even more powerful, and highly successful V2 'Green Arrow' class which superseded them. The K3's built by the L N E R

were given the advantage of a Darlington style much more commodious cab with two side windows, and the majority were coupled with Group Standard 4200 gallon tender, instead of the 3500 gallon type with coal rails. In due course, the first ten also acquired the larger capacity tender, and had a cab with side windows fitted.

Built in batches over as long as 17 years, some modifications & improvements would be expected; they were introduced, but all were comparatively minor and apart from cab and tender, barely affected appearance. Internal recognition of them led to the LNER allocating Parts 1 to 6 to the class, but modellers can comfortably ignore these variations. Part 1 was given to the original ten built to the generous G N R loading gauge, and Part 2 to the 60 which Darlington built in 1924/25, which were to the Composite Loading Gauge. Part 3 were the 20 built by Doncaster in 1929, all allocated to the North Eastern Area, and originally equipped with Westinghouse and vacuum braking; they also had 6" shorter springs for their coupled wheels. Part 4 were the nine built at Doncaster in July/August 1930, differing only from Part 2 by being slightly lighter and having flush sided tender. Part 5 engines were heavier, and were those built from March 1931, whilst Part 6, built from July 1934 had different coupled wheel springs. The L N E R recognised that so small were some of the differences that, at the end of 1935, Parts 4, 5, and 6 were all re-designated Part 2. Then, after those in Part 1 had been rebuilt

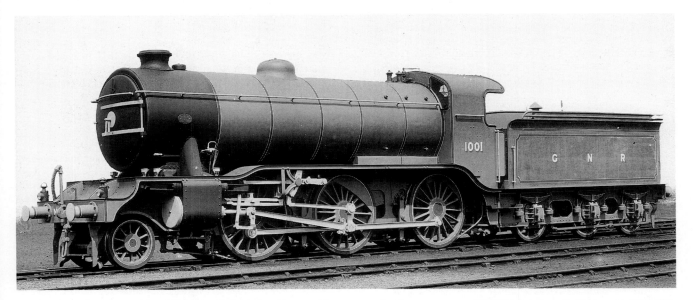

The first ten, GNR nos.1000 to 1009, were built to that Company's generous load gauge so were 13' 4" high to top of chimney, and 13' 5" to the top of the whistle because they were intended for working only on the main line between King's Cross and Doncaster. Note that they were fitted with parallel case buffers.
L.N.E.R.

1

The Grouping, effective 1st January 1923, considerably enlarged the scope for this class of engine to work, and selection of the GN design would be influenced by Gresley having been appointed C.M.E. Possibly, if that post had gone to Raven, the Group's mixed traffic design would have been the B16 class, which ultimately out-lived the K3 by at least 18 months. Darlington were given the order to build 50 Group Standard K3's, to which they gave vacant numbers in the 17 to 200 range, and there were significant differences from the first ten. Heights were cut to 13' 0" at chimney, dome, and top of safety valves, and a North Eastern cab with double windows gave much improved crew protection. A new design of tender carried 25% more coal , and 20% more water, and was adopted as a Group Standard. Buffers were changed to double case type, as used on the Pacifics, and these engines were still driven from the right hand side. *L.N.E.R.*

with side window cab, from October 1940 they joined Part 2. That left only Parts 2 and 3, and in the December 1947 Diagram Book Alterations, those Part Nos were discontinued.

TENDERS

For V2 class in Volume 4, I illustrated, and drew attention to there being some with stepped top to their tender, but the majority had the flush-sided type. Because both types were readily exchangeable, engines were photographed at some date with one type, and with the other sooner, or later. In sorrow, rather than anger, a keen modeller of LNER locomotives told me that it would have been of real assistance for absolutely correct portrayal if I had detailed when, and to which engines, the stepped-top type

had been coupled. Constructive criticism of that nature is really appreciated, and for K3 class, tender type is of even more consequence, because three quite distinctive types were coupled with them. Indeed, there was just one of the class no.28 (1811 and 61811 later) which ran with all three types for a minimum of three years with each one. The tenders used were (1) Great Northern standard class B, which carried 3500 gallons water, and was fitted with coal rails, (2) LNER Group Standard 4200 gallons with stepped-top to its side panels, and (3) that same design, but flush sided. The latter also had a minor, but noticeable, variation in that those built from November 1937 had front plate which was appreciably higher. True to form, no.1811 managed to acquire that variation from May 1947, and kept it then to withdrawal. So, in effect, that one should really be credited with four

Due to a mis-understanding as to type of tender to be used, the first two engines were ready before any new tenders were completed, so Nos.17 and 28 were sent out with borrowed GNR 3500 gallon type. Nos.184/6/91/5 were also provided from stock with that type to facilitate turning them on the smaller diameter turntables in Scottish Area. It cut the wheelbase by 12⁵/₈" and the overall length by 1' 10⁵/₈". *J.J.Cunningham.*

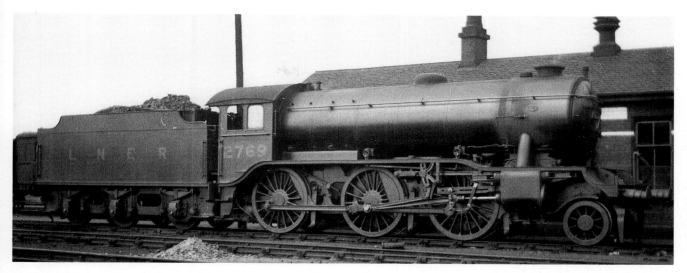

A batch of nine, nos.2761 to 2766 for Southern Area, and 2767/8/9 for Scottish Area, was built by Darlington in July/August 1930. Their cabs were the same as on 1318 (see page 6/7) which had become the standard for the rest of the class, and by then, Scottish Area had found that they were having no difficulties with the Group Standard tender. 2769 is seen on 4th August 1932 at Glasgow's Eastfield shed where it was then allocated. An order for twenty similar to 2761-69 was placed with Armstrong, Whitworth & Co. in 1930; eight numbered in the range 1100 to 1119 went to N.E.Area, and twelve from 1121 to 1166 to Southern Area.
L.Hanson.

Ten were ordered from Darlington on 9th November 1933, but on 26th February 1934 the order was transferred to Armstrong, Whitworth & Co. who built them between July and December 1934. Their numbers were 1302/4/8/10/24, 1306 and 2934-37, and their tenders did not have angle iron below their running plate. Their vertical handrails, at both ends, were noticeably taller than on all the previous tenders.
W.L.Good.

types! There were also visible differences according to whether the tender was fitted for braking by steam, Westinghouse air, or vacuum, and attention is drawn to those in the illustrations.

The original batch of ten engines was a Gresley design, built at Doncaster in 1920/21, so naturally their tender was that which had been the Doncaster standard since 1906. After the Grouping, Darlington Works were given an order on October 17th 1923 for 25 engines and tenders, and for a further 25 on November 1st, both orders saying "All engines to pass the North British gauge", and those two pieces of paper carry a superb H.N.Gresley autograph. Apart from the slight gauge clearance alterations, and change to a North Eastern style cab, the engines were similar to

those that Doncaster had built, and doubtless that works supplied Darlington with copies of the existing drawings. But Doncaster probably sent no drawing for the tender, because in line with their usual custom, the first ten had been provided with tenders from existing stock, the Great Northern working with a surplus of tenders over engines requiring them. By the time it was decided what tender type the Darlington engines were to have, progress with the engines was well on the way, and catching-up was further hindered due to the selected tender being the first new Group Standard type. For that 4200 gallons type, drawings would have to be made, approved, material specified, ordered, & then manufactured. Consequently, when Darlington

Also in February 1934 another ten were ordered outside - from Robert Stephenson & Co., numbers 1325/32/3/9/99, 1322 and 1307 for N.E.Area and 2938/9/40 for Scottish Area, all being in traffic by 15th January 1935. As 1333 shows, their tenders had the tall handrails, but they also had the customary angle iron below the running plate. *Photomatic.*

completed the first two engines, nos 17 and 28, the Group Standard tenders for them were not ready, and to get them into traffic, Doncaster sent two of their 3500 gallons coal rail type for `temporary' coupling to them.

The third engine, no.32 was the first to have Group Standard tender from new, and left Darlington before arrangements for official photograph of the class had been made, hence the fourth, instead of the customary first, engine of the class being so treated, which explains why so many people believed no. 33 to be the prototype. The Group Standard tender then continued to be coupled until March 1925, when only six more of the fifty remained to be turned out. Despite what was specified on the orders about all being made suitable for passing the North British gauge, only those remaining six were allocated to Scottish Area, and it was decided to use Great Northern type tender with them, because that reduced the total wheelbase, and overall length, which would be an advantage where they were to work. As Darlington had built the full quota of fifty G.S. tenders, they then had some spares, which came in handy for use with the engines of the original 1920/21 building, giving them an additional 700 gallons water capacity. But the arrangements for the exchange were by no means straightforward. Nos 17 and 28's expected 'temporary' use of coal rail type extended to July and December 1927 respectively. No.32 was transferred from North Eastern to Scottish Area, so in June 1925 was changed from Group Standard to Great Northern tender. Although the 49th and 50th engines were to go to Scottish Area, both left Darlington coupled with Group Standard tender, no.188 going into traffic at Carlisle shed on March 26th 1925, but at the end of May it was called to Cowlairs to have its tender changed to G N type. No.200 went straight to the L N E R stand at the 1925 British Empire Exhibition at Wembley so did not go into traffic until the following November, surprisingly keeping

its G.S.tender until as late as March 1929. Thus Scottish Area used nos 32 and 188 briefly, and no.200 for more than three years without difficulty, which rather negated the previous tender changes.

To enable any modeller of a K3 to represent it accurately, the timing of the tender type coupled is now included. Those which had the G N coal rail variety were:-

4000 new to 29/6/25	4001 new to 15/1/25
4002 new to 9/2/25	4003 new to 26/10/25
4004 new to 14/8/25	4005 new to 29/1/25
4006 new to 23/1/25	4007 new to 6/12/41
4008 new to 11/1/26	4009 new to 5/1/29
17 new to 4/4/27	28 new to 15/8/27
32 from 6/25 until withdrawal	80 from 14/3/28 to 4/42
134 from 26/8/33 to 10/12/33	140 from 14/3/28 to 26/8/33
184 from new to withdrawal	186 from new to withdrawal
188 from 28/5/25 to withdrawal	191 from new to withdrawal
195 from new to withdrawal	200 from 23/1/29 to withdrawal

The Group Standard type with stepped-out top was used (apart from the above with G N type) throughout on those which became B.R. 61800 to 61869 with the following exceptions, which were changed to the similar, but flush sided type:-

61815 from 3/8/51 to withdrawal
61816 from 27/9/40 (as no.39) to withdrawal
61818 from 12/12/58 to withdrawal
61819 from 11/57 to withdrawal
61828 from 15/4/50 to withdrawal
61869 from 28/11/59 to withdrawal
see illustration for change on page 48.

The engines which became B.R. 61870 to 61992 were all provided with the Group Standard flush sided tender which had the low front plate. Five of them changed later to the earlier type with stepped top, those being:-

61880 from 2/12/59 to withdrawal
61943 from 12/1/50 to 31/12/54
61949 from 28/1/55 to withdrawal
61969 from 28/3/56 to withdrawal
61985 from 15/4/50 to withdrawal

No.28 merits special mention; it had G N type new to 15/8/27, ex works 14/12/27 it had stepped top Group Standard which it kept to 20/2/47; then from 7/3/47 to 29/4/47 it had a flush sided type with low front, but from 31/5/47 to withdrawal it had similar type but with high front plate, that tender having previously run eight years with named V2 class 4818 ST PETER'S SCHOOL. When withdrawn, seven K3's had tenders considered fit for further service, so the opportunity was taken to change each to a less useful tender before sending those seven locomotives to be cut up. Four, nos. 61931/83/88/91 took tenders from K4 class with them; 61909 took a stepped top type, first used by J39 class 2787, but 61881/2 got ex North Eastern tenders also from J39 class. The one which accompanied 61882 was no less than the one which had been built for and ran nearly twelve years with Raven Pacific 2401 KINGSTON-UPON-HULL. 61881's partner had certainly earned its keep, having started work in August 1906 with B13 class 775. The last shed of all, except 61882, was St Margarets, who were responsible for changing that one whilst it was passing through there on its way from Woodford to Cowlairs to be cut up.

LIVERIES

All ten G N R built engines wore that Company's green paint, lined in black and white from new until their first heavy repair after the Grouping. Then they all became black with single red lining, with number moved from cab side on to the tender. The first three, no.1000 in March, and 1005/8 in May 1923 had L & N E R put on tender, but in June the use of the ampersand ceased, so nos 1001/6 in July just had L N E R. Three changed to black during the period when an area suffix was being used, 1007N in October, 1009N in November, and 1004N in December 1923. At an un-recorded date around that time the N was added to L & N E R 1000. The last one to retain G N R green was 1002 which went to works on October 24th 1924, and came out as 4002 in January 1925, No.4003 having had similar treatment when ex works in June 1924.

The sixty built at Darlington, and numbered from 17 to 231, had the standard black with single red lining, and as was Darlington custom, their cylinder casings had a panel of red lining. Those subsequently the responsibility of Doncaster and Cowlairs for maintenance lost those panels at their first repainting. Another detail peculiar to Darlington was their application of CLASS 2.6.0. on the front buffer beam, which Doncaster and Cowlairs erased. Doncaster did however add white lining to the ends and bottom edge of the front buffer beam.

No.1300 new from Doncaster in April 1929 was the first to have L N E R number on the cab side, and as the earlier engines came in for shopping, they were altered similarly, the tender lettering then being increased to 12 inch. Cowlairs continued to use the smaller size L N E R on those that it maintained until February

1931, but Doncaster then took them over, and that anomaly was removed at their next tender painting.

In March 1938 it became standard for all L N E R engines to have their class put on the front buffer beam, so CLASS K3 in 2" white characters began to appear. The word CLASS was dropped in 1943, to economise on labour under the difficult wartime conditions. Already the war had caused appearance to suffer; from November 1941 the red lining ceased to be applied, and from July 1942, only N E was used instead of L N E R on the tender, but still 12". It was January 1946 before L N E R was restored, and during that year, the hitherto random numbering was changed to 1800 to 1992, arranged substantially in order of building date, but with some exceptions.

Post-war the L N E R announced its intention to include the K3 class amongst those to be painted in lined green livery, but that proved to be one of the schemes which 'gang aglay'. Of the K3's, only no.1935 acquired that much improved appearance; it was ex works so painted on November 9th 1946, but it reverted to black from May 14th 1949, when it became B.R.61935.

By May 1947 supplies of the shaded transfers for letters and figures were nearing exhaustion, and were considered too expensive to replenish. In lieu, yellow painted numbers and letters, without back shading, using Gill Sans style, were substituted. No.1989 from Doncaster and no.1857 from Cowlairs were probably the first K3's to have them.

British Railways announced their standard liveries in July 1948, and recognised as mixed traffic engines, K3 qualified for red, cream, and grey lining on its black paint. In June 1949, when BRITISH RAILWAYS gave place to an emblem of a lion over a wheel, transfers for it were delayed in reaching Doncaster, and because repaired engines were badly needed to deal with the extra summer traffic, they released some K3's with plain tender sides. Then ex works on September 1st 1949, nos 61838 and 61914 were the first to have the emblem, although it had appeared from Cowlairs when 61936 went back into traffic on August 19th 1949. Finally, came the change from the emblem to the crest, effective from April 1957 at Doncaster but not until August at Cowlairs. All those done in Scotland had the lion facing the wrong way on the right hand side of the tender, and none survived for a further painting to have it corrected. Those shopped at Doncaster from October 1958 were then made legitimate.

DETAILS

There were only two substantial differences of detail. The original ten, and the first fifty built after the Grouping, had right hand drive. Starting with no.202 new in August 1925, there was a change to left hand drive, and the remainder were so fitted. The vacuum ejector exhaust pipe along the side of the boiler from cab to smokebox gives a clear indication of the driving side. Of the sixty with right hand drive, all except the nine allocated to the North Eastern Area retained it through to withdrawal. From October 1934 to May 1937, those nine (nos 17,28,33,36,38,39,46,52 and 53) were altered to left hand drive. Screw operated reversing gear was standard, except on the ten numbered 202 to 231, which had the North Eastern design of steam operated gear, and with which just one no.141 of the previous fifty had been so equipped. Then from November 1927, Darlington altered seven of the nine in the N.E.Area from screw to steam reversing gear, nos 17 and 39 missing out on that alteration. Steam reverse could readily be identified by the small diameter pipe from the cab below, but parallel to the vacuum ejector pipe. Starting in September 1930

(top) **After Darlington had built a further ten, with numbers ranging from 202 to 231, and which had left-hand drive, the next order was placed in May 1928 for twenty to be built at Doncaster, although all were allocated to North Eastern Area, and were equipped with Westinghouse brake. Each had similar tender except that the Group Standard type was now flush sided instead of having stepped out coping.** *L.N.E.R.*

(bottom) **Those twenty took numbers from 1300 to 1398 and went into traffic from April to December 1929. They were given Doncaster style cab with cut-out, but that caused quick complaints of draught at the back of the crew's seats so, starting with 1318 on 26th July 1930, all were altered to N.E. style with the straight rear edge.**
L.N.E.R.

at Doncaster, all the 18 with steam reverse were changed to screw type.

The other visible difference of significance only applied to a single engine no.227. From August 1935 it was equipped with a Gresham & Craven feed water heater, which was combined with a Hulburd boiler cleaner, the piping for them giving an untidy look. Whilst in works for general repair September to November 1940, all those extra fittings were removed.

With a class of almost 200, there was a plethora of minor alterations, additions, and removal of small details; attention to them is given in the illustrations & captions.

REGISTRATION

The first one that I recorded as seeing was no.227 due to its special fittings; the date was April 5th 1936, on a passenger train to Leeds in Doncaster station. Serious and determined observation of the class did not begin until April 23rd 1938, when I noted no.170 under repair in Doncaster works. From then I managed to record 187 of them in their original L N E R numbering, and five of the other six during the last year of that Company. The last one 2764/1893 was shedded at March, and eluded me until January 18th 1950 when I caught up with it at Doncaster shed. Just to mock me, on September 2nd 1951 it was transferred to Hull Dairycoates shed, from where it then did all its work to withdrawal on December 17th 1962. I even had a ride behind it - in the 7.10 p.m. Sheffield(Vic.) to Doncaster on February 10th 1955. I can't decide as to whether I was regarded as 'mixed traffic' or as 'fast goods' but from October 8th 1940, when 1158 took me in the 3.07 p.m. from Doncaster to Leeds (Central), I travelled by another 48 trains which had K3 haulage. In location, they varied widely, from 1333 of St.Margarets on July 14th 1941 with the 12.15 p.m. Corstorphine to Edinburgh (Wav.), to Stratford's 61817 on June 5th 1956 with the 8.16 p.m. Wickford to London (Liverpool St.).

In the 1950's at Hull, one expected to have a B1 or a D49 out of or into our Paragon station, but from Doncaster, the Hull portion of The Yorkshire Pullman was diagrammed for a Dairycoates

K3, which made stops at Goole and Brough, but did the 41 miles in 54 minutes, so it was not a case of the ridiculous following the sublime. The occasions, and the engines, when I had the real pleasure of returning from London by that train merit setting down for you.

28/4/49 A1/1 60113 GREAT NORTHERN from King's Cross, and 61892 from Doncaster
29/9/49 A1 60158 ABERDONIAN and 61892
24/1/50 A1 60114 W.P.ALLEN and 61923
15/6/50 61934 to Doncaster and A1 60133 to King's Cross
14/3/51 A4 60033 SEAGULL and 61941
6/2/52 A4 60032 GANNET and 61920
4/9/53 A4 60017 SILVER FOX and 61905 (see below)
22/9/53 A4 60006 SIR RALPH WEDGWOOD and 61922
3/5/56 A4 60006 SIR RALPH WEDGWOOD and 61923
7/5/57 A1 60149 AMADIS and 61883

61905's shed allocation was Immingham, but it was just ex works from a general repair, so was being run in pending return; all the others were at Dairycoates.

On journeys to and from Sheffield(Vic), Leeds, and York, other Dairycoates K3 class which hauled me in that period included 61899, 61965, 61871, 61844, 61819, 61908, 61847, 61874, and 61965 so clearly that shed did not single out just a few specially for passenger work. One more which hauled me was the erstwhile green painted 61935 on the 8.45 a.m. from Paragon to Doncaster, from where A2/2 class 60503 LORD PRESIDENT took us on to King's Cross. Other noteworthy K3 haulages included Stockton's 1117 on April 30th 1941 with the 2.04 p.m. Darlington to Leeds via Ripon; Colwick's 1102 on July 4th 1942 with the 2.10 p.m. New Basford to Mansfield; and 3828 of St Margarets on August 4th 1945 with the 5.10 p.m. Hawick to Galashiels. Despite the limitations of a 20 tons axle loading, class K3 were truly ubiquitous. Although debarred from working on the West Highland line, there is photographic proof that in 1946 or 1947, Eastfield's no.1855 with G N tender did penetrate as far as Crianlarich.

Twenty more were ordered in January 1935, to be built by North British Loco.Co. and were given numbers vacated by withdrawal of ex-Hull & Barnsley engines in the 2425 to 2468 range. Although not discernible, they had larger diameter steam pipes to their cylinders, but two details did show, albeit negatively; their tenders did not have angle iron, and they were the last of the class not to have front footsteps when new.

GRESLEY K3 CLASS

4000

Doncaster 1509.

To traffic 3/1920.

REPAIRS:
Don. 11/1-4/2/22. **L.**
Don. 8/1-31/3/23.**G.** *L&NER.*
Don. 29/6-24/10/25.**G.** *N added by 22/3/24.*
Don. 10/6-17/9/27.**G.**
Don. 15/10-8/11/27.**L.**
Don. 8-15/3/28.**L.**
Don. 31/8-5/10/29.**G.**
Don. 30/10-5/11/29.**L.**
Don. 19/7-20/9/30.**G.**
Don. 1-22/11/30.**L.**
Don. 4/6-9/7/32.**G.** *Mod. valve gear.*
Don. 2/12/33-13/1/34.**G.**
Don. 26/10-30/11/35.**G.**
Don. 17/4-15/5/37.**G.**
Don. 22/4-3/6/39.**G.** *S.W.cab fitted.*
Don. 8/6-20/7/40.**L.**
Don. 8/11-13/12/41.**G.**
Don. 5/2-4/3/44.**G.**
Don. 23/9-14/10/44.**L.**
Don. 13/4-1/6/46.**G.**
Don. 22/2-13/7/48.**G.**
Don. 23/5-6/7/50.**G.**
Don. 3/4-4/5/51.**C/L.**
Don. 29/10-21/11/51.**C/L.**
Don. 22/4-20/5/52.**G.**
Don. 2/7-14/8/53.**G.**
Don. 11/11-9/12/54.**G.**
Don. 21/9-21/10/56.**G.**
Don. 29/7-29/8/58.**G.**
Don. 16/6-28/7/60.**G.**
Don. 2-11/8/61.**C/L.**

BOILERS:
7421.
7425 *(ex4006)* 17/9/27.
7423 *(ex4002)* 5/10/29.
7425 *(ex spare and 4000)* 20/9/30.
8598 *(ex1135)* 15/5/37.
D1723 *(ex109)* 13/7/48.
3D/687 *(ex1821)* 6/7/50.
Renumbered 27103 9/50.
27234 *(ex61910)* 20/5/52.
27164 *(ex61833)* 14/8/53.
27290 *(new)* 9/12/54.
27194 *(ex61827)* 21/10/56.
27151 *(ex61865)* 29/8/58.
27132 *(ex61863)* 28/7/60.

SHEDS:
New England.
Doncaster 19/4/28.
Kings Cross 28/2/33.

Doncaster 28/4/33.
New England 1/8/39.
Doncaster 23/8/39.
Woodford 10/2/40.
Immingham 3/5/43.
Lincoln 13/6/43.
Immingham 1/8/43.
Gorton 3/8/43.
Immingham 4/8/43.
Doncaster 1/2/59.

RENUMBERED:
 1800 29/5/46.
61800 10/7/48.

CONDEMNED:
13/7/62.
Cut up at Doncaster.

4001

Doncaster 1513.

To traffic 6/1920.

REPAIRS:
Don. 17/3-20/5/22.**H.**
Don. 10/4-14/7/23.**G.**
Don. 15/1-9/5/25.**G.**
Don. 15/7-10/10/25.**L.**
Don. 29/4-17/8/27.**G.**
Don. 3/10-30/11/28.**G.**
Don. 10/5-19/7/30.**G.**
Don. 17/1-7/3/31.**G.**
Don. 11/2-18/3/33.**G.** *Mod.valve gear.*
Don. 5/5-9/6/34.**G.**
Don. 9/11-21/12/35.**G.**
Don. 2-23/10/37.**G.**
Gor. 26/9-1/10/38.**L.** *Front H.A.fitted.*
Don. 6/1-10/2/40.**G.** *S.W.Cab fitted.*
Don. 25/7-22/8/42.**G.**
Don. 24/6-22/7/44.**H/I.**
Don. 21/10-18/11/44.**G.**
Don. 1/12/45.**N/C.**
Don. 26/10-30/11/46.**G.**
Don. 28/12/48-17/2/49.**G.**
Don. 6/3-6/4/51.**G.**
Don. 11/1-5/2/52.**C/L.**
Don. 20/6-2/7/52.**C/L.**
Don. 10/2-18/3/53.G.
Don. 3/5-4/6/55.**G.**
Don. 20/9-24/10/57.**G.**
Don. 27/5-19/6/59.**G.**
Don. 21/4-2/7/60. **C/H.**

BOILERS:
7422.

7426 *(ex4004)* 30/11/28.
D1784 *(ex228)* 19/7/30.
7430 *(ex4007)* 18/3/33.
9626 *(new)* 30/11/46.
9374 *(ex1865)* 17/2/49.
27154 *(ex61852)* 6/4/51.
27172 *(ex61809)* 18/3/53.
27297 *(new)* 4/6/55.
27230 *(ex61861)* 24/10/57.
24921 *(ex61888)* 19/6/59.

SHEDS:
New England.
Gorton 16/3/36.
New England 11/6/36.
Gorton 6/1/38.
Annesley 30/10/43.
Colwick 12/10/47.
March 12/6/49.
Stratford 26/9/49.
Lincoln 4/7/54.
Stratford 17/10/54.
March 10/2/57.
Cambridge 6/12/59.
March 26/11/61.

RENUMBERED:
 1801 25/8/46.
61801 17/2/49.

CONDEMNED:
17/4/62.
Cut up at Doncaster.

4002

Doncaster 1514.

To traffic 9/1920.

REPAIRS:
Don. 10/8-11/11/22.**G.**
Don. 24/10/24-24/1/25.**G.**
Don. 9-16/2/25.**L.**
Don. 18/2-4/6/27.**G.**
Don. 27/7-31/8/29.**G.**
Don. 18/4-23/5/31.**G.**
Don. 30/1-5/3/32.G.
Don. 26/8-7/10/33.**G.** *Mod.valve gear.*
Don. 25/11-30/12/33.**L.**
Don. 9/2-9/3/35.**G.**
Don. 23/5-4/7/36.**G.**
Don. 11/1-28/2/37.**L.**
Don. 30/7-20/8/38.**G.**
Don. 27/4-1/6/40.**G.** *S.W.Cab fitted.*
Don. 30/1-27/2/43.**G.**
Don. 2/6-21/7/45.**G.**
Don. 4/8-8/9/45.**L.**

Don. 15/7-5/9/47.**G.**
Don. 2/4-11/5/50.**G.**
Don. 23/6-11/7/50.**C/L.**
Don. 30/3-2/5/52.**G.**
Don. 8/10-12/11/53.**G.**
Don. 20/2-23/3/55.**G.**
Don. 25/8-23/10/57.**G.**
Don. 15-23/9/59.**N/C.**
Don. 24/2/60.*Not repaired.*

BOILERS:
7423.
7422 *(ex4001)* 31/8/29.
D1693 *(ex116)* 23/5/31.
D1690 *(ex114)* 7/10/33.
7422 *(ex127)* 20/8/38.
D1727 *(ex1158)* 27/2/43.
8910 *(ex2453)* 21/7/45.
9548 *(ex1822)* 11/5/50.
27229 *(ex61822)* 2/5/52.
27274 *(ex61895)* 12/11/53.
27133 *(ex61892)* 23/3/55.
27277 *(ex61880)* 23/10/57.

SHEDS:
New England.
Kings Cross 15/5/34.
New England 16/7/34.
Colwick 20/6/40.
Immingham 8/8/48.
Lincoln 10/6/56.
March 21/6/59.
Lowestoft 28/6/59.
Lincoln 26/7/59.

RENUMBERED:
 1802 23/8/46.
61802 11/5/50.

CONDEMNED:
7/3/60.
Cut up at Doncaster.

4003

Doncaster 1515.

To traffic 10/1920.

REPAIRS:
Don. 11/7-2/9/22.**G.**
Don. 31/3-7/6/24.**G.**
Don. 26/10/25-30/1/26.**G.**
Don. 12/3-18/6/27.**G.**
Don. 20/4-8/6/29.**G.**
Don. 18/7-29/8/31.**G.**
Don. 8/4-27/5/33.**G.** *Mod.valve gear.*
Don. 26/1-23/2/35.**G.**
Don. 5/9-10/10/36.**G.**

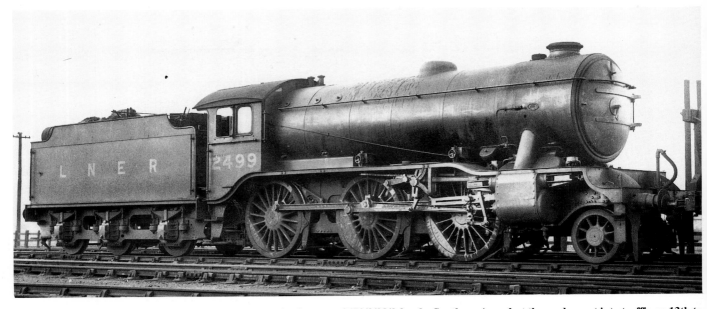

On 21st February 1935 Darlington were given an order for four, nos.2470/3/98/9 for the Southern Area, but they only went into traffic on 13th to 30th October 1936. They did have front footsteps fitted from new and their tenders had the angle iron. These four were the first of the class to be denuded of the sign of their Great Northern parentage, in that they had single, not double lamp irons at their front right hand corner. The extra iron stemmed from a G N London district lamp code which had been discarded even before the first of the class had been built in 1920. It had also survived on the rear plate of tenders to cater for running tender-first. Later in 1935, Darlington were given an order for a further twenty-one, but on 10th September 1936 that was cut to twenty, with the single engine being re-ordered as the first of the K4 class. Nos.3813 to 3832 went into traffic from 4th November 1936 to 26th February 1937. Time had then caught up with K3 class, the new V2 class already having shown enhanced capability. *W.L.Good.*

Don. 25/6-23/7/38.**G.**
Don. 28/10-9/12/39.**G.** *S.W.Cab fitted.*
Don. 8/11-20/12/41.**G.**
Don. 12/9-17/10/42.**G.**
Don. 29/9-3/11/45.**G.**
Don. 24/11-1/12/45.**L.**
Don. 4/2-22/3/47.**G.**
Don. 13/9-24/10/47.**L.**
Don. 14/4-12/5/48.**L.**
Don. 22/5-7/7/49.**G.**
Don. 23/4-25/5/51.**G.**
Don. 22/12/52-29/1/53.**G.**
Str. 3-24/9/54.**C/L.**
Don. 19/12/54-27/1/55.**G.**
Don. 3/11-6/12/56.**G.**
Don. 24/3-2/5/59.**G.**

BOILERS:
7424.
D1701 *(ex120)* 29/8/31.
D1767 *(ex206)* 9/12/39.
3217 *(new)* 20/12/41.
9996 *(new)* 7/7/49.
27166 *(ex61813)* 25/5/51.
27124 *(ex61814)* 29/1/53.
27293 *(new)* 27/1/55.
27289 *(ex61845)* 6/12/56.
27131 *(ex61950)* 2/5/59.

SHEDS:
New England.
Doncaster 3/12/36.
Woodford 10/2/40.
Immingham 3/5/43.
Lincoln 22/7/43.
Immingham 4/11/45.

Doncaster 1/2/59.

RENUMBERED:
1803 1/12/46.
61803 12/5/48.

CONDEMNED:
13/7/61.
Cut up at Doncaster.

4004

Doncaster 1517.

To traffic 12/1920.

REPAIRS:
Don. 18/11-23/12/22.**G.**
Don. 16-31/3/23.**L.**
Don. 4/10-29/12/23.**G.**
Don. 3-18/10/24.**L.**
Don. 14/8/25-8/2/26.**G.**
Don. 22-29/7/27.**L.**
Don. 1/10-3/12/27.**G.**
Don. 26/6-1/8/28.**G.**
Don. 21/12/29-25/1/30.**G.** *Mod.valve gear.*
Don. 11/4-23/5/31.**G.**
Don. 12/11-24/12/32.**G.**
Don. 29/9-27/10/34.**G.**
Don. 29/2-4/4/36.**G.**
Don. 22-29/5/37.**L.**
Don. 30/4-21/5/38.**G.**
Gor. 17-24/9/38.**L.** *Heater conn.at front.*
Don. 11/3-8/4/39.**L.**

Don. 5/10-2/11/40.**G.** *S.W.Cab.fitted.*
Don. 9/5-20/6/42.**G.**
Don. 11/7-22/8/42.**L.**
Don. 16/10-6/11/43.**L.**
Don. 18/11/44-3/2/45.**G.**
Don. 26/10-30/11/46.**G.**
Don. 8/11-11/12/47.**L.**
Don. 31/12/48-11/2/49.**G.**
Don. 29/9-10/11/50.**G.**
Don. 17/11-19/12/52.**G.**
Don. 14/4-16/5/52.**G.**
Don. 29/11/57-11/1/58.**G.**
Don. 21/10-8/12/60.**G.**

BOILERS:
7426.
7427 *(ex spare and 4005)* 3/12/27.
7428 *(ex4007)* 25/1/30.
D1766 *(ex4005)* 23/5/31.
8738 *(new)* 4/4/36.
9627 *(new)* 30/11/46.
27115 *(ex1957)* 10/11/50.
27260 *(new)* 19/12/52.
27254 *(ex61899)* 16/5/55.
24933 *(new)* 11/1/58.
27130 *(ex61969)* 8/12/60.

SHEDS:
Doncaster.
Copley Hill 8/6/31.
Doncaster 18/8/31.
Copley Hill 27/5/33.
Doncaster 13/10/37.
Colwick 12/12/37.
Gorton 24/6/38.
Annesley 6/11/43.
Lincoln 17/6/46.

Doncaster 18/8/46.
March 25/5/47.
Stratford 17/10/49.
New England 17/2/57.

RENUMBERED:
1805 30/11/46.
61805 11/2/49.

CONDEMNED:
16/9/62.
Cut up at Doncaster.

4005

Doncaster 1520.

To traffic 4/1921.

REPAIRS:
Don. 30/11-24/12/21.**L.**
Don. 20/2-12/5/23.**G.**
Don. 29/1-30/5/25.**G.**
Don. 31/7-1/9/25.**L.**
Don. 23/9-10/10/25.**L.**
Don. 4-13/2/26.**L.**
Don. 19/4-19/6/26.**L.**
Don. 1/10-10/12/27.**G.**
Don. 23/6-17/10/28.**G.**
Don. 28/6-2/8/30.**G.**
Don. 23/1-27/2/32.**G.**
Don. 23/12/33-3/2/34.**G.** *Mod.valve gear.*
Don. 11/1-8/2/36.**G.**
Don. 23/10-13/11/37.**G.**
Don. 16/9-28/10/39.**G.**

Before Darlington even began delivery of the twenty ordered in September 1935, another ten ordered from Armstrong, Whitworth & Co. in December 1935 were all earning their keep. Taking further ex-H&B numbers 2417/29/45/6/53/5/8/65/71/2, they began working from 16th May to 6th August 1936, and their tenders did not have angle iron but they did carry the long redundant double lamp irons.

S.W. Cab fitted.
Don. 31/5-12/7/41.**G.**
Don. 19/6-24/7/43.**L.**
Don. 11/9-9/10/43.**G.**
Don. 3-17/6/44.**L.**
Don. 16/12/44-20/1/45.**L.**
Don. 13/10-17/11/45.**G.**
Don. 13/4-31/5/47.**G.**
Don. 9/1-18/2/49.**G.**
Don. 21/7-25/8/50.**G.**
Don. 12/8-17/9/52.**G.**
Don. 14/2-11/3/54.**G.**
Don. 27/7-3/8/54.**N/C.**
Don. 28/10-1/12/55.**G.**
Don. 13/8-3/10/56.**N/C.**
Don. 6/12/57-16/1/58.**G.**
Don. 30/4-8/5/59.**N/C.**
Don. 1/3/60.*Not repaired.*

BOILERS:
7427.
D1766 *(new)* 30/5/25.
7427 *(ex4004)* 2/8/30.
D1693 *(ex4002)* 3/2/34.
8922 *(ex2451)* 12/7/41.
9797 *(new)* 31/5/47.
9626 *(ex1801)* 18/2/49.
3137A *(ex1827)* 25/8/50.
27100 *(ex61887)* 17/9/52.
27101 *(ex61844)* 11/3/54.
27146 *(ex61950)* 1/12/55.
24934 *(new)* 16/1/58.

SHEDS:
Doncaster.
Gorton 18/2/36.
Doncaster 17/6/36.
Woodford 30/1/40.
Immingham 3/5/43.
Lincoln 22/4/45.
Immingham 23/9/45.
Lincoln 9/11/48.

RENUMBERED:
1806 24/11/46.
61806 18/2/49.

CONDEMNED:
7/3/60.
Cut up at Doncaster.

4006

Doncaster 1516.

To traffic 11/1920.

REPAIRS:
Don. 30/6-24/9/21.**H.**
Don. 9/4-10/7/23.**G.**
Don. 23/1-13/6/25.**G.**
Don. 7-15/8/25.**L.**
Don. 26/11-5/12/25.**L.**
Don. 14/12/25-8/1/26.**L.**
Don. 12-16/4/27.**L.**
Don. 24/9-30/11/27.**G.**
Don. 21/9-26/10/29.**G.** *Mod. Valve gear.*
Don. 18/4-9/5/31.**G.**
Don. 26/11/32-14/1/33.**G.**
Don. 5/1-2/2/35.**G.**
Don. 27/6-25/7/36.**G.**
Don. 14/5-18/6/38.**G.**
Don. 22-29/10/38.**L.**
Don. 2/3-6/4/40.**G.** *S.W. Cab fitted.*
Don. 6/6-11/7/42.**G.**
Don. 20/11-4/12/43.**L.**
Don. 29/7-2/9/44.**G.**
Don. 6/7-17/8/46.**G.**
Don. 15/8-13/10/47.**L.**
Don. 19/8-8/10/48.**G.**
Don. 23/8-29/9/50.**G.**
Don. 28/3-15/5/52.**G.**
Don. 20/5-18/6/54.**G.**
Don. 19/3-27/4/56.**G.**

Don. 29/9-7/11/58.**G.**
Don. 10/6-19/7/60.**G.**
Don. 27/3/62.*Not repaired.*

BOILERS:
7425.
D1762 *(new)* 13/6/25.
D1672 *(ex91)* 9/5/31.
D1648 *(ex17)* 2/2/35.
8595 *(ex2762)* 2/9/44.
27101 *(ex61824)* 29/9/50.
27233 *(ex61889)* 15/5/52.
27317 *(ex61853)* 27/4/56.
24910 *(ex61862)* 7/11/58.
27204 *(ex61840)* 19/7/60.

SHEDS:
Doncaster.
Kings Cross 29/9/31.
Doncaster 2/3/32.
New England 22/4/45.
March 11/6/50.
New England 25/6/50.
March 20/9/50.
Lincoln 15/7/56.
Colwick 17/2/57.
Woodford 16/6/57.

RENUMBERED:
1804 12/12/46.
61804 8/10/48.

CONDEMNED:
27/3/62.
Cut up at Doncaster.

4007

Doncaster 1522.

To traffic 5/1921.

REPAIRS:
Don. 4/12/22-3/2/23.**G.**
Don. 2/7-13/10/23.**L.** *New cylinders.*
Don. 24/4-5/7/24.**G.**
Don. 5/6-26/9/25.**G.**
Don. 29/4-23/7/27.**G.**
Don. 5-25/9/28.**L.**
Don. 19/10-23/11/29.**G.**
Don. 18-25/1/30.**L.**
Don. 4/7-8/8/31.**G.** *Mod. valve gear.*
Don. 6/5-3/6/33.**G.**
Don. 27/10-8/12/34.**G.**
Don. 29/2-4/4/36.**G.**
Don. 22/1-12/2/38.**G.**
Don. 24/6-5/8/39.**G.** *S.W. Cab fitted.*
Don. 6/12/41-3/1/42.**G.**
Don. 17/6-22/7/44.**G.**
Don. 19/10-15/11/46.**G.**
Don. 16/4-31/5/48.**G.**
Don. 14/9-13/10/50.**G.**
Don. 9/6-30/7/52.**G.**
Don. 23/4-2/6/55.**G.**
Don. 21/11/57-3/1/58.**G.**
Don. 14/6-2/7/58.**C/L.**
Don. 18-29/4/59.**C/L.**
Don. 9/11/60-12/1/61.**G.**

BOILERS:
7428.
7430 *(ex spare and 4009)* 23/11/29.
D1720 *(ex146)* 8/8/31.
3214 *(new)* 3/1/42.
27108 *(ex61834)* 13/10/50.
27137 *(ex61986)* 30/7/52.
27142 *(ex61865)* 2/6/55.
27114 *(ex61895)* 3/1/58.
27135 *(ex61847)* 12/1/61.

SHEDS:
New England.
Gorton 22/9/38.
Annesley 30/11/43.
Lincoln 17/6/46.

The original Great Northern designed boiler became LNER Diagram 96, and by 1944 no less than 240 had been built (all for K3 class) and with only small detail variations. Boilers for the first ten had three washout plugs on the left hand side of the firebox above the handrail, and that arrangement was repeated on the sixty boilers which Darlington built in 1924/5 for engines numbered 17 to 231.

There were three plugs on the first ten boilers built by Doncaster in 1929 for those numbered from 1300 to 1386, but the boilers put on the other ten, as here on 1389, had firebox with expansion and sling stays instead of girder bar stays, and they had four washout plugs on each side, but with staggered pitching. That arrangement was continued on all the boilers built until August 1935. *Lens of Sutton.*

continued from page 11.

Immingham 9/2/51.
Lincoln 10/2/52.
Immingham 14/1/62.

RENUMBERED:
 1807 *22/7/46.*
 61807 *29/5/48.*

CONDEMNED:
4/11/62.
Sold for scrap to J.Cashmore, Great Bridge.

4008

Doncaster 1526.

To traffic 7/1921.

REPAIRS:
Don. 19/2-21/5/23.**G.** *L&NER.*
Don. 12/8-6/9/24.**L.**
Don. 8-27/9/24.**L.**
KX. To 4008 on 21/2/25.
Don. 11/1-9/6/26.**G.**
Don. 6/7-2/9/27.**L.**
Don. 14/2-28/6/28.**G.**
Don. 26/1-2/2/29.**L.**
Don. 27/4-8/6/29.**G.**
Don. 26/7-4/10/30.**G.**
Don. 31/10-5/12/31.**G.** *Mod.valve gear.*
Don. 14/5-16/7/32.**L.**
Don. 3/12/32-14/1/33.**G.**
Don. 26/5-21/7/34.**G.**
Don. 29/2-4/4/36.**G.**
Don. 16/1-13/2/37.**L.**
Don. 10/4-8/5/37.**G.**
Gor. 3-8/10/38.**L.** *Heater conn.at front.*
Don. 11/2-25/3/39.**G.** *S.W.Cab fitted.*
Don. 27/4-22/6/40.**G.**
Don. 26/9-7/11/42.**G.**
Don. 19/2-15/4/44.**G.**
Don. 23/2-30/3/46.**G.**
Don. 26/3-12/5/47.**G.**
Don. 22/3-6/5/49.**G.**
Don. 11/4-24/5/51.**G.**
Don. 6/7-6/8/53.**G.**
Don. 12/1-17/2/56.**G.**
Don. 6/3-27/4/56.**C/L**
Don. 15-26/7/58.**N/C.**
Don. 6/3-17/4/59.**G.**
Don. 9-17/12/59.**N/C.**
Don. 1/4-5/5/60.**C/L.**
Don. 25/9/61.*Not repaired.*

BOILERS:
 7429.
 7421 *(ex4009)* 4/10/30.
 D1673 *(ex109)* 21/7/34.
 2829 *(ex2467)* 30/3/46.
 27165 *(ex61840)* 24/5/51.
 27165 *(ex61980)* 6/8/53.
 27259 *(ex61887)* 17/2/56.

 27288 *(ex61985)* 17/4/59.

SHEDS:
Kings Cross.
Colwick 31/12/37.
Gorton 5/4/38.
Annesley 30/10/43.
Colwick 12/10/47.
Gorton 14/5/50.
Woodford 17/11/57.
Colwick 8/12/57.
March 21/6/59.
Colwick 26/7/59.

RENUMBERED:
 1808 15/9/46.
 61808 6/5/49.

CONDEMNED:
25/9/61.
Cut up at Doncaster.

4009

Doncaster 1529.

To traffic 8/1921.

REPAIRS:
Don. 14/6-6/7/22.**L.**
Don. 3/8-7/11/23.**G.** *As 1009N.*
Don. 19/5-19/9/25.**G.**
Don. 16/1-17/3/26.**L.**
Don. 15/9-17/12/26.**H.**
Don. 5/5-10/8/28.**G.**
Don. 5/1-9/2/29.**G.**
Don. 19/7-30/8/30.**G.**
Don. 26/3-7/5/32.**G.**
Don. 17/6-22/7/33.**G.**
 Mod.valve gear.

Don. 26/1-23/2/35.**G.**
Don. 6/7-17/8/35.**G.**
Don. 28/11-31/12/36.**G.**
Don. 1/10-5/11/38.**G.**
Don. 17/8-28/9/40.**G.** *S.W.Cab fitted.*
Don. 31/5-28/6/41.**L.**
Don. 23/1-13/2/43.**G.**
Don. 4/11/44-20/1/45.**G.**
Don. 26/10-20/12/46.**G.**
Don. 20/1-5/3/49.**G.**
Don. 22/5-20/6/51.**G.**
Don. 28/1-26/2/53.**G.**
Don. 26/7-16/9/54.**H/I.**
Don. 8-28/12/55.**C/L.**
Don. 16-30/1/56.**N/C.**
Don. 30/4-14/6/57.**G.**
Don. 27/7-28/8/59.**G.**
Don. 1/3/62.*Not repaired.*

BOILERS:
 7430.
 7421 *(ex4000)* 10/8/28.
 8071 *(new)* 30/8/30.
 D1748 *(ex195)* 23/2/35.
 RS4079 *(ex2425)* 20/1/45.
 9797 *(ex61806)* 5/3/49.
 27172 *(ex61883)* 20/6/51.
 27122 *(ex61831)* 26/2/53.
 27226 *(ex61863)* 14/6/57.
 27310 *(ex61857)* 28/8/59.

SHED:
Kings Cross.

RENUMBERED:
 1809 20/12/46.
 61809 5/3/49.

CONDEMNED:
1/3/62.
Cut up at Doncaster.

17

Darlington.

To traffic 25/8/24.

REPAIRS:
Ghd. 1/4-18/7/27.**G.**
Dar. 4/1-6/3/29.**L.**
Dar. 4/11/29-9/1/30.**G.**
Dar. 11/2-4/3/30.**L.**
Ghd. 31/3-10/4/31.**L.**
Dar. 25/9-9/11/31.**G.**
Dar. 22/12/32-23/1/33.**H.**
Dar. 17-24/2/33.**N/C.**
Dar. 15-26/5/33.**N/C.**
Don. 22/1-1/3/34.**G.** *Mod.valve gear.*
Don. 10/8/34.**L.** *New crank axle.*
Dar. 17/7-6/9/35.**G.** *To L.H.Drive.*
Dar. 3/1-28/2/36.**H.**
Dar. 18-30/5/36.**N/C.**
Dar. 20/1-17/3/38.**G.**
Dar. 14-20/9/39.**N/C.**
Dar. 23-27/4/40.**N/C.**
Dar. 15/8-1/10/40.**G.**
Don. 2/11-24/12/42.**G.**
Don. 22/7-19/9/43.**L.**
Don. 28/10-2/12/44.**G.**
Don. 28/1-13/2/45.**L.**
Don. 16/7-3/9/46.**G.**
Don. 10/4-13/6/47.**G.**
Don. 23/10-1/12/49.**G.**
Don. 2/5-1/6/51.**L.**
Don. 7/2-12/3/52.**G.**
Don. 26/9-4/11/54.**G.**
Don. 22/8-27/9/57.**G.**
Don. 2-19/5/58.**C/H.**
Don. 24/7-7/8/59.**C/L.**
Don. 4/4-13/5/60.**G.**
Don. 15/8/62.*Not repaired.*

Beginning with the boiler put on 2425, new 20th August 1935, all further K3 boilers built to 1944 had handholes instead of washout plugs, and domed covers were fitted. On the right hand side there were three, as seen when my Brownie box camera took this photo of 2425 at King's Cross shed on 19th March 1938.

WORKS CODES:- Cow - Cowlairs. Dar - Darlington. Don - Doncaster. Ghd - Gateshead. Gor - Gorton. Inv - Inverurie. Str - Stratford.
REPAIR CODES:- **C/H** - Casual Heavy. **C/L** - Casual Light. **G** - General. **H** - Heavy. **H/I** - Heavy Intermediate. **L** - Light. **L/I** - Light Intermediate. **N/C** - Non-Classified.

On the left hand side, these 1935 and later boilers had only two handholes, but they were pitched between those on the opposite side. *W.L.Good.*

The later Diagram 96 boilers built by Darlington had the same three and two arrangement of handhole type washout plugs, but were not fitted with the domed covers. *W.L.Good.*

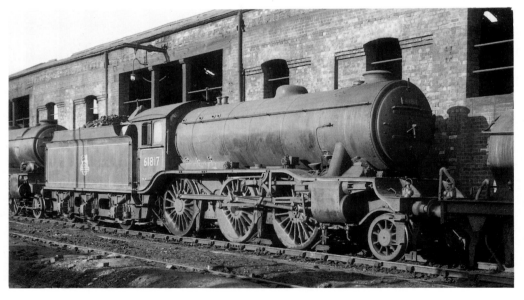

All K3 type boilers built in 1945, and subsequently, were to Diagram 96A, and were capable of working at 225 instead of 180 lb. pressure, as part of Thompson's plan to rebuild K3 class to two cylinders and so dispense with the Gresley derived valve gear. Despite 153 Diagram 96A boilers being built from 1945 to 1959, only the first one ever worked at the higher pressure, on the K5 class no.206. All used on K3 were at 180 lb.pressure. The 96A boilers were recognisable because their safety valves were 15" further forward, and on the first fifteen, built in 1945/6, there were four handholes on each side for washout. *Ken Morris.*

BOILERS:
D1645.
D1648 *(ex33)* 23/1/33.
D1730 *(ex204)* 1/3/34.
8133 *(ex1318)* 6/9/35.
8132 *(ex1394)* 17/3/38.
2909 *(ex1399)* 1/10/40.
2828 *(ex3816)* 24/12/42.
9800 *(new)* 13/6/47.
8597 *(ex1922)* 1/12/49.
27218 *(ex61938)* 12/3/52.
27238 *(ex61943)* 4/11/54.
27135 *(ex61852)* 27/9/57.

27267 *(ex61962)* 19/5/58.

SHEDS:
Blaydon.
York 25/11/27.
Retford 19/6/38.
York 28/8/38.
Gorton 17/10/40.
Woodford 30/10/43.
New England 29/6/47.
Copley Hill 12/3/50.
Stratford 9/4/50.
March 14/12/58.

Lincoln 4/12/60.
Colwick 11/12/60.
New England 17/9/61.

RENUMBERED:
1810 22/9/46.
61810 1/12/49.

CONDEMNED:
15/8/62.
Cut up at Doncaster.

28

Darlington.

To traffic 27/8/24.

REPAIRS:
Ghd. 12/8-16/12/27.**G.** *Steam reverse fitted.*
Ghd. 13-21/2/29.**L.**
Dar. 18/4-28/6/29.**G.**
Dar. 9/12/29-22/1/30.**H.**
Dar. 2-31/3/31.**N/C.**

Ghd. 23/9-5/10/31.**L.**
Dar. 20/11/31-20/1/32.**G.** *Drop grate fitted.*
Dar. 30/6-25/8/32.**H.** *New middle cyl.*
Dar. 14/11/34-7/1/35.**L.** *L.H.Drive screw rew. Mod.valve gear.*
Dar. 15/1-15/3/37.**G.** *Front footsteps fitted.*
Don. 15/8-16/9/38.**G.** *Cab side windows alt.to Drg.W434.*
Dar. 23/8-4/10/40.**G.**
Gor. 16/4-12/7/43.**G.**
Don. 27/11-3/1/45.**G.**
Don. 23/5-19/7/46.**G.**
Don. 16/2-7/3/47.**L.**
Don. 16/3-31/5/47.**G.**
Don. 19/9-8/11/47.**H.**
Don. 12/10-19/11/49.**G.**
Don. 13-31/1/50.**C/L.**
Don. 31/1-29/2/52.**G.**
Don. 19/1-18/2/54.**G.**
Don. 3-31/10/55.**G.**
Don. 14/8-21/9/57.**G.**
Don. 15-29/3/58.**C/L.** *After derailment.*
Don. 6-14/5/58.**C/L.**
Don. 5-15/5/59.**C/L.**
Don. 4/11-8/12/59.**G.**

BOILERS:
D1646.
 1658 *(ex53)* 20/1/32.
 AW81 *(ex1117)* 7/1/35.
 1652 *(ex1318)* 15/3/37.
 RS4081 *(ex1398)* 4/10/40.
 2840 *(ex1364)* 3/1/45.
 2941 *(ex1906)* 19/11/49.
 27216 *(ex61981)* 29/2/52.
 27269 *(ex61889)* 18/2/54.
 27171 *(ex61868)* 21/9/57.
 27278 *(ex61869)* 8/12/59.

SHEDS:
Blaydon.
York 25/11/27.
Colwick 23/11/40.
New England 25/6/45.
March 20/9/53.
Staveley 10/4/60.
Langwith 18/6/61.
Colwick 3/6/62.
Lincoln 17/6/62.

RENUMBERED:
 1811 9/11/46.
 1811 19/11/49.

CONDEMNED:
/11/62.
Cut up at Doncaster.

2

Darlington.

To traffic 29/8/24.

REPAIRS:
Cow. 16-30/9/26.**L.**
Cow. 2/11/26-7/3/27.**G.**
Cow. 4-19/8/27.**L.**
Cow. 17/2-6/4/28.**L.**
Cow. 17/5-28/6/28.**L.**
Cow. 9-11/8/28.**L.**
Cow. 30/11/29-25/1/30.**G.**
Don. 7/11/31-25/1/32.**G.** *Mod.valve gear.*
Don. 18/11/32-1/2/33.**L.**
Don. 8/1-12/3/34.**G.**
Don. 23/2-1/4/35.**G.**
Don. 26/2-18/4/36.**G.**
Don. 7/7-18/8/37.**G.** *Drop grate fitted.*
Cow. 17/1-16/2/39.**G.**
Cow. 6/3-15/5/40.**G.**
Cow. 10/9-23/10/41.**G.**
Cow. 18-24/12/41.**L.**
Cow. 15/1-17/2/42.**L.**
Cow. 31/3-4/4/42.**L.**
Cow. 17/11-3/12/42.**L.**
Cow. 30/4-29/5/43.**G.**
Cow. 15/6-12/7/45.**G.**
Don. 31/1-27/4/47.**G.**
Don. 21/1-13/2/48.**L.**
Don. 6/1-18/2/49.**G.**
Don. 11/4-11/5/51.**G.**
Don. 20-21/2/52.**N/C.**
Don. 5/3-8/4/53.**G.**
Don. 25/8-5/10/55.**G.**
Don. 7-10/10/55.**N/C.**
Don. 15/12/57-29/1/58.**G.**
Don. 27/7-31/8/60.**G.**

BOILERS:
D1647.
 7426 *(ex58)* 1/4/35.
 8605 *(exDonc & 1164)* 15/5/40.
 2838 *(ex186)* 12/7/45.
 9793 *(new)* 27/4/47.
 27162 *(ex61989)* 11/5/51.
 27257 *(ex spare and 61891)* 8/4/53.
 24903 *(new)* 5/10/55.
 27146 *(ex61806)* 29/1/58.
 24911 *(61930)* 31/8/60.

SHEDS:
Blaydon.
Carlisle 10/24.
St Margarets 29/1/37.
Carlisle 17/2/37.
March 8/6/38.
Carlisle 31/8/38.
St Margarets 14/3/39.
Eastfield 28/10/42.
St Margarets 4/4/43.
Carlisle 8/9/43.
St Margarets 5/3/45.
Aberdeen 20/8/45.
Doncaster 13/10/45.
Lincoln 18/6/46.
Doncaster 18/8/46.
March 25/5/47.
Norwich 6/10/48.
March 15/12/48.
Norwich 10/10/49.

Colwick 1/1/50.
Garton 10/2/52.
Lincoln 13/6/54.
Norwich 10/6/56.
Doncaster 20/1/57.

RENUMBERED:
 1812 8/11/46.
 E1812 13/2/48.
 61812 18/2/49.

CONDEMNED:
16/9/62.
Cut up at Doncaster.

33

Darlington.

To traffic 26/9/24.

REPAIRS:
Ghd. 23/9-29/12/27.**G.** *Steam reverse fitted.*
Ghd. 15/1-25/2/29.**L.**
Ghd. 16-30/10/29.**N/C.**
Ghd. 14/3-2/5/30.**G.**
Dar. 12/6-14/7/31.**H.**
Dar. 15-29/1/32.**L.**
Dar. 19/10-30/11/32.**G.**
Dar. 12-28/12/32.**N/C.**
Dar. 12/11-29/12/34.**G.** *Screw rev.l.h.drive. Mod.valve gear.*
Dar. 8/2-10/7/37.**G.** *Front footsteps fitted.*
Dar. 21/9-2/11/38.**L.** *Mid.cyl & piston fractured.*
Dar. 22/11/39-12/1/40.**G.**
Dar. 17/2-18/3/41.**L.**
Dar. 17/2-3/4/42.**G.**
Don. 5/6-5/8/44.**G.**
Don. 2-30/3/46.**H.**
Don. 2/9-16/10/48.**G.**
Don. 3-27/4/51.**G.**
Don. 3-31/3/53.**G.**
Don. 13-15/5/53.**N/C.**
Don. 29/3-2/5/55.**G.**
Don. 23/5-5/7/57.**G.**
Don. 11/8-18/9/59.**G.**
Don. 26/4-2/5/60.**N/C.**
Don. 26/3/62.*Not repaired.*

BOILERS:
D1648.
D1655 *(ex53)* 30/11/32.
D1646 *(ex52)* 29/12/34.
AW82 *(ex52)* 10/7/37.
 8123 *(ex1389)* 12/1/40.
AW83 *(ex1322)* 3/4/42.
C1824 *(ex2940)* 5/8/44.
 9549 *(new)* 30/3/46.
 27159 *(ex61867)* 27/4/51.
 27154 *(ex61801)* 31/3/53.
 27295 *(new)* 2/5/55.
 27250 *(ex61892)* 5/7/57.
 27273 *(ex61921)* 18/9/59.

SHEDS:
Blaydon.
Heaton 12/24.
Blaydon 30/9/37.
Heaton 19/6/43.
Darlington 10/8/43.
Neville Hill 25/6/45.
Hull Dairycoates 5/10/47.

RENUMBERED:
 1813 20/10/46.
 61813 15/10/48.

CONDEMNED:
9/4/62.
Cut up at Doncaster.

36

Darlington.

To traffic 26/9/24.

REPAIRS:
Ghd. 26/11-15/12/24.**L.**
Ghd. 16/8-16/12/27.**G.** *Steam reverse.*
Ghd. 5-14/3/29.**L.**
Ghd. 1/11/29-15/1/30.**G.**
Dar. 20/10-27/11/31.**L.**
Ghd. 10/5-16/6/32.**L.**
Dar. 1/3-23/5/33.**G.** *Drop grate fitted.*
Dar. 11/6-21/8/35.**G.** *Screw rev.l.h.drive. Mod.valve gear.*
Dar. 2/7-15/9/36.**L.** *After derailment.*
Dar. 13/12/37-18/2/38.**G.** *Front footsteps fitted.*
Dar. 24/6/40-13/2/41.**G.**
Dar. 12-24/5/41.**L.**
Dar. 8/12/42-13/1/43.**H.**
Don. 18/8-22/9/45.**G.**
Ghd. 30/1-19/2/47.**L.**
Don. 20/9-23/10/48.**G.**
Don. 2-30/11/50.**G..**
Don. 3/12/52-2/1/53.**G.**
Don. 20/8-16/9/53.**L.**
Don. 20/1-22/2/55.**G.**
Don. 30/8-21/9/55.**C/L.**
Don. 25/7-22/8/57.**G.**
Don. 13-16/11/57.**N/C.**
Don. 28/5-14/6/58.**C/L.**
Don. 13/8-17/9/59.**G.**
Don. 23-28/4/60.**N/C.**
Don. 5/12/61.*Not repaired.*

BOILERS:
D1649.
D1650 *(ex38)* 23/5/33.
 8121 *(ex1331)* 21/8/35.
RS4080 *(ex1398)* 18/2/38.
D1652 *(ex28)* 13/2/41.
 8127 *(ex1119)* 13/1/43.
 8921 *(ex2466)* 22/9/45.
 27124 *(ex61966)* 30/11/50.
 27148 *(ex61875)* 2/1/53.
 27155 *(ex61905)* 22/2/55.
 27127 *(ex61856)* 22/8/57.

WORKS CODES:- Cow - Cowlairs. Dar - Darlington. Don - Doncaster. Ghd - Gateshead. Gor - Gorton. Inv - Inverurie. Str - Stratford.
REPAIR CODES:- **C/H** - Casual Heavy. **C/L** - Casual Light. **G** - General. **H** - Heavy. **H/I** - Heavy Intermediate. **L** - Light. **L/I** - Light Intermediate. **N/C** - Non-Classified.

15

27262 *(ex61891)* 17/9/59.

SHEDS:
Blaydon.
Heaton 12/24.
Gateshead 10/7/43.
Neville Hill 23/7/45.
Hull Dairycoates 5/10/47.

RENUMBERED:
1814 24/11/46.
61814 22/10/48.

CONDEMNED:
27/12/61.
Cut up at Doncaster.

38

Darlington.

To traffic 30/9/24.

REPAIRS:
Ghd. 26/11-15/12/24.**L.**
Ghd. 6/12/27-17/3/28.**G.** *Steam rev.*
Ghd. 29/4-19/6/30.**G.**
Ghd. 24/2-15/5/31.**H.**
Dar. 2-22/2/32.**L.**
Dar. 13/2-24/3/33.**G.** *Drop grate fitted.*
Dar. 21/8-26/10/34.**G.** *Screw rev.L.H.drive. Mod.valve gear.*
Dar. 2/7-1/9/36.**G.**
Dar. 23/9-28/10/36.**L.**

Dar. 7/11-1/12/36.**L.**
Dar. 11/4-24/6/38.**G.**
Dar. 27/2-4/4/40.**L.**
Dar. 18/11-27/12/40.**G.**
Dar. 30/12/42-16/2/43.**G.**
Dar. 8-29/9/45.**G.**
Cow. 10/12/47-16/3/48.**H.**
Don. 15/10-4/11/48.**L.**
Don. 4/8-14/9/50.**G.**
Don. 29/7-3/8/51.**C/L.**
Don. 14/10-14/11/52.**G.**
Don. 18-27/8/54.**C/L.**
Don. 4/7-4/8/55.**G.**
Don. 28/12/57-1/2/58.**G.**
Don. 25/3-15/4/59.**C/L.**
Don. 27/6/60.*Not repaired.*

BOILERS:
D1650.
D1645 *(ex17)* 24/3/33.
8074 *(ex53)* 26/10/34.
8130 *(ex1398)* 1/9/36.
8121 *(ex36)* 24/6/38.
8140A *(ex1118)* 27/12/40.
8871 *(ex53)* 16/2/43.
8801 *(ex61925)* 14/9/50.
27261 *(new)* 14/11/52.
27177 *(ex61961)* 4/8/55.
27279 *(ex61864)* 1/2/58.

SHEDS:
Blaydon.
Heaton 4/6/25.
Blaydon 30/9/37.
Gateshead 24/1/40.
Blaydon 28/3/43.

Heaton 23/6/43.
Gateshead 8/7/43.
Neville Hill 23/7/45.
March 23/3/47.
Stratford 30/9/49.
Lincoln 4/7/54.
Stratford 26/9/54.
Parkeston 9/3/58.
Stratford 8/11/59.

RENUMBERED:
1815 25/8/46.
61815 4/11/48.

CONDEMNED:
11/7/60.
Cut up at Doncaster.

39

Darlington.

To traffic 30/9/24.

REPAIRS:
Dar. 15/2-8/5/28.**G.**
Dar. 20/1-30/4/30.**G.**
Dar. 7/6-3/8/32.**G.**
Dar. 4/10-10/11/34.**G.** *L.H.Drive & Mod.valve gear.*
Dar. 3/3-9/7/37.**G.**
Dar. 12-16/7/37.**N/C.**
Dar. 13/8-6/9/37.**L.**
Dar. 27/10-16/12/39.**G.**
Don. 24/7-25/9/41.**G.**

Don. 2/10-4/11/43.**G.**
Don. 10/3-11/5/46.**G.**
Don. 20/9-3/11/48.**G.**
Don. 22/11-21/12/50.**G.**
Don. 26/3-30/4/52.**G.**
Don. 3/11-5/12/53.**C/H.**
Don. 18/2-24/3/55.**G.**
Don. 18/3-26/4/57.**G.**
Don. 23/12/58-30/1/59.**G.**
Don. 14-24/9/59.**C/L.**

BOILERS:
D1652.
8074 *(new)* 30/4/30.
8073 *(ex52)* 3/8/32.
D1645 *(ex38)* 10/11/34.
8118 *(ex1345)* 9/7/37.
8116 *(ex1387)* 16/12/39.
8120 *(ex1367)* 11/5/46.
9988 *(new)* 3/11/48.
27127 *(ex61865)* 21/12/50.
27228 *(ex61956)* 30/4/52.
27112 *(ex61964)* 26/4/57.
27194 *(ex61800)* 30/1/59.

SHEDS:
York.
Gorton 27/9/40.
Woodford 4/11/43.
Colwick 26/5/46.
March 11/6/50.
Colwick 20/8/50.
March 20/9/53.
Sheffield 15/3/59.

Diagram 96A boilers built from March 1947 had the washing-out handholes increased to five on each side, clearly seen on 61802 photographed **March shed on 4th May 1952. Note that this 1920 built engine still has original parallel case buffers, and that they had circular flange, all those wi** **double case, and Group Standard having a square flange.** *L.W.Perkins.*

RENUMBERED:
1816 11/5/46.
61816 3/11/48.

CONDEMNED:
31/5/62.
Cut up at Doncaster.

46

Darlington.

To traffic 11/10/24.

REPAIRS:
Dar. 28/9-22/10/26.**L.**
Ghd. 6/12/27-13/3/28.**G.** *Steam reverse fitted.*
Ghd. 5/4-3/6/29.**L.**
Dar. 17/9-15/11/29.**L.**
Ghd. 7/7-22/8/30.**G.**
Dar. 2/5-3/7/33.**G.**
Dar. 9/3-28/4/36.**G.** *Screw rev. L.H.Drive. Mod.valve gear.*
Dar. 10/3-29/4/37.**H.**
Dar. 20/8-9/9/37.**N/C.**
Dar. 14/4-25/5/39.**G.**
Dar. 11/4-27/5/41.**G.**
Dar. 26/6-13/8/43.**G.**
Dar. 28/12/43-22/1/44.**L.**
Don. 2/1-20/2/45.**G.**
Don. 20/7-4/10/46.**G.**
Don. 27/9-12/11/48.**G.**
Don. 20/11-20/12/50.**G.**
Don. 2/11-7/12/51.**C/L.**
Don. 29/7-29/9/52.**G.**
Don. 2-6/3/53.**L.**
Str. 10-15/12/53.**N/C.**
Don. 12/5-17/6/55.**G.**
Don. 10-29/8/56.**C/L.**
Don. 22/10-23/11/57.**G.**
Don. 25/3-5/4/58.**N/C.**
Don. 22/4-1/5/59.**C/L.**
Don. 18/2-18/3/60.**G.**
Don. 26/9-22/10/60.**C/L.**

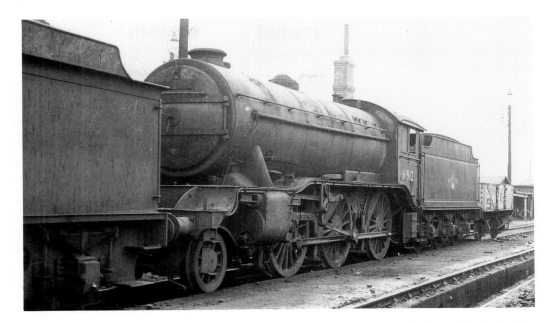

The last K3's were withdrawn from traffic in December 1962, but three taken out in the previous September, **61835, 61912** and **61943**, served further as Stationary Boilers, the last one until October 1965. This one on **61912** worked at King's Cross until Top Shed closed on 16th June 1963 and was then hauled to Grantham shed (as seen here on 13th July 1963) to work until it was condemned in March 1965. *A.G.Ellis.*

BOILERS:
D1654.
D1649 *(ex36)* 3/7/33.
RS4076 *(ex1332)* 28/4/36.
 2848 *(ex3827)* 25/5/39.
 8121 *(ex38)* 27/5/41.
8136A *(ex1392)* 13/8/43.
 8928 *(ex2427)* 20/2/45.
 8916 *(ex2443)* 4/10/46.
27128 *(ex61869)* 20/12/50.
27298 *(new)* 17/6/55.
24927 *(new)* 23/11/57.
27177 *(ex61914)* 18/3/60.

SHEDS:
Blaydon.
Heaton 12/24.
Blaydon 30/9/37.
Gateshead 24/1/40.
Heaton 29/10/41.
Darlington 3/8/43.
Doncaster 29/5/44.
March 25/5/47.
Stratford 30/9/49.
Cambridge 14/12/58.
March 26/11/61.

RENUMBERED:
1817 28/4/46.
61817 12/11/48.

CONDEMNED:
16/9/62.
Sold for scrap to Central Wagon Co. Ince.

No.227 here in 1930 did not then differ from its fellows, but some details are worthy of mention. Note that it was still as built with left hand drive, and that it was one of those fitted with Darlington design steam reversing gear. Front footsteps, and cab sight screens have yet to be added, and the redundant double lamp iron to be taken off. Another Doncaster feature which proved surplus to requirements is the carrying of guard irons both on the front end of the frame, and on the pony truck. Every K3 was so fitted although by 1930 Doncaster had realised that those on the frame were in the 'belt and braces' category, yet it was into BR years ere a determined effort then removed them.

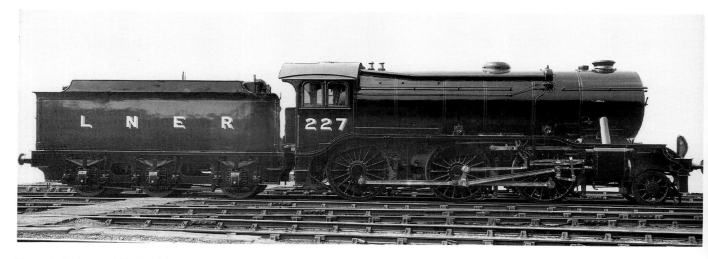

Ex-works in August 1935, No.227 had been fitted with a Gresham & Craven feed water heater combined with a Hulburd boiler cleaner, actually a blow-down apparatus. The operating rod from the cab for the latter needed part of the handrail to be removed on the fireman's side. *L.N.E.R.*

The apparatus appreciably extended the period between washouts, but failed to eliminate priming, so on 20th June 1936, a Gunderson electrical foam detector was fitted. The two connections and the wiring to the cab from them can be seen to the rear of the dome cover. *B.W.Anwell.*

52

Darlington.

To traffic 11/10/24.

REPAIRS:
Dar. 28/8-21/9/25.**L.**
Dar. 9/8-30/11/27.**G.** *Steam reverse fitted.*
Ghd. 24/5-24/6/29.**L.**
Dar. 27/1-29/3/30.**G.**
Dar. 8/8/30.**N/C.**
Dar. 18-21/5/31.**N/C.**
Dar. 23/5-2/7/32.**G.**
Dar. 20/7-4/8/33.**L.**
Dar. 5/10-17/11/34.**G.** *Screw Rev. L.H.Drive. Mod.valve gear.*
Dar. 25/8-24/9/36.**L.**
Dar. 12/12/36-28/4/37.**G.** *New rear frames.*
Dar. 25/8-24/9/37.**L.**
Dar. 29/8-13/10/39.**G.** *New cab windows fitted.*
Dar. 29/7-3/10/41.**G.**
Dar. 17/3-1/5/42.**L.**
Dar. 6/10-11/11/43.**H.**
Don. 15/12/45-19/1/46.**G.**
Don. 10/10-6/12/47.**G.**

Ghd. 19/8-24/9/49.**C/L.**
Don. 10/10-19/11/49.**G.**
Don. 27/11-27/12/51.**G.**
Don. 14/9-12/10/53.**G.**
Don. 27/9-22/10/54.**C/L.**
Don. 1/11-2/12/55.**G.**
Don. 21/11-24/12/57.**G.**
Don. 1-12/12/58.**C/L.**
Don. 10/9-8/10/59.**G.**
Don. 20/2/62.*Not repaired.*

BOILERS:
D1655.
  8073 *(new)* 29/3/30.
D1646 *(ex28)* 2/7/32.
  AW82 *(ex1118)* 17/11/34.
  8871 *(new)* 28/4/37.
  8073 *(ex1395)* 13/10/39.
  8133 *(ex3826)* 11/11/43.
  8741 *(ex1881)* 6/12/47.
  8909 *(ex1929)* 19/11/49.
  27201 *(ex61819)* 27/12/51.
  27270 *(ex61918)* 12/10/53.
  24930 *(new)* 24/12/57.
  27122 *(ex61927)* 8/10/59.

SHEDS:
Blaydon.
York 10/24.

Heaton 14/5/40.
Tyne Dock 4/12/60.
Thornaby 18/12/60.
Hull Dairycoates 11/6/61.

RENUMBERED:
  1818 5/5/46.
61818 18/11/49.

CONDEMNED:
15/3/62.
Cut up at Doncaster.

53

Darlington.

To traffic 24/10/24.

REPAIRS:
Dar. 19/1-21/4/28.**G.** *Steam reverse fitted.*
Dar. 28/6-17/7/29.**L.**
Dar. 5/2-2/5/30.**G.**
Dar. 16/5-13/6/30.**N/C.**
Dar. 5/7-23/8/32.**G.**
Don. 8/33.**L.** *New crank axle.*
Dar. 7/7-20/9/34.**G.** *Screw rev.&*

mod.valve gear.
Dar. 8/3-11/5/37.**G.** *L.H.Drive.*
Dar. 20/9-28/10/39.**G.**
Dar. 6/12/39-3/1/40.**H.**
Dar. 11/5-13/6/42.**G.**
Dar. 27/9-14/10/43.**L.**
Don. 24/7-2/9/44.**G.**
Don. 9-23/3/46.**L.**
Don. 1/2-15/3/47.**H.**
Don. 5-27/12/47.**L.**
Ghd. 15/9-4/10/48.**L.**
Don. 12/9-29/10/49.**G.**
Don. 5-29/11/51.**G.**
Don. 31/1-13/2/52.**L.**
Don. 2-19/9/52.**L.**
Don. 15/12/53-15/1/54.**G.**
Don. 8/12/55-17/1/56.**G.**
Don. 16/6-25/7/58.**G.**
Don. 22/2-5/4/61.**G.**

BOILERS:
D1658.
D1655 *(ex52)* 2/5/30.
  8074 *(ex39)* 23/8/32.
D1654 *(ex46)* 20/9/34.
  8871 *(ex52)* 28/10/39.
  8117 *(ex1302)* 13/6/42.
D1666 *(ex156)* 2/9/44.
  2796 *(ex3820)* 15/3/47.

'his August 1939 photograph in the yard at York North Shed shows that the foam detector had been taken off, actually at the February 1937
eneral repair, when the crew would have more benefit from the addition of front footsteps and sight screens on the cab. The feed water heating
·ial was not extended beyond No.227, and all the apparatus was removed when 227 was in works for general repair September/November 1940.

0533 *(new)* 29/10/49.
7271 *(new)* 29/11/51.
7178 *(ex61874)* 15/1/54.
7229 *(ex61867)* 17/1/56.
4905 *(ex61958)* 25/7/58.

HEDS:
ork.
laydon 5/7/40.
eaton 21/6/43.
arlington 27/7/43.
ull Dairycoates 23/7/45.

ENUMBERED:
819 24/11/46.
819 4/10/48.

ONDEMNED:
/12/62.
ut up at Doncaster.

B

arlington.

traffic 23/10/24.

EPAIRS:
on. 15/10-31/12/27.**G.**
on. 3/6-31/7/29.**G.**
on. 11/11/30-8/1/31.**G.**

Mod.valve gear.
Don. 28/2-18/5/33.**G.**
Don. 14-26/2/35.**G.**
Don. 7/6-15/7/36.**G.**
Don. 20/4-30/5/38.**G.**
Don. 13-20/5/39.**L.**
Don. 17/2-23/3/40.**G.**
Don. 17/5-21/6/41.**L.**
Don. 27/6-15/8/42.**G.**
Don. 4/11-23/12/44.**G.**
Don. 20/7-24/8/46.**G.**
Don. 8/7-20/8/48.**G.**
Don. 19/10-23/11/48.**L.**
Don. 2-30/5/49.**C/L.**
Don. 25/7-1/9/49.**C/L.**
Don. 30/11/50-4/1/51.**G.**
Don. 17/2-19/3/53.**G.**
Str. 24/2-3/3/55.**N/C.**
Don. 18/5-8/7/55.**G.**
Don. 23/10-10/11/55.**N/C.**
Don. 15/9-11/10/57.**G.**
Don. 16/12/58-8/1/59.**N/C.**
Don. 11/12/59-8/1/60.**G.**
Don. 12-25/8/60.**C/L.**

BOILERS:
D1659.
D1679 *(ex111)* 31/7/29.
7426 *(ex4001)* 8/1/31.
D1742 *(ex186)* 26/2/35.
7429 *(ex228)* 30/5/38.
D1737 *(ex92)* 23/3/40.

2814 *(ex2473)* 23/12/44.
27130 *(ex61836)* 4/1/51.
27135 *(ex61893)* 19/3/53.
27299 *(new)* 8/7/55.
27224 *(ex61913)* 11/10/57.
27156 *(ex61849)* 8/1/60.

SHEDS:
Doncaster.
Annesley 11/7/31.
Doncaster 27/6/33.
March 26/6/39.
Stratford 17/10/49.
Parkeston 16/3/58.
Stratford 8/11/59.
Staveley 3/4/60.
Mexborough 12/6/60.
Millhouses 9/7/61.
Canklow 31/12/61.
Colwick 3/6/62.
Lincoln 17/6/62.

RENUMBERED:
1820 8/12/46.
61820 20/8/48.

CONDEMNED:
4/11/62.
Sold for scrap to T.W.Ward,
Broughton Lane, Sheffield.

69

Darlington.

To traffic 31/10/24.

REPAIRS:
Don. 24/1-22/4/27.**G.**
Don. 20/10-22/12/28.**G.**
Don. 3/4-7/7/30.**G.**
Don. 21/11/31-3/2/32.**G.** *Mod.valve*
gear.
Don. 2/11/33-19/1/34.**G.**
Don. 19/7-19/9/35.**G.**
Don. 12/2-23/4/38.**G.** *Heater conn.at*
front.
Don. 19/8-23/9/39.**L.**
Gor. 25/5-8/6/40.**L.**
Don. 23/8-27/9/41.**G.**
Don. 7-21/2/42.**L.**
Don. 8/1-5/2/44.**G.**
Don. 6/10-3/11/45.**G.**
Don. 7/1-13/4/48.**G.**
Don. 22/11-6/12/48.**L.**
Don. 1/1-24/2/50.**G**
Don. 18/9-23/10/51.**G.**
Don. 29/7-27/8/53.**G.**
Don. 12/11-9/12/54.**C/L.**
Don. 12/9-14/10/55.**G.**
Don. 22/2-28/3/58.**G.**
Don. 20-24/12/58.**N/C.**
Don. 9-18/12/59.**N/C.**

Don. 30/8-7/10/60.**G.**

BOILERS:
D1663.
D1727 *(ex159)* 7/7/30.
D1776 *(ex203)* 3/2/32.
 8606 *(ex1166)* 23/4/38.
3D/687 *(ex1897)* 13/4/48.
RS4076 *(ex1856)* 24/2/50.
27196 *(ex1864)* 23/10/51.
27204 *(ex61905)* 27/8/53.
24904 *(new)* 14/10/55.
24908 *(ex61887)* 28/3/58.

24902 *(ex61944)* 7/10/60.

SHEDS:
Kings Cross.
Gorton 22/9/35.
Woodford 24/10/43.
Neasden 27/4/46.
Colwick 26/5/46.
Immingham 8/7/62.

RENUMBERED:
 1821 19/5/46.
61821 13/4/48.

CONDEMNED:
16/9/62.
Sold for scrap to J.Cashmore, Great Bridge.

73

Darlington.

To traffic 31/10/24.

REPAIRS:
Don. 13/5-10/8/27.**G.**
Don. 15/12/28-6/2/29.**G.**
Don. 12/6-5/9/30.**G.**
Don. 12/12/31-8/3/32.**G.** *Mod.valve gear.*
Don. 24/8-16/10/33.**G.**
Don. 1/3-4/4/35.**G.**
Don. 16/4-30/5/36.**G.**
Don. 19/1-19/2/38.**G.**
Don. 9/3-20/4/40.**G.**
Don. 21/3-2/5/42.**G.**
Don. 31/10-21/11/42.**L.**

This Doncaster official photograph was taken in March 1939 to record that 2934 had been fitted with new driving wheel axleboxes which had Friedman bearings. No details of them are known, except that they were removed in July 1942. *L.N.E.R.*

Don. 25/9-16/10/43.**L.**	*BOILERS:*	*SHEDS:*	Colwick 3/6/62.
Don. 3/6-15/7/44.**G.**	D1664.	New England.	Lincoln 17/6/62.
Don. 16/2-23/3/46.**G.**	D1666 *(ex75)* 6/2/29.	Colwick 24/6/40.	
Don. 21/9-30/10/47.**G.**	D1734 *(ex206)* 16/10/33.	Annesley 13/10/40.	*RENUMBERED:*
Don. 12/2-21/4/50.**G.**	D1722 *(ex121)* 19/2/38.	Sheffield 3/5/43.	**1822** 6/10/46.
Don. 11/5-1/6/51.**C/L.**	D1672 *(ex146)* 15/7/44.	New England 25/6/45.	**61822** 21/4/50.
Don. 12/3-10/4/52.**G.**	9548 *(new)* 23/3/46.	Lincoln 11/8/46.	
Don. 19/9-14/10/52.**C/L.**	10807 *(new)* 21/4/50.	Colwick 15/10/50.	*CONDEMNED:*
Don. 10/5-15/6/54.**G.**	27224 *(ex61810)* 10/4/52.	March 27/9/53.	4/11/62.
Don. 25/1-2/3/56.**G.**	27192 *(ex61982)* 15/6/54.	Staveley 24/4/60.	*Sold for scrap to T.W.Ward,*
Don. 1-17/4/56.**C/L.**	27254 *(ex61805)* 25/1/58.	Mexborough 12/6/60.	*Broughton Lane, Sheffield.*
Don. 23/12/57-25/1/58.**G.**	27265 *(ex61965)* 16/12/59.	Millhouses 9/7/61.	
Don. 17/11-16/12/59.**G.**		Canklow 31/12/61.	

75

Darlington.

To traffic 6/11/24.

REPAIRS:
Don. 17/8-12/12/25.**L.**
Don. 4/2-13/3/26.**L.**
Don. 3/1-8/4/27.**G.**
Don. 14/11/28-12/1/29.**G.**
Don. 9/7-22/8/30.**G.**
Don. 15/3-28/4/32.**G.**
Don. 14/12/33-26/1/34.**G.** *Mod.valve gear.*
Don. 9/11-12/12/34.**L.**
Don. 9/1-6/2/35.**G.**
Don. 17/2-28/3/36.**G.**
Don. 25/2-26/3/38.**G.**
Don. 28/10-9/12/39.**G.**
Don. 7/3-11/4/42.**G.**
Cow. 9/6/44.**G.**
Cow. 8/3-11/5/46.**G.**
Cow. 17/9-20/12/47.**G.**
Cow. 19/8-7/10/49.**G.**
Cow. 1/6-4/7/51.**L/I.**
Cow. 7-29/11/52.**G.**
Cow. 13/4-29/6/54.**H/I.**
Cow. 27/11-18/12/54.**C/L.**
Cow. 1/2-5/3/55.**C/L.**
Cow. 18/4-14/5/55.**C/L.**
Cow. 20/1-3/3/56.**L/I.**
Cow. 1/10-14/11/57.**G.**
Cow. 29/9-9/10/58.**C/L.**
Cow. 11/2-21/3/59.**H/I.**

BOILERS:
D1666.
  7992 *(new)* 12/1/29.
D1726 *(ex158)* 26/1/34.
  8927 *(ex2467)* 11/4/42.
C1822 *(ex2938)* 20/12/47.
Renumbered 27318 4/7/51.
27329 *(ex61936)* 29/11/52.
27318 *(ex61955)* 14/11/57.

SHEDS:
Doncaster.
St Margarets 30/9/42.
Carlisle 10/43.
St Margarets 5/3/45.

RENUMBERED:
  1823 22/9/46.
61823 7/10/49.

CONDEMNED:
29/12/59.
Cut up at Cowlairs.

80

Darlington.

To traffic 8/11/24.

REPAIRS:
Don. 1/7-4/9/26.**G.**
Don. 21/12/27-14/3/28.**G.**
Don. 18/12/29-14/2/30.**G.**
Don. 26/10/31-11/1/32.**G.** *Mod.valve gear.*
Don. 6/12/32-2/2/33.**G.**
Don. 28/4-30/6/34.**G.**
Don. 3/9-19/10/35.**G.**
Don. 26/4-16/7/37.**G.**
Gor. 13-17/6/38.**H.** *Front heater conn.*
Don. 5-19/11/38.**L.**
Don. 21/10-25/11/39.**G.**
Don. 20/12/41-31/1/42.**G.**
Don. 20/12/42-30/1/43.**L.**
Don. 19/2-18/3/44.**G.**
Don. 29/9-27/10/45.**G.**
Don. 27/5-9/7/48.**G.**
Don. 2/3-27/4/50.**G.**
Don. 18/8/51-25/9/51.**G.**
Don. 12/6-15/7/52.**H.**
Don. 1/4-7/5/53.**G.**
Don. 21-27/5/54.**N/C.**
Don. 18/1-23/2/55.**G.**
Don. 14/6-20/7/57.**G.**
Don. 11-30/7/58.**C/L.**
Don. 16/9-14/10/59.**G.**
Don. 24/2-12/3/60.**C/L.**
Don. 7-13/10/60.**C/L.**
Don. 5/7/61.*Not repaired.*

BOILERS:
D1668.
D1659 *(ex58)* 14/2/30.
D1668 *(ex140)* 17/6/38.
10504 *(new)* 9/7/48.
10809 *(new)* 27/4/50.
27190 *(ex61880)* 25/9/51.

27107 *(ex61975)* 7/5/53.
27176 *(ex61883)* 20/7/57.
27296 *(ex61839)* 14/10/59.

SHEDS:
New England.
Gorton 19/10/35.
Trafford Park 9/9/37.
Gorton 22/5/39.
Woodford 30/10/43.
Annesley 29/6/47.
Colwick 13/7/47.
March 27/9/53.
Colwick 20/12/53.
Woodford 5/1/58.

RENUMBERED:
  1824 15/9/46.
61824 9/7/48.

CONDEMNED:
5/7/61.
Cut up at Doncaster.

91

Darlington.

To traffic 13/11/24.

REPAIRS:
Don. 4/3-12/6/27.**G.**
Don. 23/1-29/3/29.**G.**
Don. 6/12/30-10/2/31.**G.**

Between October 1934 and May 1937, the nine 1924 built engines in the N.E.Area numbered 17 to 52 were altered from original right-hand to left hand drive as seen on No.39 at York on 24th August 1935. Note it still has the original cab sides with a horizontal handrail above the windows, bu a coil spring between the middle and rear coupled wheels indicates that it had been fitted with a drop grate. *Photomatic.*

No.32, the first of the Darlington built engines to be coupled with Group Standard 4200 gallon tender went new to Blaydon shed, but after only five weeks moved to Carlisle (Canal) shed to work a Glasgow goods via the Waverley route. It was changed to the shorter GN type 3500 gallon tender which it has here outside Eastfield shed, and the original right hand drive position will be noted. Unlike its contemporaries in N.E.Area, it was never changed to left hand, nor was it altered to steam reversing gear, as they were.

Mod. valve gear.
Don. 15/10-9/12/32.**G.**
Don. 30/5-10/8/34.**G.**
Don. 27/1-7/3/36.**G.**
Don. 7/10-8/11/37.**G.**
Don. 25/5-15/6/40.**G.**
Don. 20/3-17/4/43.**G.**
Don. 9-30/12/44.**G.**
Don. 18/5-6/7/46.**G.**
Don. 5/3-16/4/48.**G.**
Don. 25/5-13/7/50.**G.**
Don. 14-29/10/51.**C/L.**
Don. 13/5-16/6/52.**G.**
Don. 17/12/53-26/1/54.**G.**
Don. 9/11-4/12/54.**C/L.**
Don. 23/4-20/5/55.**G.**
Don. 12/3-27/4/57.**G.**
Don. 16/7-14/8/59.**G.**

BOILERS:
D1672.
D1715 *(ex141)* 10/2/31.
D1713 *(ex114)* 8/11/37.
  8969 *(ex2465)* 6/7/46.
A8139 *(ex1867)* 13/7/50.
27239 *(ex61846)* 16/6/52.
27284 *(new)* 26/1/54.
27296 *(new)* 20/5/55.
27208 *(ex61837)* 27/4/57.
27120 *(ex61915)* 14/8/59.

SHEDS:
Kings Cross.
Ardsley 8/11/37.
Copley Hill 30/10/38.
Ardsley 16/4/39.
Copley Hill 6/8/39.
Ardsley 26/7/42.
Copley Hill 6/9/42.
Doncaster 27/2/44.
New England 22/4/45.

Immingham 1/5/49.
Sheffield 17/11/57.
New England 29/10/61.

RENUMBERED:
  1825 22/9/46.
  61825 16/4/48.

CONDEMNED:
16/9/62.
Cut up at Doncaster.

92

Darlington.

To traffic 19/11/24.

REPAIRS:
Don. 26/1-24/5/27.**G.**
Don. 1/7-27/8/29.**G.**
Don. 18/3-18/5/31.**G.**
Don. 5/11-30/12/32.**G.** *Mod.valve gear.*
Don. 24/2-17/5/34.**G.**
Don. 19/7-22/9/34.**G.**
Don. 31/12/35-14/2/36.**G.**
Don. 24/8-1/9/37.**G.**
Don. 15/4-20/5/39.**G.**
Don. 20/9-25/10/41.**G.**
Don. 23/10-20/11/43.**G.**
Don. 22/12/45-26/1/46.**G.**
Don. 20/2-11/4/47.**G.**
Don. 19/7-28/8/48.**G.**
Don. 25/9-27/10/50.**G.**
Don. 15/8-26/9/52.**G.**
Don. 10/5-8/7/54.**G.**
Don. 29/2-6/4/56.**G.**
Don. 16-25/4/57.**N/C.**
Don. 29/7-17/8/57.**C/L.**

Don. 12/3-18/4/58.**G.**
Don. 2/1-4/2/60.**G.**

BOILERS:
D1673.
D1716 *(ex143)* 27/8/29.
D1737 *(ex178)* 30/12/32.
5D/687 *(ex113)* 20/5/39.
  8740 *(ex1166)* 20/11/43.
  8923 *(ex2459)* 26/1/46.
27112 *(ex61877)* 27/10/50.
27126 *(ex61845)* 26/9/52.
27248 *(ex61948)* 8/7/54.
27118 *(ex61808)* 6/4/56.
27142 *(ex61807)* 18/4/58.

SHEDS:
New England.
Doncaster 25/10/37.
Gorton 3/12/39.
Woodford 18/11/43.
Colwick 26/5/46.
March 20/9/53.
Norwich 8/6/58.
Staveley 31/1/60.
Colwick 3/6/62.

RENUMBERED:
  1826 6/10/46.
  61826 28/8/48.

CONDEMNED:
16/9/62.
Sold for scrap to J.Cashmore, Great Bridge.

109

Darlington.

To traffic 21/11/24.

REPAIRS:
Don. 17/4-17/7/26.**G.**
Don. 18/9-15/10/26.**L.**
Don. 10/3-7/28.**G.**
Don. 11/11/29-11/1/30.**G.**
  Mod.valve gear.
Don. 25/3-1/8/31.**G.**
Don. 18/9-20/11/33.**G.**
Don. 30/4-15/6/35.**G.**
Don. 26/3-17/4/36.**L.**
Don. 3/11-17/12/36.**G.**
Don. 19/6-4/8/38.**G.**
Don. 15/6-6/7/40.**G.**
Don. 29/8-26/9/42.**G.**
Don. 27/11/43.**N/C.**
Don. 18/11-16/12/44.**G.**
Don. 11/5-8/6/46.**G.**
Don. 22/6-24/7/47.**L.**
Don. 18/2-7/5/48.**G.**
Don. 15-31/1/49.**C/L.**
Don. 16/6-4/8/50.**G.**
Don. 11/6-24/7/52.**G.**
Don. 8/7-12/8/54.**G.**
Don. 15/5-20/6/56.**G.**
Don. 17/4-23/5/58.**G.**
Don. 19/1-18/2/60.**G.**

BOILERS:
D1678.
D1673 *(ex92)* 11/1/30.
D1785 *(ex231)* 20/11/33.
  8601 *(ex2765)* 6/7/40.
D1723 *(ex126)* 26/9/42.
8137A *(ex1830)* 7/5/48.
  9379 *(ex61843)* 4/8/50.

27246 (ex61943) 24/7/52.
27194 (ex61864) 12/8/54.
27225 (ex61951) 20/6/56.
24904 (ex61821) 23/5/58.
27334 (ex61854) 18/2/60.

SHEDS:
New England.
Doncaster 16/8/26.
Annesley 1/8/31.
Doncaster 6/2/34.
New England 22/4/45.
Immingham 1/5/49.
March 27/9/53.
Lincoln 4/12/60.
Colwick 11/12/60.

RENUMBERED:
1827 7/6/46.
61827 7/5/48.

CONDEMNED:
16/9/62.
Sold for scrap to J.Cashmore, Great Bridge.

111

Darlington.

To traffic 25/11/24.

REPAIRS:
Don. 13-24/10/25.**L.**
Don. 17/2-13/3/26.**L.**
Don. 3/4-5/6/26.**L.**
Don. 1/12/26-12/3/27.**G.**
Don. 27/1-28/3/28.**L.**
Don. 11/1-21/2/29.**G.**
Don. 24/2-29/3/30.**H.**
Don. 27/10-30/11/31.**G.** *Mod.valve gear.*
Don. 20/7-28/8/33.**G.**
Don. 25/3-28/4/35.**G.**
Don. 1-30/7/36.**H.**
Don. 19/11-17/12/37.**H.**
Don. 8/7-26/8/39.**G.**
Don. 17/5-21/6/41.**G.**
Don. 5/6-17/7/43.**G.**
Don. 20/1-24/2/45.**G.**
Don. 20/7-24/8/46.**G.**
Don. 30/6-9/8/48.**G.**
Gor. 9-15/4/50.**N/C.**
Don. 2/10-2/11/50.**G.**
Don. 20/9-23/10/51.**C/L.**
Don. 11/1-10/2/53.**G.**
Don. 13/5-5/7/55.**G.**
Don. 22/1-15/2/58.**G.**
Don. 9-14/5/59.**N/C.**
Don. 16/3/61.*Not repaired.*

BOILERS:
D1679.
D1695 (ex118) 21/2/29.
D1687 (ex180) 30/11/31.
 8737 (new) 28/4/35.
 9555 (new) 24/8/46.
10503 (new) 9/8/48.
27114 (ex1902) 2/11/50.
27161 (ex61838) 10/2/53.

27152 (ex61860) 5/7/55.
27205 (ex61842) 15/2/58.

SHEDS:
Doncaster.
Ardsley 30/7/44.
New England 25/6/45.
March 16/6/46.
New England 16/10/46.
Gorton 23/1/49.
London Mid.Reg. 29/5/49.
Gorton 5/6/49.
Lincoln 13/6/54.

RENUMBERED:
1828 31/3/46.
61828 7/8/48.

CONDEMNED:
20/3/61.
Cut up Doncaster.

112

Darlington.

To traffic 4/12/24.

REPAIRS:
Don. 27/9/26-22/1/27.**G.**
Don. 6/11/28-11/1/29.**G.**
Don. 19/3-26/4/30.**G.**
Don. 30/4-8/6/31.**H.**
Don. 24/1-27/2/33.**G.** *Mod.valve gear.*
Don. 19/7-29/8/34.**G.**
Don. 18/2-7/3/35.**L.**
Don. 27/12/35-22/1/36.**H.**
Don. 27/9-22/10/37.**G.**
Don. 26/8-14/10/39.**G.**
Don. 6/1-17/2/40.**L.**
Don. 12-26/10/40.**L.**
Don. 4/4-9/5/42.**G.**
Don. 24/10-14/11/42.**G.**
Don. 11/9-9/10/43.**G.**
Don. 11/5-15/6/46.**G.**
Don. 2/2-15/3/49.**G.**
Don. 7/10-22/11/50.**G.**
Don. 4/12/52-9/1/53.**G.**
Don. 4/9-19/10/53.**C/L.**
Don. 26/8-5/10/54.**C/L.**
Don. 3/8-1/9/55.**G.**
Don. 26/10-4/12/57.**G.**
Don. 1/1-6/2/60.**G.**

BOILERS:
D1682.
 7991 (new) 11/1/29.
 7427 (ex4005) 29/8/34.
 8918 (ex2447) 15/6/46.
RS4079 (ex1809) 15/3/49.
27121 (ex1842) 22/11/50.
27105 (ex61899) 9/1/53.
27201 (ex61895) 1/9/55.
27258 (ex61973) 4/12/57.
27284 (ex61935) 6/2/60.

SHEDS:
New England.
Stratford 7/5/38.

Gorton 23/9/38.
Woodford 30/10/43.
Gorton 19/6/49.
Sheffield 13/6/54.
Lincoln 17/10/54.
Norwich 10/6/56.
Doncaster 20/1/57.

RENUMBERED:
1829 5/5/46.
61829 15/3/49.

CONDEMNED:
28/2/62.
Cut up at Doncaster.

113

Darlington.

To traffic 3/12/24.

REPAIRS:
Don. 26/1-7/5/27.**G.**
Don. 26/11-10/12/27.**L.**
Don. 22/11/28-24/1/29.**G.**
Don. 17/7-29/8/30.**G.**
Don. 15/4-27/5/31.**L.**
Don. 28/4-3/6/32.**G.**
Don. 26/11-7/12/33.**G.** *Mod.valve gear.*
Don. 9/4-5/6/35.**G.**
Don. 21/1-19/2/37.**H.**
Don. 17/12/38-28/1/39.**G.**
Don. 28/12/40-8/2/41.**G.**
Don. 7/4/41.**L.**
Don. 7/8-11/9/43.**G.**
Don. 5/8-2/9/44.**L.**
Don. 22/12/45-26/1/46.**G.**
Don. 22/6-28/7/47.**L.**
Don. 26/5-26/6/48.**G.**
Don. 25/8-16/9/48.**L.**
Don. 13/10-13/11/50.**G.**
Don. 20/3-8/4/52.**C/L.**
Don. 13/12/52-21/1/53.**G.**
Don. 1/6-15/7/54.**C/L.**
Don. 9/2-10/3/55.**G.**
Don. 11/10-16/11/57.**G.**
Don. 30/9-4/11/60.**G.**

BOILERS:
D1687.
 8072 (new) 24/1/29.
8D/687 (ex2766) 5/6/35.
5D/687 (ex2767) 19/2/37.
D1715 (ex91) 28/2/39.
10502 (new) 26/6/48.
27117 (ex61828) 13/11/50.
27255 (ex61944) 21/1/53.
27175 (ex61967) 10/3/55.
27162 (ex61870) 16/11/57.
27209 (ex61970) 4/11/60.

SHEDS:
New England.
March 26/6/39.
Stratford 24/2/49.
New England 17/2/57.
Doncaster 16/9/62.

RENUMBERED:
1830 7/4/46.
61830 22/6/48.

CONDEMNED:
4/11/62.
Cut up at Doncaster.

114

Darlington.

To traffic 11/12/24.

REPAIRS:
Don. 31/1-26/5/27.**G.**
Don. 4/1-5/3/29.**G.**
Don. 12/11/30-9/1/31.**G.** *Mod.valve gear.*
Don. 26/1-23/4/31.**G.**
Don. 23/11/32-21/1/33.**G.**
Don. 16/6-25/8/34.**G.**
Don. 7/11-7/12/35.**G.**
Don. 2/4-15/5/37.**G.**
Don. 3/12/38-14/1/39.**G.**
Don. 24/2-2/3/40.**L.**
Don. 7/9-5/10/40.**G.**
Don. 17/10-28/11/42.**G.**
Don. 7/10-4/11/44.**G.**
Don. 26/1-9/2/46.**L.**
Don. 25/11/46-10/1/47.**G.**
Don. 4/8-1/10/48.**G.**
Don. 8/6-22/7/49.**C/L.**
Don. 14/10-24/11/50.**G.**
Don. 17/5-6/6/51.**C/L.**
Don. 12/1-7/2/53.**G.**
Don. 7/3-15/4/55.**G.**
Don. 3-27/7/56.**C/L.**
Don. 8/11-13/12/57.**G.**
Don. 20/10-14/11/59.**G.**

BOILERS:
D1690.
D1713 (ex135) 21/1/33.
 7991 (ex186) 15/5/37.
 9282 (ex1978) 1/10/48.
27122 (ex61805) 24/11/50.
27117 (ex61830) 7/2/53.
24929 (new) 13/12/57.
27275 (61842) 14/11/59.

SHEDS:
New England.
Mexborough 3/5/43.
Doncaster 25/8/46.
March 25/5/47.
Stratford 24/2/49.
March 17/2/57.
Lincoln 4/12/60.
Colwick 11/12/60.

RENUMBERED:
1831 7/4/46.
61831 1/10/48.

CONDEMNED:
16/9/62.
Sold for scrap to J.Cashmore, Great Bridge.

The improved performance of the Pacifics given by modified valve gear led to trials on K3 class, and ex works on 20th October 1928, No.134 had similar modifications. Evidence of this is seen in the appreciably longer slot in the reversing link to give increased maximum valve travel. It quickly showed considerable economy in coal consumption.

116

Darlington.

To traffic 15/12/24.

REPAIRS:
Don. 20/12/26-26/3/27.**G.**
Don. 28/2-16/4/28.**L.**
Don. 2/3-25/4/29.**G.**
Don. 25/3-1/5/31.**G.**
Don. 23/7-27/8/31.**L.**
Don. 12/12/32-14/1/33.**G.** *Mod.valve gear.*
Don. 28/3-28/4/34.**G.**
Don. 18/5-14/6/34.**L.**
Don. 6/6-6/7/35.**G.**
Don. 7/1-13/2/37.**H.**
Don. 14/1-18/2/39.**G.**
Don. 6-13/4/40.**L.**
Don. 26/10-30/11/40.**G.**
Don. 6/2-6/3/43.**G.**
Don. 20/1-10/3/45.**G.**
Don. 9-23/6/45.**L.**
Don. 3/3-12/5/47.**G.**
Don. 24/10-7/12/49.**G.**
Don. 18/12/50-16/1/51.**C/L.**
Don. 24/3-30/4/52.**G.**
Don. 26/8-5/10/54.**G.**
Don. 6/1-7/2/58.**G.**
Don. 27/2-13/4/61.**G.**
Don. 1/5-6/6/61.**C/L.**

BOILERS:
D1693.
 7423 *(ex4000)* 1/5/31.
 8600 *(ex1141)* 13/2/37.
 8800 *(ex1976)* 12/5/47.

8741 *(ex1818)* 7/12/49.
Renumbered 27136 16/1/51.
27227 *(ex61867)* 30/4/52.
24903 *(ex61812)* 7/2/58.

SHEDS:
Ardsley.
New England 23/1/25.
Colwick 25/10/41.
New England 25/6/45.
Gorton 23/1/49.
London Mid.Reg. 29/5/49.
Gorton 12/6/49.
Woodford 18/7/59.

RENUMBERED:
1832 26/5/46.
61832 7/12/49.

CONDEMNED:
29/10/62.
Cut up at Doncaster.

118

Darlington.

To traffic 22/12/24.

REPAIRS:
Don. 15/2-16/4/26.**L.**
Don. 6/12/26-4/3/27.**G.**
Don. 15/11/28-12/1/29.**G.**
Don. 29/5-8/8/30.**G.**
Don. 29/4-10/6/32.**G.**
Don. 11/4-9/5/33.**L.**
Don. 2/10-6/11/33.**H.**

Mod.valve gear.
Don. 30/4-31/5/35.**G.**
Don. 2/12/36-9/1/37.**H.**
Don. 8-31/8/38.**H.**
Don. 6/7-10/8/40.**G.**
Don. 10/10-14/11/42.**G.**
Don. 4/11/44-20/1/45.**G.**
Don. 19/11/46-8/2/47.**G.**
Don. 9/3-11/4/49.**G.**
Don. 4/4-18/5/51.**G.**
Don. 10/7-12/8/53.**G.**
Don. 12/5-30/6/55.**G.**
Don. 8/4-17/5/57.**G.**
Don. 8-22/10/57.**C/L.**
Don. 18/4-16/5/59.**G.**
Don. 17-24/12/59.**N/C.**

BOILERS:
D1695.
 7990 *(new)* 12/1/29.
D1735 *(ex170)* 6/11/33.
AW83 *(ex33)* 20/1/45.
RS4080 *(ex1972)* 11/4/49.
27164 *(ex61958)* 18/5/51.
27176 *(ex61886)* 12/8/53.
27172 *(ex61801)* 30/6/55.
27159 *(ex61975)* 17/5/57.
24935 *(new)* 16/5/59.

SHEDS:
Ardsley.
New England 12/1/25.
Doncaster 3/5/26.
New England 23/8/35.
March 12/6/49.
Norwich 10/10/49.
Colwick 3/1/50.
March 11/6/50.

Colwick 27/8/50.

RENUMBERED:
1833 19/5/46.
61833 11/4/49.

CONDEMNED:
20/9/61.
Cut up at Doncaster.

120

Darlington.

To traffic 30/12/24.

REPAIRS:
Don. 3/2-20/5/27.**G.**
Don. 1/1-8/3/29.**G.**
Don. 13/10-27/12/30.**G.** *Mod.valve gear.*
Don. 21/8-9/11/32.**G.**
Don. 6/2-6/4/33.**G.**
Don. 13/7-30/8/34.**G.**
Don. 21/12/35-28/1/36.**G.**
Don. 16/4-19/6/37.**G.**
Don. 18/2-1/4/39.**G.**
Don. 26/4-31/5/41.**G.**
Don. 29/1-19/2/44.**G.**
Don. 4/5-8/6/46.**G.**
Don. 10/3-22/4/48.**G.**
Don. 28/8-12/10/50.**G.**
Don. 23/10-19/11/52.**G.**
Don. 27/8-13/10/54.**G.**
Don. 29/4-1/6/57.**G.**
Don. 8/10-6/11/59.**G.**
Don. 2-21/5/60.**C/L.**

In June 1929 Doncaster was instructed to alter the valve gear on another five, and in August 1930 it was decided to alter all the others. When 140 was altered in June 1931, it still retained the Ashcroft cut-off control gear fitted in February 1928.

BOILERS:
D1701.
D1663 *(ex69)* 27/12/30.
D1785 *(ex109)* 31/5/41.
 8740 *(ex92)* 8/6/46.
27106 *(ex61967)* 12/10/50.
27252 *(ex61806)* 19/11/52.
27145 *(ex61875)* 13/10/54.
27161 *(ex61839)* 1/6/57.
27127 *(ex61814)* 6/11/59.

SHEDS:
Ardsley.
New England 22/1/25.
Colwick 16/9/40.
Annesley 13/10/40.
Sheffield 3/5/43.
New England 25/6/45.
March 12/6/49.
Stratford 17/10/49.
Parkeston 9/3/58.
Cambridge 10/8/58.
March 8/10/61.

RENUMBERED:
 1834 7/6/46.
61834 22/4/48.

CONDEMNED:
15/5/62.
Cut up at Doncaster.

121

Darlington.

To traffic 9/1/25.

REPAIRS:
Don. 17/6-4/7/25.**L.**
Don. 1-10/10/25.**L.**
Don. 3/3-3/4/26.**L.**
Don. 15/6-26/8/27.**G.**
Don. 21/8-9/10/29.**G.**
Don. 17/5-1/8/31.**G.**
Don. 13/2-27/4/33.**G.**

 Mod.valve gear.
Don. 20/10-8/12/34.**G.**
Don. 25/3-4/5/36.**G.**
Don. 31/12/37-31/1/38.**G.**
Don. 23/12/39-3/2/40.**G.**
Don. 29/3-10/5/41.**G.**
Don. 25/7-15/8/42.**G.**
Don. 15/5-19/6/43.**G.**
Don. 18/3-20/5/44.**G.**
Don. 13/10-24/11/45.**G.**
Don. 20/10-5/12/47.**G.**
Don. 27/11/49-6/1/50.**G.**
Don. 8/1-7/2/52.**G.**
Don. 26/9-29/10/54.**G.**
Don. 13/2-9/3/56.**C/L.**
Don. 28/11/56-5/1/57.**G.**
Don. 12-25/4/58.**C/L.**
Don. 12/11-23/12/58.**G.**
Don. 20/2-23/3/61.**G.**
Don. 12-18/8/61.**N/C.**

BOILERS:
D1703.
D1722 *(ex153)* 27/4/33.
8D/687 *(ex113)* 31/1/38.
D1726 *(ex75)* 15/8/42.
 8925 *(ex2425)* 20/5/44.
2799 *(ex1930)* 6/1/50.
27211 *(ex61847)* 7/2/52.
27252 *(ex61834)* 29/10/54.
27293 *(ex61803)* 5/1/57.
27285 *(ex61901)* 23/12/58.
27233 *(ex61862)* 23/3/61.
Renumbered SB4520.

SHEDS:
Ardsley.
Doncaster 20/2/25.
New England 3/5/26.
Colwick 22/6/40.
Annesley 13/10/40.
Sheffield 20/6/43.
New England 25/6/45.
March 16/6/46.
New England 19/10/46.
March 16/2/47.
Norwich 7/10/48.

March 17/12/48.
Stratford 17/10/49.
March 27/9/53.
Lincoln 4/12/60.
Colwick 11/12/60.
Immingham 17/9/61.
New England 15/4/62.

RENUMBERED:
 1835 2/6/46.
61835 6/1/50.

CONDEMNED:
16/9/63.
Cut up at Doncaster.

125

Darlington.

To traffic 10/1/25.

REPAIRS:
Don. 7/2-20/5/27.**G.**
Don. 25/1-21/3/29.**G.**
Don. 2/3-15/4/31.**G.** *Mod.valve gear.*
Don. 13/10-15/11/32.**G.**
Don. 11/6-3/8/34.**G.**
Don. 12/11-18/12/35.**G.**
Don. 21/4-24/5/37.**G.**
Don. 20/1-25/2/39.**G.**
Don. 21-23/6/40.**N/C.**
Don. 24/8-5/10/40.**G.**
Don. 24/10-28/11/42.**G.**
Don. 30/9-21/10/44.**G.**
Don. 31/3-21/4/45.**L.**
Don. 22/6-27/7/46.**G.**
Don. 8/8-23/9/48.**G.**
Don. 21-30/9/49.**C/L.**
Don. 5/10-10/11/50.**G.**
Don. 25/7-28/8/52.**G.**
Don. 6/7-19/8/54.**G.**
Don. 22/9-15/10/55.**C/H.**
Don. 12/6-25/7/56.**G.**
Don. 2/5-6/6/58.**G.**
Don. 1/2/60.*Not repaired.*

BOILERS:
D1706.
D1789 *(ex207)* 3/8/34.
8886 *(ex153)* 21/10/44.
27116 *(ex1850)* 10/11/50.
27104 *(ex1902)* 28/8/52.
27203 *(ex61981)* 19/8/54.
27100 *(ex61838)* 25/7/56.
24907 *(ex61929)* 6/6/58.

SHEDS:
Ardsley.
New England 5/2/25.
Woodford 30/3/43.
Immingham 3/5/43.
Lincoln 13/6/43.
Immingham 22/7/43.
Mexborough 1/2/59.
Doncaster 14/6/59.

RENUMBERED:
 1836 26/5/46.
61836 23/9/48.

CONDEMNED:
8/2/60.
Cut up at Doncaster.

126

Darlington.

To traffic 19/1/25.

REPAIRS:
Don. 2-21/10/25.**L.**
Don. 16/6-20/8/26.**L.**
Don. 15/5-10/8/27.**G.**
Don. 23/2-17/4/29.**G.**
Don. 1/10-8/11/30.**G.**
Don. 14/6-16/7/32.**G.** *Mod.valve gear.*
Don. 9/8-25/9/33.**G.**
Don. 7/12/34-10/1/35.**G.**
Don. 23/4-27/5/36.**H.**
Don. 17/3-28/4/37.**H.**

WORKS CODES:- Cow - Cowlairs. Dar - Darlington. Don - Doncaster. Ghd - Gateshead. Gor - Gorton. Inv - Inverurie. Str - Stratford.
REPAIR CODES:- **C/H** - Casual Heavy. **C/L** - Casual Light. **G** - General. **H** - Heavy. **H/I** - Heavy Intermediate. **L** - Light. **L/I** - Light Intermediate. **N/C** - Non-Classified.

Don. 1-22/10/38.**L.**
Don. 3/6-8/7/39.**G.**
Don. 20/4-8/6/40.**G.**
Don. 25/7-22/8/42.**G.**
Don. 12/2-11/3/44.**G.**
Don. 13/5-3/6/44.**L.**
Don. 21/4-2/6/45.**G.**
Don. 25/11-8/12/45.**L.**
Don. 22/1-1/3/47.**G.**
Don. 18/6-5/8/49.**G.**
Don. 12/6-18/7/51.**G.**
Don. 14/3-17/4/53.**G.**
Don. 3/8-15/9/54.**G.**
Don. 26/5-13/7/55.**C/H.**
Don. 21/2-27/3/57.**G.**
Don. 29/5-17/7/59.**G.**
Don. 29/12/59-7/1/60.**C/L.**

BOILERS:
D1709.
D1778 *(ex207)* 8/11/30.
D1723 *(ex156)* 10/1/35.
 3218 *(new)* 22/8/42.
27177 *(ex61808)* 18/7/51.
27132 *(ex61973)* 17/4/53.
27208 *(ex61929)* 15/9/54.
24919 *(new)* 27/3/57.
27159 *(ex61833)* 17/7/59.

SHEDS:
Ardsley.
Doncaster 26/1/25.
New England 12/6/31.
Woodford 25/3/43.
Immingham 3/5/43.
Lincoln 13/6/43.
Immingham 14/11/43.
Lincoln 17/6/45.
Immingham 23/9/45.
Colwick 5/1/58.

RENUMBERED:
 1837 23/6/46.
61837 5/8/49.

CONDEMNED:
27/4/62.
Cut up at Doncaster.

127

Darlington.

To traffic 23/1/25.

REPAIRS:
Don. 10/2-4/6/27.**G.**
Don. 13/2-4/4/29.**G.**
Don. 20/8-9/10/30.**G.**
Don. 4/7-12/8/32.**G.**
Don. 23/5-5/7/33.**H.** *Mod.valve gear.*
Don. 16/11-19/12/34.**G.**
Don. 26/8-29/9/36.**H.**
Don. 16/6-27/8/38.**H.**
Don. 2-9/3/40.**L.**
Don. 15/6-6/7/40.**G.**
Don. 14-28/6/41.**L.**
Don. 20/6-25/7/42.**G.**
Don. 17/7-14/8/43.**L.**
Don. 28/4-9/6/45.**G.**
Don. 27/7-10/8/46.**L.**
Don. 29/6-15/8/47.**G.**
Don. 10/7-1/9/49.**G.**
Don. 2/4-4/5/51.**G.**
Don. 7/1-6/2/53.**G.**
Don. 15/7-27/8/54.**G.**
Don. 29/8-4/10/55.**C/H.**
Don. 22/5-23/6/56.**G.**
Don. 2-8/2/57.**C/L.**
Don. 16/4-15/5/58.**G.**
Don. 10/3/60.*Not repaired.*

BOILERS:
D1710.
 7422 *(ex4002)* 12/8/32.
D1690 *(ex4002)* 27/8/38.
 2845 *(ex1318)* 15/8/47.
 9280 *(ex61892)* 1/9/49.
27161 *(ex61944)* 4/5/51.
27256 *(ex61894)* 6/2/53.
27100 *(ex61806)* 27/8/54.
27255 *(ex61830)* 23/6/56.
24913 *(ex61948)* 15/5/58.

SHEDS:
Ardsley.
New England 9/2/25.

Woodford 24/3/43.
Immingham 3/5/43.
Colwick 17/2/57.
Woodford 16/6/57.

RENUMBERED:
 1838 16/6/46.
61838 1/9/49.

CONDEMNED:
21/3/60.
Cut up at Doncaster.

134

Darlington.

To traffic 28/1/25.

REPAIRS:
Don. 26/11/25-9/1/26.**L.**
Don. 28/11/26-12/2/27.**G.**
Don. 18/9-3/11/27.**L.**
Don. 30/8-20/10/28.**G.** *Mod.valve gear.*
Don. 7/5-26/6/30.**G.**
Don. 2-29/10/30.**L.**
Don. 26/4-25/6/32.**G.**
Don. 21/12/33-5/2/34.**G.**
Don. 26/8-4/10/35.**G.**
Don. 2-4/8/37.**L.**
Don. 21/8-25/9/37.**H.**.
Don. 22/11-10/12/37.**H**
Don. 14-24/2/38.**L.** *Heater conn.front.*
Don. 25/3-6/5/39.**G.**
Don. 25/4-30/5/42.**G.**
Don. 5-12/2/44.**L.**
Don. 18/11-44-13/1/45.**G.**
Don. 29/12/47-5/3/48.**G.**
Gor. 7/1/50.*Weigh.*
Don. 9/5-15/6/50.**G.**
Don. 5-29/5/52.**G.**
Don. 6/1-15/2/54.**G.**
Don. 18/5-18/6/54.**C/L.**
Don. 23/5-13/7/55.**G.**
Don. 3/4-10/5/57.**G.**

Don. 5/8-4/9/59.**G.**

BOILERS:
D1712.
 8070 *(new)* 20/10/28.
D1778 *(ex126)* 4/10/35.
 8126 *(ex1307)* 13/1/45.
RS4075 *(ex1987)* 5/3/48.
 8910 *(ex1802)* 15/6/50.
27236 *(ex61957)* 29/5/52.
27283 *(new)* 15/2/54.
27161 *(ex61828)* 13/7/55.
27296 *(ex61825)* 10/5/57.
27190 *(ex61986)* 4/9/59.

SHEDS:
Ardsley.
Doncaster 2/3/25.
New England 20/10/28.
Kings Cross 26/6/30.
Gorton 4/10/35.
Trafford Park 22/5/39.
Gorton 11/10/40.
Woodford 30/10/43.
Gorton 19/6/49.
Immingham 27/5/51.
Mexborough 1/2/59.
Doncaster 14/6/59.

RENUMBERED:
 1839 5/1/47.
E1839 5/3/48.
61839 7/1/50.

CONDEMNED:
9/1/62.
Cut up at Doncaster.

135

Darlington.

To traffic 4/2/25.

REPAIRS:
Don. 1/10-1/12/27.**G.**
Don. 9/3-16/5/29.**G.**

Beginning with 1302, new in July 1934, it was standard to fit five of the joints in the valve gear with Ransome & Marles roller bearings. From when the first engine was new, all had been fitted with Skefko ball bearings in their eccentric cranks. 2939 is included (not for those details) **but to show** Darlington's style for official photographs. Despite front lamps being those for a Royal train, they had no significance, but were normally fitted for official photos. The painting was grey lined in white, with numbers and letters in white, back shaded in black. 2939 when new, did not have either front footsteps, or cab sight screens fitted, but extra lamp iron was omitted.

Don. 1/11/30-19/1/31.**G.** *Mod.valve gear.*
Don. 7/5-10/8/32.**G.**
Don. 29/12/33-19/2/34.**G.**
Don. 4/7-10/8/35.**G.**
Don. 7/12/36-30/1/37.**G.**
Don. 16/2-2/4/37.**L.**
Don. 3/6-8/7/39.**G.**
Don. 4-11/5/40.**L.**
Don. 16/5-13/6/42.**G.**
Don. 17/10-14/11/42.**L.**
Don. 19/8-23/9/44.**G.**
Don. 3/12/46-11/1/47.**G.**
Don. 3/2-11/3/49.**G.**
Don. 23/2-30/3/51.**G.**
Don. 14/5-18/6/53.**G.**
Don. 3/8-13/9/55. **G.**
Don. 1-23/5/56.**C/L.**
Don. 7/2-7/3/58.**G.**
Don. 18/5-29/9/60.**G.**
Don. 30/12/60-12/1/61.**C/L.**

BOILERS:
D1713.
D1712 *(ex159)* 10/8/32.
D1703 *(ex204)* 13/6/42.
 8928 *(ex1817)* 11/1/47.
27152 *(ex61828)* 30/3/51.
27130 *(ex61820)* 18/6/53.
27204 *(ex61853)* 7/3/58.
27305 *(Cow and 61991)* 29/9/60.

SHEDS:
Ardsley.
Doncaster 2/3/25.
Kings Cross 5/11/25.
Copley Hill 9/9/35.
Ardsley 14/9/35.
Copley Hill 12/10/35.
Ardsley 9/10/37.
Copley Hill 31/7/39.
Ardsley 24/8/41.
Copley Hill 26/7/42.
Doncaster 15/2/43.
New England 27/6/45.
Stratford 9/4/50.
Parkeston 14/12/58.
March 8/2/59.

RENUMBERED:
 1840 17/10/46.
61840 11/3/49.

CONDEMNED:
16/9/62.
Cut up at Doncaster.

140

Darlington.

To traffic 7/2/25.

REPAIRS:
Don. 13/12/27-14/3/28.**G.** *Ashcroft Cut-off control.*
Don. 8/10-9/11/29.**G.**
Don. 14/5-30/6/31.**G.** *Mod.valve gear.*
Don. 27/1-3/3/33.**G.**
Don. 15/8-21/9/34.**G.**
Don. 2-29/7/36.**G.**
Don. 22/2-19/3/38.**G.**
Don. 5/8-16/9/39.**G.**
Don. 26/4-31/5/41.**G.**
Don. 30/1-6/3/43.**G.**
Don. 24/3-9/6/45.**G.**
Don. 9-30/3/46.**L.**
Don. 19/10-2/11/46.**L.**
Don. 17/6-1/8/47.**G.**
Don. 5/8-28/9/49.**G.**
Don. 4/3-2/4/52.**G.**
Don. 11/5-9/6/54.**G.**
Don. 21/12/55-20/1/56.**G.**
Don. 5/2-6/3/58.**G.**
Don. 12/12/59-15/1/60.**G.**

BOILERS:
D1714.
D1668 *(ex141)* 3/3/33.
D1772 *(ex1154)* 19/3/38.
 8914 *(ex2439)* 6/3/43.
8136A *(ex46)* 9/6/45.
 3217 *(ex61803)* 28/9/49.

27221 *(ex61923)* 2/4/52.
27230 *(ex61853)* 9/6/54.
27178 *(ex61819)* 20/1/56.
27154 *(ex61914)* 6/3/58.
24920 *(ex61856)* 15/1/60.

SHEDS:
Ardsley.
Kings Cross 19/2/25.
Annesley 30/9/39.
Colwick 1/3/40.
New England 25/6/45.
March 16/6/46.
New England 16/10/46.
March 20/9/53.
Woodford 16/9/56.

RENUMBERED:
 1841 30/3/46.
61841 28/9/49.

CONDEMNED:
27/3/62.
Cut up at Doncaster.

141

Darlington.

To traffic 7/2/25.

No.4000 has just passed under Holgate Bridge at York and is going south with one of the 12-coach sets of green-and-cream painted excursion coaches sometime in 1938. It shows that the first ten of the class were still to the generous GNR gauge as to heights of chimney and cab roof. War portents then indicated the wisdom of bringing those ten within the Composite Load Gauge to give them wider operational scope.

REPAIRS:
Don. 13-24/10/25.**L.**
Don. 1-20/3/26.**L.**
Don. 6/7-23/10/26.**G.**
Don. 19/4-25/7/28.**G.**
Don. 1/5-21/6/30.**G.**
Don. 4-27/2/31.**G.** *Alt.to screw reverse.*
Don. 18/7-20/9/32.**G.**
Don. 16/4-18/5/34.**G.** *Mod.valve gear.*
Don. 24/5-29/6/35.**G.**
Don. 15/10-7/11/36.**G.**
Don. 21/6-23/9/38.**G.**
Don. 23-30/3/40.**L.**
Don. 6/7-17/8/40.**G.**
Don. 1-29/8/42.**G.**
Don. 27/11/43-1/1/44.**G.**
Don. 23/6-7/7/45.**L.**
Don. 1-22/9/45.**L.**
Don. 1/6-3/8/46.**G.**
Don. 21-28/9/46.**L.**
Don. 12/9-2/11/48.**G.**
Don. 21/9-20/10/50.**G.**
Don. 10-22/3/51.**C/L.**
Don. 19/9-18/10/51.**C/L.**
Don. 29/4-29/5/52.**G.**
Don. 17/2-24/3/54.**G.**
Don. 8-16/12/54.**C/L.**
Don. 21/3-26/4/56.**G.**
Don. 12-22/1/57.**C/L.**
Don. 17/12/57-24/1/58.**G.**
Don. 29/9-28/10/59.**G.**
Don. 29/12/59-5/1/60.**C/L.**

BOILERS:
D1715.
D1668 *(ex80)* 21/6/30.
D1727 *(ex69)* 20/9/32.
D1766 *(ex4004)* 7/11/36.
D1779 *(ex159)* 23/9/38.
 8131 *(ex1386)* 17/8/40.
 8739 *(ex229)* 29/8/42.
C1824 *(ex33)* 3/8/46.
27109 *(ex61861)* 20/10/50.
27235 *(ex61853)* 29/5/52.
27209 *(ex61922)* 24/3/54.
27205 *(ex61844)* 26/4/56.
27275 *(ex61877)* 24/1/58.
27325 *(ex spare and 61988)* 28/10/59.

SHEDS:
Ardsley.
Doncaster 18/2/25.
New England 12/6/31.
Woodford 24/3/43.
Immingham 3/5/43.
March 27/9/53.
Woodford 16/9/56.

RENUMBERED:
1842 1/8/46.
61842 2/11/48.

CONDEMNED:
21/8/61.
Cut up at Doncaster.

143

Darlington.

To traffic 13/2/25.

REPAIRS:
Don. 20/7-5/10/27.**G.**
Don. 15/12/28-6/2/29.**G.**
Don. 14/2-22/3/30.**G.** *Mod.valve gear.*
Don. 25/9-5/11/31.**G.**
Don. 17/8-2/10/33.**G.**
Don. 2-26/1/35.**G.**
Don. 2/7-30/8/35.**L.**
Don. 17/1-15/2/36.**H.**
Don. 12/7-7/8/37.**G.**
Don. 20/1-5/2/38.**H.**
Don. 23/9-11/11/39.**G.**
Don. 20/4-18/5/40.**L.**
Don. 16/8-20/9/41.**G.**
Don. 11/12/43-15/1/44.**G.**
Don. 1/6-13/7/46.**G.**
Don. 6/2-2/3/48.**G.**
Don. 7-23/9/48.**L.**
Don. 19/4-26/5/50.**G.**
Don. 11/6-2/7/52.**G.**
Don. 10/2-18/3/53.G.
Don. 27/7-31/8/54.**G.**
Don. 10/4-19/5/56.**G.**
Don. 12-23/3/57.**G.**
Don. 14/8-23/9/58.**G.**
Don. 2/3-14/4/61.**G.**

BOILERS:
D1716.
D1682 *(ex112)* 6/2/29.
 7428 *(ex4004)* 5/11/31.
D1687 *(ex111)* 15/2/36.
 9379 *(new)* 15/1/44.
 8925 *(ex1835)* 26/5/50.
27245 *(ex61825)* 2/7/52.
27209 *(ex61842)* 19/5/56.
27202 *(ex61867)* 23/9/58.
27285 *(ex61835)* 14/4/61.

SHEDS:
Doncaster.
Kings Cross 30/10/25.
Doncaster 14/10/37.
Copley Hill 6/8/44.
New England 25/6/45.
March 20/9/53.
Woodford 16/9/56.

RENUMBERED:
1843 20/12/46.
E1843 12/3/48.
61843 26/5/50.

CONDEMNED:
29/10/62.
Cut up at Doncaster.

146

Darlington.

To traffic 26/2/25.

REPAIRS:
Don. 13/11-26/12/25.**L.**
Don. 3/4-29/5/26.**L.**
Don. 12/5-12/8/27.**G.**
Don. 30/4-11/6/29.**G.**
Don. 18/9-28/10/30.**G.**
Don. 15/6-22/7/32.**G.** *Mod.valve gear.*
Don. 19/1-7/2/33.**L.**
Don. 13/12/33-20/1/34.**G.**
Don. 25/9-5/11/35.**G.**
Don. 29/1-27/2/37.**G.**
Don. 5-26/11/38.**L.**
Don. 11/2-8/4/39.**G.**
Don. 18/1-15/2/41.**G.**
Don. 13/6-15/7/42.**L/I.**
Don. 21/8-18/9/43.**G.**
Don. 6/7-17/8/46.**G.**
Don. 21/7-2/8/47.**L.**
Don. 5-18/12/47.**L.**
Don. 28/1-20/2/48.**L.**
Don. 9/11-10/12/48.**G.**
Don. 25/7-1/9/50.**G.**
Don. 30/4-29/5/52.**G.**
Don. 20/1-23/2/54.**G.**
Don. 20/9-14/10/54.**C/L.**
Don. 16/2-22/3/56.**G.**
Don. 31/1-27/2/58.**G.**
Don. 29/1-20/2/59.**C/L.**
Don. 18/11-18/12/59.**G.**
Don. 18/5/61.*Not repaired.*

BOILERS:
D1720.
D1772 *(ex204)* 28/10/30.
D1672 *(ex4006)* 5/11/35.
D1646 *(ex2465)* 18/9/43.
 9554 *(new)* 17/8/46.
 9378 *(ex61846)* 1/9/50.
27101 *(ex61804)* 29/5/52.
27205 *(ex61847)* 23/2/54.
24911 *(new)* 22/3/56.
27227 *(ex61832)* 27/2/58.
27270 *(ex61918)* 18/12/59.

SHEDS:
Copley Hill.
Doncaster 21/8/28.
Copley Hill 26/9/29.
Doncaster 10/3/30.
New England 20/11/35.
Doncaster 17/6/36.
Copley Hill 27/2/44.
New England 26/11/44.
March 11/6/50.
Lowestoft 8/10/50.
March 10/12/50.
Hull Dairycoates 2/9/51.
Heaton 23/9/56.
Tweedmouth 11/9/60.
Heaton 4/12/60.
Thornaby 18/12/60.

RENUMBERED:
1844 14/8/46.
E1844 20/2/48.
61844 10/12/48.

CONDEMNED:
5/6/61.
Cut up at Doncaster.

153

Darlington.

To traffic 21/2/25.

REPAIRS:
Don. 2-20/3/26.**L.**
Don. 6/6-6/9/27.**G.**
Don. 8/5-5/7/29.**G.**
Don. 1/2-12/5/31.**G.**
Don. 29/9-24/11/32.**G.** *Mod.valve gear.*
Don. 19/3-9/6/34.**G.**
Don. 22/8-11/10/35.**G.**
Don. 4-30/10/37.**G.**
Gor. 20-23/4/38.**N/C.** *Front heater conn.*
Gor. 8-9/8/38.**N/C.** *Fluid container fitted.*
Don. 18/11/39-6/1/40.**G.**
Don. 28/2-11/4/42.**G.**
Don. 11/3-1/4/44.**G.**
Don. 24/11-22/12/45.**G.**
Don. 30/11/47-4/2/48.**L.**
Don. 7/11-20/12/48.**G.**
Don. 8/11-13/12/50.**G.**
Don. 21/9-16/10/51.**C/L.**
Don. 17/7-21/8/52.**G.**
Don. 18/2-25/3/54.**C/L.**
Don. 23/10-25/11/54.**G.**
Don. 16/8-5/10/56.**G.**
Don. 25/7-6/9/58.**G.**
Don. 7/7-11/8/60.**G.**
Don. 25/5-1/6/61.**N/C.**

BOILERS:
D1722.
 7424 *(ex4003)* 24/11/32.
 8886 *(new)* 6/1/40.
D1772 *(ex140)* 1/4/44.
 8123 *(ex1332)* 22/12/45.
 9991 *(new)* 20/12/48.
27126 *(ex61830)* 13/12/50.
27108 *(ex61807)* 21/8/52.
27289 *(new)* 25/11/54.
27203 *(ex61836)* 5/10/56.
27268 *(ex61952)* 6/9/58.
27157 *(ex61910)* 11/8/60.

SHEDS:
Ardsley.
Doncaster 29/6/25.
New England 19/4/28.
Kings Cross 25/10/30.
Gorton 11/10/35.
Liverpool 8/1/38.
Gorton 9/2/38.

WORKS CODES:- Cow - Cowlairs. Dar - Darlington. Don - Doncaster. Ghd - Gateshead. Gor - Gorton. Inv - Inverurie. Str - Stratford.
REPAIR CODES:- **C/H** - Casual Heavy. **C/L** - Casual Light. **G** - General. **H** - Heavy. **H/I** - Heavy Intermediate. **L** - Light. **L/I** - Light Intermediate. **N/C** - Non-Classified.

29

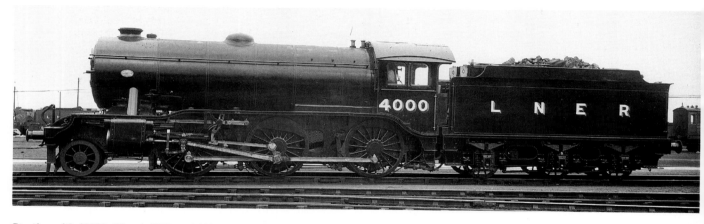

Starting with 4008 in March 1939, and 4000 in June, all the GNR built engines were fitted with reduced boiler mountings to bring the height from rail to 13 feet maximum. The opportunity was also taken to provide them with the improved double window cab, and 4004's alteration in November 1940 completed that transformation. *L.N.E.R.*

Stratford 22/9/38.
Immingham 23/11/40.
Lincoln 29/3/53.
March 27/9/53.
Norwich 28/6/59.
March 26/7/59.
Colwick 18/12/60.
Lincoln 26/3/61.

RENUMBERED:
  1845 1/12/46.
  E1845 4/2/48.
  61845 20/12/48.

CONDEMNED:
16/9/62.
Cut up at Doncaster.

156

Darlington.

To traffic 24/2/25.

REPAIRS:
Don. 26/8-17/9/25.**L.**
Don. 25/6-23/9/27.**G.**
Don. 9/7-15/8/29.**G.**
Don. 16/7-14/8/30.**H.**
Don. 11/5-30/6/32.**G.** *Mod.valve gear.*
Don. 4/1-9/2/34.**G.**
Don. 7/5-7/6/35.**G.**
Don. 15/12/36-15/1/37.**H.**
Don. 3-31/12/38.**G.**
Don. 25/5-27/7/40.**L.**
Don. 14/12/40-25/1/41.**G.**
Don. 22/3-19/4/41.**L.**
Don. 7/2-11/4/42.**G.**
Don. 2-23/10/43.**G.**
Don. 2/2-2/3/46.**G.**
Don. 9-21/12/46.**L.**
Don. 20/2-22/3/48.**G.**
Don. 13-21/1/49.**L.**
Don. 24/1-31/3/50.**G.**
Don. 15/4-16/5/52.**G.**
Don. 24/10-6/11/52.**L.**
Don. 1-7/7/53.**L.**

Don. 25/1-11/2/54.**C/L.**
Don. 15/6-23/7/54.**G.**
Don. 3/5-16/6/56.**G.**
Don. 21/9-19/10/56.**C/L.**
Don. 4/12/58-15/1/59.**G.**
Don. 23-27/5/60.**N/C.**
Don. 9/6-27/7/61.**G.**

BOILERS:
D1723.
D1666 *(ex73)* 9/2/34.
  9378 *(new)* 23/10/43.
  8913 *(ex1847)* 31/3/50.
27136 *(ex1832)* 16/5/52.
27102 *(ex61902)* 23/7/54.
24912 *(new)* 16/6/56.
27293 *(ex61835)* 15/1/59.
27269 *(ex61913)* 27/7/61.

SHEDS:
Doncaster.
Kings Cross 3/11/25.
New England 14/8/30.
Doncaster 25/7/40.
March 21/7/41.
Stratford 16/5/47.
March 23/5/47.
Lowestoft 6/10/48.
Norwich 4/12/48.
March 16/12/48.
Hull Dairycoates 2/9/51.

RENUMBERED:
  1846 22/10/46.
  61846 22/3/48.

CONDEMNED:
17/12/62.
Cut up at Doncaster.

158

Darlington.

To traffic 27/2/25.

REPAIRS:
Don. 14-29/8/25.**L.**
Don. 16/10/27-19/1/28.**G.**

Don. 11/1-23/2/29.**G.**
Don. 30/6-8/8/30.**G.**
Don. 17/7-31/8/31.**H.** *Mod.valve gear.*
Don. 10/8-18/9/33.**G.**
Don. 20/3-4/5/35.**G.**
Don. 28/9-24/10/36.**G.**
Don. 12/10-5/11/38.**G.**
Don. 18/11-30/12/39.**G.**
Don. 18/4-23/5/42.**G.**
Don. 17/6-15/7/44.**G.**
Don. 17/8-21/9/46.**G.**
Don. 6/11-10/12/47.**G.**
Don. 27/11-31/12/48.**G.**
Don. 20/12/49-26/1/50.**G.**
Don. 12/12/51-15/1/52.**G.**
Don. 31/12/53-29/1/54.**G.**
Don. 18-24/2/54.**N/C.**
Don. 29/11/55-5/1/56.**G.**
Don. 29/10-11/12/58.**G.**
Don. 8/12/60-18/1/61.**G.**

BOILERS:
D1726.
D1714 *(ex140)* 18/9/33.
D1776 *(ex69)* 30/12/39.
  8913 *(ex2766)* 21/9/46.
6D/687 *(ex1927)* 26/1/50.
27205 *(ex61837)* 15/1/52.
27189 *(ex61915)* 29/1/54.
24906 *(new)* 5/1/56.
27135 *(ex61810)* 11/12/58.
27255 *(ex61960)* 18/1/61.

SHEDS:
Doncaster.
Kings Cross 2/11/25.
March 29/6/38.
Norwich 9/10/48.
March 16/12/48.
Hull Dairycoates 2/9/51.

RENUMBERED:
  1847 15/12/46.
  61847 31/12/48.

CONDEMNED:
10/12/62.
Cut up at Doncaster.

159

Darlington.

To traffic 2/3/25.

REPAIRS:
Don. 14-29/8/25.**L.**
Don. 22/11/26-18/2/27.**G.**
Don. 23/10-15/12/28.**G.**
Don. 7/6-6/7/29.**H.**
Don. 26/2-3/4/30.**H.**
Don. 22/9-28/10/31.**G.** *Mod.valve gear.*
Don. 14/6-18/7/33.**G.**
Don. 22/3-27/4/35.**G.**
Don. 22/3-22/4/37.**G.**
Gor. 17-21/3/38.**N/C.** *Front heater conn.*
Don. 11/7-3/8/38.**H.**
Don. 13/5-8/7/39.**L.**
Don. 1-29/3/41.**G.**
Don. 13/12/41-28/3/42.**G.**
Don. 23/10-20/11/43.**G.**
Don. 26/2-11/3/44.**H.**
Don. 20/5-22/7/44.**G.**
Don. 10/4-25/5/46.**G.**
Don. 10/2-17/3/48.**G.**
Don. 21/7-18/8/49.**C/H.**
Don. 13-21/9/49.**N/C.**
Don. 13/2-21/3/51.**G.**
Don. 17/10-28/11/52.**H/I.**
Don. 13/4-12/5/55.**G.**
Don. 18-21/6/57.**C/L.**
Don. 5/3-11/4/58.**G.**
Don. 23/9-1/10/59.**N/C.**
Don. 14/10-18/11/60.**G.**

BOILERS:
D1727.
D1712 *(ex134)* 15/12/28.
D1779 *(ex228)* 28/10/31.
D1766 *(ex141)* 3/8/38.
  9382 *(new)* 11/3/44.
27151 *(ex61978)* 21/3/51.
27251 *(ex61870)* 12/5/55.
27193 *(ex61917)* 11/4/58.
24933 *(ex61805)* 18/11/60.

Following the Munich political crisis at the end of September 1938, air raid precautions deemed it prudent to diminish glare when a firebox door had to be opened. Ex-works on 8th October 1938, No.3816 had been fitted with tarpaulin screen from rear edge of cab roof to front of tender, and that device was universal throughout the 1939-45 war. *L.N.E.R.*

SHEDS:
Ardsley.
Doncaster 23/3/25.
Annesley 10/10/31.
Gorton 30/10/35.
Colwick 5/4/38.
Annesley 16/7/41.
Sheffield 3/5/43.
New England 25/6/45.
Gorton 23/1/49.
Sheffield 13/6/54.
Lincoln 26/9/54.

RENUMBERED:
1848 25/5/46.
61848 17/3/48.

CONDEMNED:
16/9/62.
Cut up at Doncaster.

163

Darlington.

To traffic 7/3/25.

REPAIRS:
Don. 18/6-24/9/27.**G.**
Don. 26/7-6/9/28.**G.**
Don. 16/2-12/4/30.**G.**
Don. 9/1-19/3/32.**G.** *Mod.valve gear.*
Don. 6/10-1/12/33.**G.**
Don. 5/4-23/5/35.**G.**
Don. 6/10-13/11/36.**G.**
Don. 16/8-23/9/38.**G.**
Don. 18/5-29/6/40.**G.**
Don. 18/1-15/2/41.**G.**
Don. 25/4/41.**L.**
Don. 21/6-12/7/41.**L.** *Front heater conn.*
Don. 27/3-1/5/43.**G.**
Don. 22/7-5/8/44.**L.**

Don. 30/12/44-3/3/45.**G.**
Don. 10-17/11/45.**L.**
Don. 11/5-6/7/46.**G.**
Don. 21-28/9/46.**L.**
Don. 11/3-14/4/47.**L.**
Don. 19/7-26/8/48.**G.**
Don. 2/11-8/12/50.**G.**
Don. 17/12/51-29/1/52.**C/L.**
Don. 7/1-6/2/53.**G.**
Str. 16-24/11/54.**N/C.**
Don. 8/8-14/9/55.**G.**
Don. 11/7-2/8/56.**C/L.**
Don. 26/11-21/12/57.**G.**
Don. 8/10-7/11/59.**G.**
Don. 17/4/61.*Not repaired.*

BOILERS:
D1730.
D1664 *(ex73)* 12/4/30.
D1682 *(ex143)* 19/3/32.
D1647 *(ex1141)* 29/6/40.
  8598 *(ex1800)* 26/8/48.
27125 *(ex1980)* 8/12/50.
27121 *(ex61829)* 6/2/53.
24902 *(new)* 14/9/55.
24931 *(new)* 21/12/57.
27250 *(ex61813)* 7/11/59.

SHEDS:
Ardsley.
Doncaster 21/3/25.
Kings Cross 29/10/25.
March 19/11/38.
Stratford 26/2/49.
Parkeston 14/12/58.
Cambridge 1/3/59.

RENUMBERED:
1849 5/7/46.
61849 26/8/48.

CONDEMNED:
17/4/61.
Cut up at Doncaster.

167

Darlington.

To traffic 10/3/25.

REPAIRS:
Don. 2/10-28/11/25.**L.**
Don. 13-23/1/26.**L.**
Don. 5-19/3/26.**L.**
Don. 25/5-24/7/26.**L.**
Don. 2/8-6/10/27.**G.**
Don. 7/7-23/8/29.**G.**
Don. 20/1-28/2/31.**G.**
Don. 7/7-11/8/32.**H.**
Don. 1/12/32-7/1/33.**H.**
Don. 6/4-12/5/34.**G.** *Mod.valve gear.*
Don. 6/6-13/7/35.**G.**
Don. 9/11-11/12/36.**H.**
Don. 22/8-19/9/38.**G.**
Don. 24/8-12/10/40.**G.**
Don. 15/2-8/3/41.**L.**
Don. 2-23/1/43.**G.**
Don. 16/12/44-3/2/45.**G.**
Don. 17/8-19/10/46.**G.**
Don. 31/8-8/10/48.**G.**
Don. 28/9-27/10/50.**G.**
Don. 2-30/10/52.**G.**
Don. 7/7-6/8/54.**G.**
Don. 21/9-12/10/55.**C/L.**
Don. 19/3-4/5/56.**G.**
Don. 13/1-18/2/59.**G.**

BOILERS:
D1734.
D1736 *(ex178)* 23/8/29.
D1664 *(ex163)* 11/8/32.
D1770 *(ex208)* 12/5/34.
  8131 *(ex1118)* 19/10/46.
27111 *(ex61804)* 27/10/50.
27116 *(ex61836)* 30/10/52.
27136 *(ex61846)* 6/8/54.
24909 *(new)* 4/5/56.
27291 *(ex61890)* 18/2/59.

SHEDS:
Ardsley.
Doncaster 17/3/25.
New England 16/8/26.
March 20/9/53.
Mexborough 16/9/56.
Doncaster 14/6/59.

RENUMBERED:
1850 19/10/46.
61850 8/10/48.

CONDEMNED:
30/6/61.
Cut up at Doncaster.

170

Darlington.

To traffic 14/3/25.

REPAIRS:
Don. 5/5-30/7/27.**G.**
Don. 13/4-23/5/29.**G.**
Don. 16/4-21/5/31.**G.**
Don. 22/11/32-8/2/33.**G.** *Mod.valve gear.*
Don. 7/5-9/6/34.**G.**
Don. 1-31/7/35.**G.**
Don. 15/2-13/3/37.**H.**
Don. 14/4-5/5/38.**G.**
Don. 15/4-1/7/39.**L.**
Don. 13/4-18/5/40.**G.**
Don. 24/2/42.**L.**
Don. 9/5-6/6/42.**G.**
Cow. 15/11-21/12/45.**G.**
Cow. 14/2/47.**L.**
Cow. 7/1-7/2/48.**G.**
Cow. 24/1-25/2/50.**H/I.**
Cow. 25/6-20/8/51.**C/H.**
Cow. 17/1-1/3/52.**G.**
Cow. 10/4-10/5/53.**H/I.**

WORKS CODES:- Cow - Cowlairs. Dar - Darlington. Don - Doncaster. Ghd - Gateshead. Gor - Gorton. Inv - Inverurie. Str - Stratford.
REPAIR CODES:- **C/H** - Casual Heavy. **C/L** - Casual Light. **G** - General. **H** - Heavy. **H/I** - Heavy Intermediate. **L** - Light. **L/I** - Light Intermediate. **N/C** - Non-Classified.

Cow. 26/11-19/12/53.**C/L.**
Cow. 30/12/54-4/2/55.**H/I.**
Car. 24/10-24/11/55.**C/L.**
Cow. 10/5-26/6/56.**G.**
Cow. 2-4/7/56.**N/C.**
Cow. 9/7-27/8/58.**H/I.**

BOILERS:
D1735.
D1736 *(ex167)* 8/2/33.
9284 *(new)* 6/6/42.
8927 *(ex1823)* 7/2/48.
Renumbered 27316 20/8/51.
27334 *(new)* 1/3/52.
27342 *(new)* 26/6/56.

SHEDS:
New England.
Doncaster 22/11/35.
New England 17/6/36.
Colwick 7/7/40.
Doncaster 27/7/40.
St Margarets 5/9/42.
Carlisle 8/9/43.
March 28/6/59.
Carlisle 14/2/60.
Woodford 18/6/60.

RENUMBERED:
1851 25/8/46.
61851 19/9/48.

CONDEMNED:
22/11/61.
Cut up at Cowlairs.

178

Darlington.

To traffic 17/3/25.

REPAIRS:
Don. 17/8-5/9/25.**L.**
Don. 26/5-20/8/27.**G.**
Don. 22/6-2/8/29.**G.**
Don. 2/10-11/11/30.**G.**
Don. 16/6-29/7/32.**G.**
Don. 23/11-30/12/33.**G.** *Mod.valve gear.*
Don. 20/3-16/4/35.**G.**
Don. 12/8-19/9/36.**G.**
Don. 18/7-10/8/38.**G.**
Don. 18/5-15/6/40.**G.**
Don. 24/10-21/11/42.**G.**
Don. 26/2-11/3/44.**L.**
Don. 10-17/6/44.**H/I.**
Don. 3/3-14/4/45.**G.**
Don. 16/2-24/4/47.**G.**
Don. 16/1-2/3/49.**G.**
Don. 7/2-7/3/51.**G.**
Don. 4/2-5/3/53.**G.**
Don. 12/2-30/3/54.**C/H.**
Don. 16/6-29/7/55.**G.**
Don. 8/8-5/9/57.**G.**
Don. 20/10-20/11/59.**G.**
Don. 14-21/1/60.**N/C.**

BOILERS:
D1736.
D1737 *(ex180)* 2/8/29.

D1695 *(ex111)* 29/7/32.
D1679 *(ex203)* 10/8/38.
9794 *(new)* 24/4/47.
27147 *(ex61914)* 7/3/51.
27114 *(ex61828)* 5/3/53.
27135 *(ex61820)* 29/7/55.
27147 *(ex61915)* 5/9/57.
24931 *(ex61849)* 20/11/59.

SHEDS:
Ardsley.
New England 1/4/25.
Doncaster 17/7/40.
Lincoln 18/6/46.
Gorton 21/5/50.
Lincoln 13/6/54.
Immingham 8/5/55.
Colwick 5/1/58.

RENUMBERED:
1852 1/12/46.
61852 2/3/49.

CONDEMNED:
18/7/61.
Cut up at Doncaster.

180

Darlington.

To traffic 21/3/25.

REPAIRS:
Don. 16/6-15/9/27.**G.**

Don. 6/6-9/7/29.**G.**
Don. 10/6-25/7/31.**G.** *Mod.valve gear.*
Don. 7/11-15/12/32.**G.**
Don. 5/2-9/3/34.**G.**
Don. 13/4-18/5/35.**G.**
Don. 10/8-18/9/36.**G.**
Don. 2-28/7/38.**G.**
Don. 15/6-6/7/40.**G.**
Don. 5/9-10/10/42.**G.**
Don. 21/10-18/11/44.**G.**
Don. 23/12/44-13/1/45.**L.**
Don. 21/4-12/5/45.**L.**
Don. 29/12/45-26/1/46.**G.**
Don. 6-13/7/46.**L.**
Don. 17-24/8/46.**L.**
Don. 17/5-10/7/47.**G.**
Don. 12/11-16/12/49.**G.**
Don. 8/4-7/5/52.**G.**
Don. 20/4-21/5/54.**G.**
Don. 14-27/1/55.**C/L.**
Don. 24/1-25/2/56.**G.**
Don. 16/1-12/2/58.**G.**
Don. 30/12/59-3/2/60.**G.**

BOILERS:
D1737.
D1687 *(ex113)* 9/7/29.
D1709 *(ex126)* 25/7/31.
D1742 *(ex58)* 28/7/38.
8596 *(ex2767)* 10/7/47.
8800 *(ex1832)* 16/12/49.
27230 *(ex61841)* 7/5/52.
27317 *(ex61992)* 21/5/54.
27204 *(ex61821)* 25/2/56.

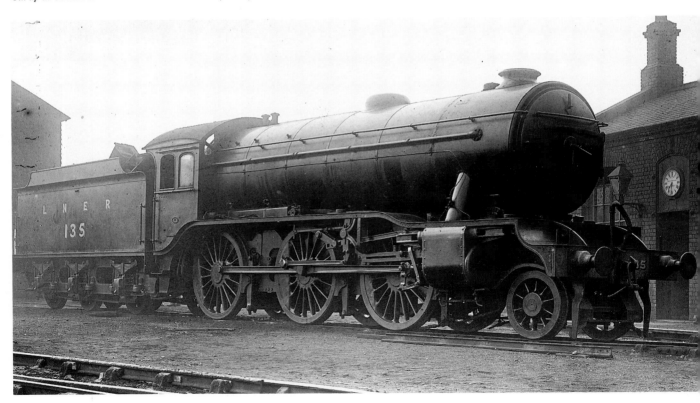

The Darlington designed cab had the side windows too low for the liking of GN Section crews, whose complaints led to an alteration being made. The thirty built to No.134 had windows in the original position, but starting with 135, the other thirty had windows 3½" higher, although the cross rail above them was retained. On the second thirty, the vertical handrail at the cab entrance was also made 2' 7½" instead of 2' 4" between pillar centres.

27105 *(ex61940)* 12/2/58.
27298 *(ex61948)* 3/2/60.

SHEDS:
Ardsley.
New England 1/4/25.
March 20/9/53.
Woodford 16/9/56.
Ardsley 17/5/59.
Low Moor 11/6/61.
Ardsley 10/9/61.

RENUMBERED:
1853 13/7/46.
61853 16/12/49.

CONDEMNED:
18/12/62.
Cut up at Doncaster.

184

Darlington.

To traffic 24/3/25.

REPAIRS:
Cowlairs repairs not located.
Don. 14/5-24/6/31.**G.** *Mod.valve gear.*
Don. 16/2-23/3/33.**G.**
Don. 5/4-11/5/34.**G.**
Don. 31/5-29/6/35.**G.**
Don. 24/3-23/4/37.**G.**
Cow. 15/4/38.**L.**
Cow. 26/7/38.**H.**
Cow. 14/2/40.**G.**
Cow. 11/8/40.**L.**
Cow. 2/8/41.**G.**
Cow. 8-29/5/43.**G.**
Cow. 14/6/44.**L.**
Cow. 11/4-5/5/45.**G.**
Cow. 4/11/46-11/1/47.**G.**
Cow. 23/9-18/11/48.**G.**
Cow. 23/3-28/4/50.**G.**
Cow. 10-24/6/50.**C/L.**
Cow. 5/3-10/5/52.**G.**
Cow. 4/3-8/4/54.**L/I.**
Cow. 29/8-1/10/55.**H/I.**
Cow. 24/11-22/12/56.**G.**
Don. 19/9-10/10/58.**C/L.**
Don. 4/1-12/2/60.**G.**

BOILERS:
D1740.
D1710 *(ex127)* 23/3/33.
9372 *(new)* 29/5/43.
27335 *(new)* 10/5/52.
27334 *(ex61851)* 22/12/56.
27297 *(ex61895)* 12/2/60.

SHEDS:
Carlisle.
St Margarets 14/3/39.
Haymarket 5/41.
Eastfield 28/10/42.
St Margarets 4/4/43.
Carlisle 17/9/43.
Hull Dairycoates 25/2/57.
Tweedmouth 8/6/58.
Hull Dairycoates 10/9/61.

RENUMBERED:
1854 13/10/46.
61854 18/11/48.

CONDEMNED:
29/10/62.
Cut up at Doncaster.

186

Darlington.

To traffic 25/3/25.

REPAIRS:
Cowlairs repairs not located.
Don. 25/6-9/10/31.**G.**
Don. 21/9-14/10/32.**L.**
Don. 15/6-24/7/33.**G.** *Mod.valve gear.*
Don. 6/11-5/12/34.**G.**
Don. 16/7-8/8/36.**G.**
Don. 27/1-19/2/38.**G.**
Cow. 9/12/38.**L.**
Cow. 15/4/39.**N/C.**
Cow. 26/8/39.**G.**
Cow. 15/2/41.**G.**
Cow. 22/5/43.**G.**
Cow. 13/4-7/5/45.**G.**
Cow. 9/5/46.**L.**
Cow. 16/7-30/8/47.**G.**
Cow. 30/3-14/5/49.**L/I.**
Cow. 7/10-17/12/49.**G.**
Cow. 16/8-29/9/51.**L/I.**
Cow. 15/5-14/6/52.**H/I.**
Cow. 5/5-26/6/54.**G.**
Cow. 5-6/7/54.**N/C.**
Cow. 11/2-17/3/56.**L/I.**
Cow. 8/7-30/8/57.**H/I.**

BOILERS:
D1742.
7991 *(ex112)* 5/12/34.
8599 *(ex1137)* 8/8/36.
2838 *(ex3828)* 15/2/41.
8599 *(ex188)* 7/5/45.
8071 *(ex1955)* 17/12/49.
Renumbered 27308 29/9/51.
27336 *(new)* 26/6/54.

SHEDS:
Carlisle.
Polmont by 11/5/28 .
Eastfield by 11/9/31.
Polmont by 12/32.
St Margarets 8/40.
Haymarket 5/41.
St Margarets 28/10/42.
Carlisle 8/9/43.
Eastfield 18/5/46.
St Margarets 31/8/47.

RENUMBERED:
1855 9/5/46.
61855 14/5/49.

CONDEMNED:
6/7/59.
Cut up at Cowlairs.

188

Darlington.

To traffic 26/3/25.

REPAIRS:
Cow. 26/5-3/6/25.**L.** *"New Tender" on card.*
Cow. 14/10-23/12/26.**L.**
Cow. 23/5-6/8/27.**G.**
Cow. 16/1-6/4/29.**G.**
Cow. 19/6-17/7/30.**G.**
Don. 4/11/31-30/1/32.**G.** *Mod.valve gear.*
Don. 13/6-18/8/33.**G.**
Don. 5/9-20/10/34.**G.**
Don. 10/12/35-11/1/36.**G.**
Don. 27/3-1/5/36.**L.**
Don. 17/7-13/8/37.**G.** *Drop grate fitted.*
Cow. 1/3-28/4/39.**G.**
Cow. 31/1-2/4/40.**L.**
Cow. 23/5-26/6/41.**G.**
Cow. 12/4-17/5/43.**H.**
Cow. 29/3-21/4/45.**H.**
Don. 9/10-17/12/46.**G.**
Don. 7/7-23/8/47.**G.**
Don. 18/12/49-4/2/50.**G.**
Don. 3/4-14/5/52.**G.**
Don. 21/10-19/11/54.**G.**
Don. 15/2-1/3/55.**C/L.**
Don. 25/9-8/10/56.**C/L.**
Don. 26/2-29/3/57.**G.**
Don. 2/12/59-1/1/60.**G.**

BOILERS:
D1743.
D1740 *(ex184)* 18/8/33.
8599 *(ex186)* 26/6/41.
D1710 *(ex184)* 21/4/45.
RS4076 *(ex1918)* 23/8/47.
8967 *(ex61871)* 4/2/50.
27231 *(ex61926)* 14/5/52.
27127 *(ex61974)* 19/11/54.
24920 *(new)* 29/3/57.
27186 *(ex61923)* 1/1/60.

SHEDS:
Carlisle.
Eastfield 15/8/30.
Carlisle 30/1/32.
St Margarets 5/3/45.
Aberdeen 20/8/45.
Doncaster 13/10/45.
Gorton 14/5/50.
Colwick 13/6/54.
Annesley 30/1/55.
Ardsley 17/5/59.

RENUMBERED:
1856 7/12/46.
61856 4/2/50.

CONDEMNED:
17/12/62.
Cut up at Doncaster.

191

Darlington.

To traffic 1/4/25.

REPAIRS:
Cow. 7/26.**G.**
Cow. 3-5/27.**G.**
Cow. 29/9/27.**L.**
Cow. 8-9/30.**G.**
Don. 3/6-28/7/32.**G.** *Mod.valve gear.*
Don. 16/11-29/12/33.**G.**
Don. 10/1-2/2/35.**G.**
Don. 20/5-20/6/36.**G.**
Don. 21/6-15/7/37.**G.**
Cow. 2/2/39.**G.**
Cow. 2/8/40.**G.**
Cow. 16/8/40.**L.**
Cow. 12/9/42.**G.**
Cow. 2/9/44.**G.**
Cow. 30/8-27/9/45.**G.**
Cow. 1/5-12/6/47.**G.**
Cow. 22/11-31/12/49.**H/I.**
Cow. 7/11-5/12/51.**G.**
Cow. 10/8-9/9/53.**H/I.**
Cow. 11/3-16/4/55.**L/I.**
Cow. 27/10-1/12/56.**G.**
Don. 18/6-31/7/59.**G.**
Don. 2-6/5/60.**N/C.**

BOILERS:
D1746.
D1781 *(ex227)* 2/2/35.
D1695 *(ex1858)* 12/6/47.
27333 *(new)* 5/12/51.
27310 *(ex61879)* 1/12/56.
24923 *(ex61932)* 31/7/59.

SHEDS:
Carlisle.
St Margarets 29/1/37.
Carlisle 17/2/37.
St Margarets 14/3/39.
Haymarket 5/41.
St Margarets 30/9/42.
Eastfield 28/10/42.
St Margarets 4/4/43.
Carlisle 17/9/43.
Eastfield 15/6/46.
St Margarets 31/8/47.
Hull Dairycoates 25/2/57.

RENUMBERED:
1857 20/10/46.
61857 18/9/48.

CONDEMNED:
3/12/62.
Cut up at Doncaster.

195

Darlington.

To traffic 4/4/25.

REPAIRS:
Cowlairs repairs not located.
Don. 11/2-27/3/31.**G.**

Even with the 3½" lift to the cab windows, Southern Area still complained, so between January 1930 (No.227) and August 1931 (No.203) all that Area's K3's had their windows lifted - by 6½" on those to 134, and by 3" on the later engines, with the cross rail above them being discarded. From March 1931 Doncaster also altered the Scottish Area engines, whose maintenance they had taken over, and did likewise to N.E.Area engines after they too became Doncaster's responsibility. No.186 at Polmont shed on 15th September 1935 shows that alteration, but it was only completed on N.E.Area engines in 1943-46. *W.A.Camwell.*

Don. 12/1-16/2/33.**G.** *Mod.valve gear.*
Don. 11/5-5/7/34.**G.**
Don. 26/11-28/12/35.**G.**
Dar. 10-31/1/36.**N/C.**
Don. 18/5-18/6/37.**G.**
Cow. 2/11/38.**G.** *Front footsteps fitted.*
Cow. 14/3/40.**L.**
Cow. 28/5/40.**G.**
Cow. 16/1/42.**G.**
Cow. 26/6/43.**H.**
Cow. 6/9-6/10/45.**G.**
Cow. 23/1-26/4/47.**G.**
Cow. 13/10-19/11/48.**G.**
Cow. 17/5-17/6/50.**G.**
Cow. 25/6-8/8/51.**H/I.**
Cow. 28/10-23/11/52.**L/I.**
Cow. 14/12/53-20/1/54.**H/I.**
Cow. 25/5-3/7/54.**C/L.**
Cow. 1/3-4/4/55.**G.**
Cow. 13-31/12/55.**C/L.**
Cow. 1/9-15/10/56.**H/I.**
Cow. 30/7-2/9/58.**H/I.**
Cow. 27/10-8/11/58.**C/L.**
Cow. 4/2-4/3/59.**C/L.**

BOILERS:
D1748.
 7992 *(ex75)* 5/7/34.
D1695 *(exDonc)* 28/5/40.
 2861 *(ex1990)* 26/4/47.
27305 *(ex1983)* 8/8/51.
27327 *(ex61885)* 4/4/55.

SHEDS:
Carlisle.
St Margarets 15/3/39.
Carlisle 11/39.
Sheffield 23/11/40.
Carlisle 5/5/41.

RENUMBERED:
1858 25/8/46.
61858 19/9/48.

CONDEMNED:
26/4/61.
Cut up at Cowlairs.

200

Darlington.

To traffic 10/4/25.

REPAIRS:
Dar. 17/11-3/12/25.**L.** *Back from Wembley.*
Cow. 10/8-19/10/27.**G.**
Cow. 8/3-28/4/28.**G.**
Cow. 30-31/5/28.**N/C.**
Cow. 23/1-21/3/29.**G.**
Don. 14/1-5/3/31.**G.**
Don. 29/9-25/11/32.**G.** *Mod.valve gear.*
Don. 7/2-28/3/34.**G.**
Don. 24/8-11/10/35.**G.**

Don. 9/1-26/2/37.**G.** *Drop grate fitted.*
Cow. 22/9-16/11/38.**G.**
Cow. 22/11-11/12/39.**L.**
Cow. 16-21/2/40.**L.**
Cow. 11/6-6/7/40.**G.**
Cow. 1-7/4/41.**L.**
Cow. 13-21/5/41.**L.**
Cow. 4/11-23/12/41.**G.**
Cow. 11-30/5/42.**L.**
Cow. 14/11/42-14/1/43.**H.**
Cow. 19-21/1/43.**L.**
Cow. 12/12/44-17/1/45.**H.**
Don. 24/10-13/12/45.**G.**
Don. 6/7-13/9/46.**H.**
Don. 18/1-23/2/48.**G.**
Don. 15/10-5/11/48.**L.**
Don. 16/6-21/7/50.**G.**
Don. 1/9-15/10/52.**G.**
Don. 17/3-15/4/53.**N/C.**
Don. 21/10-9/12/54.**G.**
Don. 1-29/12/55.**N/C.**
Don. 15-30/11/56.**C/L.**
Don. 3-10/12/56.**N/C.**
Don. 15/10-13/11/57.**G.**
Don. 14-24/3/59.**C/L.**
Don. 6/10-11/11/60.**G.**

BOILERS:
D1750.
7D/687 *(ex2763)* 26/2/37.
D1740 *(ex188)* 21/5/41.
C1421 *(ex188)* 23/12/41.
AW76 *(ex1368)* 14/1/43.

RS4075 *(ex61839)* 21/7/50.
27262 *(ex61869)* 15/10/52.
27109 *(ex61972)* 9/12/54.
27133 *(ex61802)* 13/11/57.
27101 *(ex61867)* 11/11/60.

SHEDS:
Wembley exhibition.
Eastfield 4/12/25.
Carlisle 2/11/31.
St Margarets 15/3/39.
Eastfield 28/10/42.
St Margarets 5/4/43.
Carlisle 17/9/43.
Doncaster 13/10/45.
Lincoln 18/6/46.

RENUMBERED:
1859 31/3/46.
E1859 23/2/48.
61859 5/11/48.

CONDEMNED:
4/11/62.
Sold for scrap to T.W.Ward, Broughton Lane, Sheffield.

202

Darlington.

To traffic 7/8/25.

GRESLEY K3

No.4007 - the odd one which hung on to its GN tender - had cab sight screens fitted in December 1934, but it was found that on its style of cab they slightly fouled the load gauge, and that shorter ones were needed. Note the square end to front buffer beam, and that the redundant lamp iron has been removed.

No.4002 shows the solution to the problem with the sight screen - the same length of glass was able to be used by adopting a lower fitting position. Note cut corners to buffer beam. *C.C.B.Herbert.*

The quadrant cut-outs from the front buffer beam first appeared on 1300, seen here 'no old at all' in Doncaster paint shop. Making quite sure of clearance, they were of 9" radius, although it was found that 4^1/$_2$" sufficed when some of the earlier engines received that treatment. The Westinghouse brake pump will be noted, and the front end connection was below the buffer beam, and not by swan-neck pipe as for the vacuum brake.

Neasden 27/10/25.
Doncaster 26/1/27.
Copley Hill 8/10/27.
Doncaster 15/2/43.
New England 22/4/45.
March 16/2/47.
Colwick 18/12/60.

RENUMBERED:
1860 24/3/46.
61860 30/9/49.

CONDEMNED:
16/11/61.
Cut up at Doncaster.

204

Darlington.

To traffic 26/8/25.

REPAIRS:
Don. 19/11/27-11/2/28.**G.**
Don. 2/5-19/6/28.**L.**
Don. 11/3-9/5/30.**G.**
Don. 15/1-17/2/31.**G.** *Steam to screw
rev.*
Don. 31/3-16/6/32.**G.** *Mod.valve
gear.*
Don. 12/9-3/11/33.**G.**
Don. 19/12/34-26/1/35.**G.**
Don. 30/4-18/6/36.**G.**
Don. 24/4-7/7/38.**G.**
Don. 6/7-10/8/40.**G.**
Don. 29/8-10/10/42.**G.**
Don. 7-28/10/44.**G.**
Don. 24/2-31/3/45.**G.**
Don. 17/8-5/10/46.**G.**
Don. 13/12/48-22/1/49.**G.**
Don. 26/1-23/2/51.**G.**
Don. 5-8/3/51.**C/L.**
Don. 21/11-11/12/51.**C/L.**
Don. 8/4-13/5/53.**G.**
Don. 13/4-13/5/54.**G.**
Don. 20/2-23/3/56.**G.**
Don. 28/3-5/4/56.**N/C.**
Don. 8/8-11/10/58.**G.**

Don. 31/7-27/8/59.**C/H.**
Don. 2/11-20/12/60.**G.**

BOILERS:
D1772.
D1730 *(ex163)* 9/5/30.
D1703 *(ex121)* 3/11/33.
D1734 *(ex206)* 10/8/40.
  9556 *(new)* 5/10/46.
27144 *(ex61825)* 23/2/51.
27186 *(ex61954)* 13/5/54.
24910 *(new)* 23/3/56.
27233 *(ex61946)* 11/10/58.
27226 *(ex61809)* 20/12/60.

SHEDS:
Gorton.
Neasden 2/2/26.
Doncaster 17/6/27.
Copley Hill 10/7/30.
Doncaster 12/9/30.
New England 5/6/31.
Lincoln 22/6/52.
Stratford 5/10/52.
Parkeston 14/12/58.
March 12/6/60.

RENUMBERED:
1862 8/4/46.
61862 22/1/49.

CONDEMNED:
16/1/62.
Cut up at Doncaster.

206

Darlington.

To traffic 2/9/25.

REPAIRS:
Don. 27/8-5/11/27.**G.**
Don. 14/9-28/10/29.**G.**
Don. 25/7-10/11/30.**G.**
Steam to screw rev.
Don. 24/2-11/5/33.**G.**
Mod.valve gear.

Don. 7/9-18/10/34.**G.**
Don. 21/1-28/2/36.**G.**
Don. 27/11/36-15/1/37.**L.**
Don. 25/1-21/3/38.**G.**
Don. 11/5-15/6/40.**G.**
Don. 16/8-20/9/41.**G.**
Don. 13/2-6/3/43.**G.**
Don. 24/2/45. *for rebuilding.*

BOILERS:
D1776.
D1734 *(ex167)* 28/10/29.
D1767 *(ex202)* 11/5/33.
D1734 *(ex73)* 21/3/38.
D1678 *(ex202)* 15/6/40.

SHEDS:
Gorton.
Neasden 2/2/26.
Doncaster 31/5/27.
Copley Hill 18/7/30.
Doncaster 20/7/30.
New England 12/6/31.

*Rebuilt to 2 cylinders &
made Class K5 from 13/10/45.*

207

Darlington.

To traffic 17/9/25.

REPAIRS:
Don. 2/3-17/5/28.**G.**
Don. 28/6-4/7/28.**L.**
Don. 23/4-6/6/30.**G.**
Don. 23/4-22/5/31.**L.** *Steam to screw
rev.*
Don. 14/3-28/4/32.**G.** *Mod.valve
gear.*
Don. 21/7-3/8/32.**H.**
Don. 13/12/33-18/1/34.**G.**
Don. 17/5-19/6/35.**G.**
Don. 25/1-25/2/37.**G.**
Don. 24/12/38-4/2/39.**G.**
Don. 28/9-26/10/40.**G.**
Don. 8/2-1/3/41.**L.**

Don. 3/4-1/5/43.**G.**
Don. 19/2-4/3/44.**L.**
Don. 31/3-5/5/45.**G.**
Don. 1/7-17/8/47.**G.**
Don. 12/4-26/5/49.**G.**
Don. 29/8-9/10/51.**G.**
Don. 1-3/1/52.**N/C.**
Don. 5-31/1/53.**C/L.**
Don. 8/12/53-7/1/54.**G.**
Don. 19/10-19/11/55.**G.**
Don. 1/12/57-4/1/58.**G.**
Don. 14/6-27/7/60.**G.**

BOILERS:
D1778.
D1789 *(ex231)* 6/6/30.
D1743 *(ex188)* 18/1/34.
  8962 *(ex1974)* 17/8/47.
27194 *(ex61824)* 9/10/51.
27279 *(new)* 7/1/54.
27109 *(ex61859)* 4/1/58.
24910 *(ex61804)* 27/7/60.

SHEDS:
Gorton.
Cambridge 22/5/26.
Doncaster 3/1/27.
New England 5/6/31.
March 16/6/46.
New England 21/10/46.
March 25/6/50.
Lowestoft 8/10/50.
Colwick 10/12/50.
March 20/9/53.
New England 4/11/56.

RENUMBERED:
1864 24/3/46.
61864 26/5/49.

CONDEMNED:
16/9/62.
*Sold for scrap to A.King & Son,
Norwich.*

208

Darlington.

To traffic 19/9/25.

REPAIRS:
Don. 27/2-10/5/28.**G.**
Don. 17/12/29-18/1/30.**G.**
Don. 4-28/6/30.**L.**

**Like 4002, 4004 had been change~~d~~
from GN type to a Group Stand~~-~~
ard tender which had a stepped ou~~t~~
coping. 4004 had one of the ear~~-~~
lier ones with short vertical rail a~~t~~
each end, whereas that with 400~~2~~
was built in 1925, and they ha~~d~~
taller rails, but both have the nor~~-~~
mal style of boiler handrail whic~~h~~
curved round to end on the fron~~t~~
plate of the smokebox. All kept tha~~t~~
arrangement at least until 1950.
W.Clark.**

Don. 3/3-10/4/31.**L.**
Steam to screw rev.
Don. 25/2-15/4/32.**G.**
Mod.valve gear.
Don. 12/10-14/11/33.**G.**
Don. 18/10-23/11/34.**G.**
Don. 20/6-24/7/36.**G.**
Don. 11/3-19/4/38.**G.**
Don. 31/8-12/10/40.**G.**
Don. 6/3-3/4/43.**G.**
Don. 9/6-21/7/45.**G.**
Don. 2/1-14/2/47.**G.**
Don. 15/10-10/12/48.**G.**
Don. 20/10-8/12/50.**G.**
Gor. 20-22/4/52.**N/C.**
Don. 12/11-5/12/52.**G.**
Don. 19/4-24/5/55.**G.**
Don. 18/3-24/4/58.**G.**

BOILERS:
D1779.
D1770 *(ex203)* 18/1/30.
D1784 *(ex4001)* 14/11/33.
9374 *(new)* 3/4/43.
9990 *(new)* 10/12/48.
27260 *(new)* 8/12/50.
27142 *(ex61904)* 5/12/52.
27151 *(ex61848)* 24/5/55.
27283 *(ex61944)* 24/4/58.

SHEDS:
Gorton.
Cambridge 25/5/26.
Doncaster 12/1/27.
Kings Cross 18/10/30.
March 14/5/38.
Kings Cross 7/7/38.
Retford 19/7/39.
Kings Cross 31/8/39.
Annesley 30/9/39.
Colwick 1/3/40.
March 27/5/48.
Colwick 31/10/48.
Gorton 14/5/50.
Woodford 2/4/60.

RENUMBERED:
1865 5/5/46.
61865 10/12/48.

CONDEMNED:
30/6/61.
Cut up at Doncaster.

227

Darlington.

To traffic 5/10/25.

REPAIRS:
Don. 19/12/27-3/3/28.**G.**
Don. 27/11/29-16/1/30.**G.**
Don. 16/3-28/4/31.**G.** *Steam to screw*
rev. and mod.valve gear.
Don. 16/11/32-3/1/33.**G.**
Don. 14/3-17/4/34.**G.**
Don. 5/7-10/8/35.**G.** *Feed water*
heater fitted.
Don. 6-20/6/36.**L.**

Foam detector fitted.
Don. 29/12/36-6/2/37.**G.**
Don. 8-29/10/38.**G.**
Don. 28/9-2/11/40.**G.** *Feed heater*
removed.
Don. 1/3-5/4/41.**L.**
Don. 17/7-21/8/43.**G.**
Don. 24/3-5/5/45.**G.**
Don. 17/2-3/4/47.**G.**
Don. 8/11-17/12/48.**G.**
Don. 11/5-14/6/51.**G.**
Don. 18/2-17/3/53.**G.**
Don. 22/11-17/12/54.**G.**
Don. 14/2-16/3/57.**G.**
Don. 8-11/2/59.**N/C.**
Don. 6/4-7/5/59.**G.**

BOILERS:
D1781.
7990 *(ex118)* 17/4/34.
9380 *(new)* 21/8/43.
27170 *(ex61838)* 14/6/51.
27167 *(ex61886)* 17/3/53.
27262 *(ex61859)* 17/12/54.
27126 *(ex61967)* 16/3/57.
24938 *(new)* 7/5/59.

SHEDS:
Gorton.
Cambridge 29/5/26.
Doncaster 3/1/27.
New England 9/5/31.
Doncaster 10/8/35.
March 11/7/41.
Woodford 16/9/56.
Immingham 5/1/58.
Lincoln 18/12/60.

RENUMBERED:
1866 13/4/46.
61866 17/12/48.

CONDEMNED:
19/10/61.
Cut up at Doncaster.

228

Darlington.

To traffic 13/10/25.

REPAIRS:
Don. 24/11/27-10/3/28.**G.**
Don. 30/12/29-7/2/30.**G.**
Don. 9/4-16/5/31.**G.** *Steam to screw*
rev. and mod.valve gear.
Don. 3/2-13/3/33.**G.**
Don. 24/9-24/10/34.**G.**
Don. 16/1-15/2/36.**G.**
Don. 13/11-11/12/37.**G.**
Don. 16/9-28/10/39.**G.**
Don. 12/7-23/8/41.**G.**
Don. 9/10-6/11/43.**G.**
Don. 15/12/45-12/1/46.**G.**
Don. 18/12/47-4/3/48.**G.**
Don. 5-19/8/48.**L.**
Don. 20/12/48-7/1/49.**C/L.**
Don. 17/3-28/4/50.**G.**
Don. 22/2-26/3/52.**G.**

Don. 5/2-4/3/54.**G.**
Don. 16/3-5/4/55.**C/L.**
Don. 30/11/55-7/1/56.**G.**
Don. 13/5-18/6/58.**G.**
Don. 14/10-25/11/60.**G.**
Don. 18/9-4/10/61.**C/L.**

BOILERS:
D1784.
D1779 *(ex208)* 7/2/30.
7429 *(ex4008)* 16/5/31.
D1750 *(ex200)* 11/12/37.
8139A *(ex1909)* 4/3/48.
10800 *(new)* 28/4/50.
27219 *(ex61835)* 26/3/52.
27229 *(ex61867)* 4/3/54.
27202 *(ex61957)* 7/1/56.
27101 *(ex61908)* 18/6/58.
27225 *(ex61963)* 25/11/60.

SHEDS:
Gorton.
Cambridge 21/5/26.
Doncaster 3/1/27.
March 11/5/30.
Doncaster 17/5/30.
New England 2/6/31.
Colwick 16/9/40.
Annesley 13/10/40.
Sheffield 3/5/43.
New England 25/6/45.
March 20/9/53.
Mexborough 16/9/56.
Doncaster 14/6/59.
March 21/6/59.
Doncaster 26/7/59.

RENUMBERED:
1867 31/3/46.
E1867 4/3/48.
61867 19/8/48.

CONDEMNED:
4/11/62.
Cut up at Doncaster.

229

Darlington.

To traffic 22/10/25.

REPAIRS:
Don.19/11/27-9/2/28.**G.**
Don. 17/12/29-1/2/30.**G.**
Don. 25/9-3/11/30.**L.** *Steam to screw*
rev.
Don. 5/1-8/2/32.**G.** *Mod.valve gear.*
Don. 23/2-28/3/33.**G.**
Don. 6/9-10/10/34.**G.**
Don. 23/3-25/4/36.**G.**
Don. 19/11-21/12/37.**G.**
Don. 4/11-16/12/39.**G.**
Don. 30/3-6/4/40.**L.**
Don. 27/9-8/11/41.**G.**
Cow. 11/4-25/6/43.**G.**
Don. 24/2-31/3/45.**G.**
Don. 28/7-25/8/45.**L.**
Don. 27/1-27/3/47.**G.**
Don. 12/11-22/12/48.**G.**

Don. 18/12/50-19/1/51.**G.**
Don. 15/2-19/3/51.**C/L.**
Don. 17-30/5/51.**C/L.**
Don. 10/3-9/4/53.**G.**
Don. 26/10-23/11/53.**N/C.**
Don. 13/1-15/2/55.**G.**
Don. 24/7-27/8/57.**G.**
Don. 4/4-11/5/60.**G.**

BOILERS:
D1785.
D1678 *(ex109)* 1/2/30.
D1762 *(ex4006)* 8/2/32.
8739 *(new)* 25/4/36.
9279 *(new)* 8/11/41.
27133 *(ex61845)* 19/1/51.
27162 *(ex61812)* 9/4/53.
27171 *(ex61896)* 15/2/55.
27260 *(ex61891)* 27/8/57.
27277 *(ex61802)* 11/5/60.

SHEDS:
Gorton.
Cambridge 20/5/26.
New England 3/1/27.
Kings Cross 6/3/27.
Colwick 16/12/39.
Annesley 13/10/40.
Gorton 3/7/43.
Woodford 24/10/43.
New England 29/6/47.
March 20/9/53.
Mexborough 16/9/56.
Doncaster 14/6/59.

RENUMBERED:
1868 2/6/46.
61868 22/12/48.

CONDEMNED:
10/5/62.
Cut up at Doncaster.

231

Darlington.

To traffic 14/12/25.

REPAIRS:
Don. 20/9-31/10/26.**L.**
Don. 14/2-28/4/28.**G.**
Don. 16/1-21/2/30.**G.**
Don. 24/2-28/3/31.**L.**
Don. 7/10-9/11/31.**G.** *Steam to screw*
rev.and mod.valve gear.
Don. 24/5-1/7/33.**G.**
Don. 18/10-16/11/34.**G.**
Don. 24/6-24/7/36.**G.**
Don. 3-24/12/38.**G.**
Don. 3/5-21/6/41.**G.**
Don. 5/2-4/3/44.**G.**
Don. 30/12/44-27/1/45.**L.**
Don. 10-17/11/45.**L.**
Don. 14/11-21/12/46.**G.**
Don. 2/9-15/10/48.**G.**
Don. 14/11-14/12/50.**G.**
Don. 3/7-8/8/52.**G.**
Don. 12/4-14/5/54.**G.**
Don. 21/3-28/4/56.**G.**

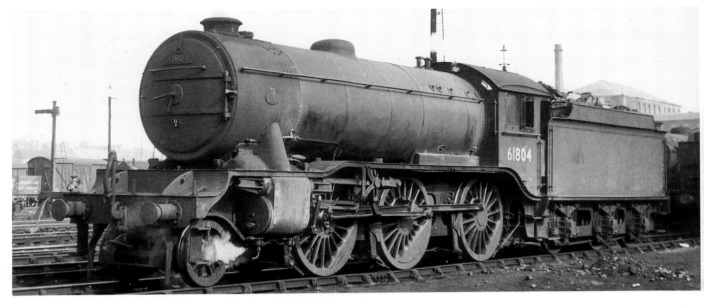

61804, at Lincoln GN shed on 27th September 1953, has had the boiler handrails cut back to terminate on the side of the smokebox, and many (but not all) were so treated. It still carries both pairs of guard irons, but its buffer beam cut-outs are less than on 4002. Note that there is a single stop between the hinge straps on the smokebox door, and that the BR cast number plate is between the cross rail and the top lamp iron.

Don. 17/2-15/3/58.**G.**
Don. 30/10-28/11/59.**G.**
Don. 11-14/4/60.**N/C.**

BOILERS:
D1789.
D1785 *(ex229)* 21/2/30.
D1716 *(ex92)* 1/7/33.
D1714 *(ex158)* 21/6/41.
 9629 *(new)* 21/12/46.
27262 *(new)* 14/12/50.
27247 *(ex61964)* 8/8/52.
27223 *(ex61910)* 14/5/54.
27186 *(ex61862)* 28/4/56.
27278 *(ex61938)* 15/3/58.
27137 *(ex61872)* 28/11/59.

SHEDS:
Gorton.
Cambridge 3/6/26.
Kings Cross 3/1/27.
Copley Hill 3/8/36.
New England 25/6/45.
March 31/1/49.
Hull Dairycoates 2/9/51.
Heaton 23/9/56.
Hull Dairycoates 17/1/60.

RENUMBERED:
 1869 24/3/46.
61869 15/10/48.

CONDEMNED:
3/12/62.
Cut up at Doncaster.

1300

Doncaster 1711.

To traffic 20/4/29.

REPAIRS:
Dar. 6-21/12/29.**L.**
Dar. 8/8-11/9/30.**L.**
Dar. 23/1-13/2/31.**N/C.**
Ghd. 6-20/1/32.**N/C.**
Dar. 21/1-7/3/32.**G.** *West.brake off.*
Dar. 14/3-25/4/34.**G.**
Dar. 30/3-26/6/36.**G.**
Dar. 5-26/10/37.**L.**
Dar. 22/11/37-4/2/38.**G.**
Dar. 7-17/2/38.**N/C.**
Dar. 31/8-2/9/39.**N/C.**
Dar. 12-18/3/40.**N/C.**
Dar. 26/6-7/8/40.**G.**
Don. 14/10-19/11/42.**G.**
Don. 18/9-4/11/44.**G.**
Don. 8/6-27/7/47.**G.**
Don. 2/5-10/6/49.**G.**
Don. 18/9-2/11/50.**L/I.**
Don. 24/9-19/10/51.**C/L.**
Don. 6/10-5/11/52.**G.**
Don. 24/3-9/5/55.**G.**
Don. 27/9-1/11/57.**G.**
Don. 19/9-22/10/59.**G.**
Don. 7-13/1/60.**N/C.**

BOILERS:
 8130.
 8115 *(ex1364)* 25/4/34.
RS4077 *(ex1333)* 26/6/36.
 8139A *(ex1324)* 4/2/38.
RS4079 *(ex1367)* 7/8/40.
 9286 *(new)* 19/11/42.
 9283 *(ex1873)* 10/6/49.
Renumbered 27113 2/11/50.
27251 *(ex61859)* 5/11/52.
27162 *(ex61868)* 9/5/55.
24925 *(new)* 1/11/57.
24917 *(61903)* 22/10/59.

SHEDS:
York.
Retford 19/6/38.

York 6/8/38.
Blaydon 1/6/40.
Colwick 23/11/40.
Annesley 28/11/40.
Gorton 3/5/43.
Woodford 30/10/43.
Gorton 26/6/49.
Colwick 13/6/54.

RENUMBERED:
 1870 25/3/46.
61870 10/6/49.

CONDEMNED:
12/7/62.
Cut up at Doncaster.

1312

Doncaster 1712.

To traffic 8/5/29.

REPAIRS:
Dar. 26/1-15/3/32.**G.** *West.brake off.*
Ghd. 13-17/6/32.**N/C.**
Dar. 29/7-6/9/32.**N/C.**
Dar. 13-28/9/33.**N/C.**
Dar. 10/7-7/9/34.**G.**
Dar. 16/8-1/11/35.**L.**
Dar. 28/4-12/6/36.**G.**
Dar. 19/6-1/7/36.**N/C.**
Dar. 1/3-27/5/37.**G.**
Dar. 5/5-27/6/39.**G.**
Dar. 24/4-25/6/40.**H.**
Don. 19/10-16/11/40.**G.**
Don. 18/9-17/10/42.**G.**
Don. 24/11-5/12/42.**L.**
Dar. 31/3-14/5/43.**H.**
Dar. 30/6-16/7/43.**L.**
Dar. 2-24/8/44.**L.**
Don. 9/6-14/7/45.**H.**

Don. 28/9-5/10/46.**L.**
Don. 22/9-25/10/47.**G.**
Ghd. 2-23/2/49.**L/I.**
Don. 7/11-17/12/49.**G.**
Don. 12-28/3/51.**L.**
Don. 4-29/2/52.**G.**
Don. 11/2-11/3/54.**G.**
Don. 20-26/4/54.**N/C.**
Don. 3/1-8/2/56.**G.**
Don. 12/3-17/4/58.**G.**
Don. 29/8-22/9/58.**C/L.**
Don. 29/8-19/9/59.**C/L.**
Don. 5/7-6/8/60.**G.**

BOILERS:
 8131.
 8126 *(ex1395)* 7/9/34.
RS4079 *(ex1399)* 12/6/36.
 8870 *(new)* 27/5/37.
 8135A *(ex1117)* 27/6/39.
 8967 *(ex2455)* 17/10/42.
10537 *(new)* 17/12/49.
27217 *(ex61930)* 29/2/52.
27271 *(ex61819)* 11/3/54.
27180 *(ex61874)* 8/2/56.
27152 *(ex61828)* 17/4/58.
27151 *(ex61800)* 6/8/60.

SHEDS:
York.
Gorton 21/9/40.
York 17/10/40.
Gateshead 1/9/41.
Heaton 28/3/43.
Hull Dairycoates 12/5/46.

RENUMBERED:
 1871 20/1/46.
61871 23/2/49.

CONDEMNED:
3/12/62.
Cut up at Doncaster.

GRESLEY K3

1318

Doncaster 1713.

To traffic 12/6/29.

REPAIRS:
Don. 22/5-26/7/30.**L.**
Dar. 13/8-7/9/31.**N/C.**
Dar. 23/2-13/4/33.**G.** *West.brake off.*
Dar. 9/8-2/9/34.**L.**
Dar. 24/5-17/7/35.**G.**
Dar. 20/10/36-14/1/37.**G.**
Dar. 16/3-19/5/39.**G.**
Dar. 8-10/4/40.**N/C.**
Dar. 9/6-29/7/41.**G.**
Dar. 31/3-29/4/42.**L.**
Dar. 23/12/42-14/1/43.**L.**
Don. 11/12/43-15/1/44.**H.**
Don. 24/11/44-6/1/45.**G.**
Don. 30/3-27/4/46.**L.**
Don. 22/2-29/3/47.**G.**
Ghd. 22/6-8/7/48.**L.**
Don. 22/8-1/10/49.**G.**
Don. 8-9/2/51.**N/C.**
Don. 21/8-27/9/51.**G.**
Don. 12/5-12/6/53.**G.**
Don. 7/2-9/3/55.**G.**
Don. 9-31/5/55.**G.**
Don. 28/9-10/10/55.**C/L.**
Don. 6/8-5/9/57.**G.**
Don. 9/10-12/11/59.**G.**
Don. 11-19/4/60.**N/C.**

BOILERS:
8133.
D1652 *(ex1367)* 17/7/35.
8119 *(ex1395)* 14/1/37.

8125 *(ex1102)* 19/5/39.
2845 *(ex3825)* 29/7/41.
2788 *(ex3817)* 29/3/47.
27191 *(ex61888)* 27/9/51.
27150 *(ex61965)* 12/6/53.
27110 *(ex61890)* 9/3/55.
27137 *(ex61927)* 5/9/57.
24925 *(ex61870)* 12/11/59.

SHEDS:
York.
Gateshead 7/6/37.
Stockton 16/10/39.
Blaydon 14/6/41.
Heaton 19/6/43.
Darlington 16/7/43.
Neville Hill 25/6/45.
Hull Dairycoates 5/10/47.

RENUMBERED:
1872 25/4/46.
61872 8/7/48.

CONDEMNED:
3/12/62.
Cut up at Doncaster.

1331

Doncaster 1714.

To traffic 29/6/29.

REPAIRS:
Dar. 2/9-20/10/31.**G.** *West.brake off.*
Ghd. 11-21/4/32.**N/C.**
Dar. 23/10-29/11/33.**G.**

Dar. 1/5-19/6/35.**G.**
Dar. 11/5-28/7/26.**L.**
Dar. 7/6-6/8/37.**G.**
Dar. 7-13/8/37.**N/C.**
Dar. 28/9-10/11/39.**G.**
Don. 21/10/41-21/1/42.**G.**
Don. 19-30/3/42.**L.**
Don. 8/8-12/9/43.**L.**
Don. 22/4-23/5/44.**G.**
Don. 9/10-6/11/45.**G.**
Don. 9/6-13/8/47.**G.**
Don. 27/4-2/6/49.**G.**
Don. 15-26/10/49.**C/L.**
Don. 14/8-19/9/51.**G.**
Don. 16/10-5/11/51.**C/L.**
Don. 20/9-22/10/53.**G.**
Don. 4/2-7/3/55.**C/L.**
Don. 24/7-26/8/55.**G.**
Don. 11/4-25/5/57.**G.**
Don. 29/7-2/9/59.**G.**
Don. 18-22/1/60.**N/C.**

BOILERS:
8132.
8121 *(ex1388)* 29/11/33.
8116 *(ex1387)* 19/6/35.
8117 *(ex1117)* 6/8/37.
D1649 *(ex1307)* 10/11/39.
9283 *(new)* 21/1/42.
AW83 *(ex118)* 2/6/49.
27188 *(ex61951)* 19/9/51.
27120 *(ex61966)* 22/10/53.
27228 *(ex61816)* 25/5/57.
27337 *(ex spare and 61931)* 2/9/59.

SHEDS:
Tweedmouth.
York 19/3/39.

Sheffield 11/9/40.
New England 25/6/45.
March 16/6/46.
New England 19/10/46.
March 16/2/47.
Colwick 16/9/56.

RENUMBERED:
1873 24/3/46.
61873 2/6/49.

CONDEMNED:
8/5/62.
Cut up at Doncaster.

1345

Doncaster 1715.

To traffic 6/7/29.

REPAIRS:
Ghd. 16-23/11/29.**L.**
Ghd. 10/8-7/9/31.**L.**
Dar. 14/12/31-8/2/32.**G.** *West.brake off.*
Dar. 18/4-20/6/33.**G.**
Dar. 1/8-3/9/34.**L.**
Dar. 16/1-31/10/35.**G.**
Dar. 2/4-4/6/37.**G.**
Don. 20/2-18/3/39.**G.**
Dar. 24/5-3/6/40.**N/C.**
Dar. 7/2-5/4/41.**G.**
Don. 11/12/43-8/1/44.**G.**
Dar. 16/11/44-8/1/45.**L.**
Don. 8/9-13/10/45.**G.**
Don. 27/7-17/8/46.**L.**

61867 seen running through York station in July 1958 has a smokebox door differing in two respects. Each strap has been extended beyond the hinge to form a door stop, and the cross rail is above the cast number plate, which was unusual, the only other K3 so noted being 61924. The boiler handrails have been cut back, and the guard irons have been taken off the frame ends, but it has had Automatic Warning System installed. Repainted in June 1958 it would be one of the last to get the discredited BR emblem which had the lion facing the wrong way, but correction was made at a November 1960 repair.

No.1300 was also the first K3 fitted with Group Standard instead of double case buffers and this photograph was taken after March 1932 when the Westinghouse brake was taken off. Two other front end details are worth pointing out; the addition of CLASS K3 to the buffer beam is evidence of a shopping by Darlington - the other workshops did not make it until March 1938 onwards. Note the elliptical hole in the vertical plate to permit access to the 2 to 1 levers, but its usefulness was outweighed by smokebox char being able to get at them when the door was open for cleaning.

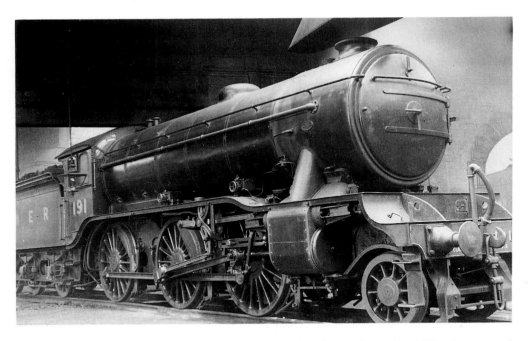

It was the middle 1930's before protection was provided against char getting at the middle valve gear, and as seen on 191 in Gateshead shed on 18th March 1939, the effective remedy was the fitting of a small hinged cover to the access hole. The difference between 191's double case, and 1300's Group Standard buffers is readily discernible.

27166 *(ex61945)* 24/1/58.
27154 *(ex61841)* 29/1/60.

SHEDS:
Tweedmouth.
York 19/3/39.
Neville Hill 20/1/43.
Heaton 28/3/43.
Hull Dairycoates 12/5/46.

RENUMBERED:
1874 17/8/46.
61874 24/12/48.

CONDEMNED:
22/5/61.
Cut up at Doncaster.

1364

Doncaster 1716.

To traffic 13/7/29.

REPAIRS:
Dar. 3/10-28/11/31.**G.** *West.brake off.*
Ghd. 24/8-10/9/32.**L.**
Ghd. 17-24/12/32.**N/C.**
Dar. 13/1-17/2/34.**G.**
Dar. 28/9-23/11/35.**G.**
Dar. 3/4-12/6/37.**G.**
Dar. 24/9/38-14/1/39.**L.**
Dar. 3/6-5/8/39.**G.**
Dar. 24-27/4/40.**N/C.**
Dar. 8/2-1/3/41.**L.**
Dar. 3/1-14/2/42.**G.**
Dar. 15/8-12/9/42.**L.**
Dar. 23/10-18/12/43.**H.**

Don. 11/11-31/12/47.**G.**	Don. 19/11/59-29/1/60.**G.**	8118 *(ex1386)* 20/6/33.
Don. 13-24/12/48.**L.**	Don. 28/3-2/4/60.**N/C.**	AW81 *(ex28)* 4/6/37.
Don. 20/9-12/11/49.**G.**	Don. 3-11/5/60.**N/C.**	2808 *(ex3822)* 5/4/41.
Don. 12/6-17/7/51.**G.**	Don. 12/5/61.*Not repaired.*	8919 *(ex1949)* 31/12/47.
Don. 4-28/8/53.**G.**		27178 *(ex61812)* 17/7/51.
Don. 18/7-23/8/55.**G.**	*BOILERS:*	27180 *(ex61953)* 28/8/53.
Dar. 10/12/57-24/1/58.**G.**	8134.	24901 *(new)* 23/8/55.

For the axleboxes, a Wakefield mechanical lubricator was provided, and it was mounted on the running plate above the middle coupled wheel on the right hand side. Lubrication for the motion was by sight feed from the cab, with the piping on the left hand side seen clearly on the lower photograph on page 2.

Dar. 8-17/3/45.**L.**
Don. 12/9-20/10/45.**G.**
Don. 15/7-10/8/46.**L.**
Don. 5/8-1/10/47.**G.**
Ghd. 27/2-9/4/48.**H.**
Don. 18/7-14/9/49.**G.**
Ghd. 9/6-4/7/50.**C/L.**
Don. 12/2-13/3/51.**G.**
Don. 17/11-12/12/52.**G.**
Don. 30/8-12/10/54.**G.**
Don. 7/6-19/7/56.**G.**
Don. 19/3-6/4/57.**C/L.**
Don. 16-24/8/57.**C/L.**
Don. 28/5-18/7/58.**G.**
Don. 17/5-15/6/60.**G.**

BOILERS:
8115.
8132 (ex1331) 17/2/34.
8120 (ex1364) 23/11/35.
8870 (ex1312) 5/8/39.
2840 (ex3827) 14/2/42.
D1645 (ex3827) 18/12/43.
2828 (ex17) 1/10/47.
27148 (ex1905) 13/3/51.
27145 (ex61978) 12/12/52.
27286 (new) 12/10/54.
27247 (ex61948) 19/7/56.
27170 (ex61919) 18/7/58.
24934 (ex61806) 15/6/60.

SHEDS:
Tweedmouth.
Heaton 19/3/39.
Stockton 1/4/40.
Blaydon 14/6/41.
Gateshead 26/6/43.
March 30/5/48.
Heaton 31/10/48.
Hull Dairycoates 17/1/60.

RENUMBERED:
1875 10/8/46.
61875 9/4/48.

CONDEMNED:
10/12/62.
Cut up at Doncaster.

1365

Doncaster 1717.

To traffic 27/7/29.

REPAIRS:
Dar. 26/5-19/8/31.**G.**
Ghd. 9-17/9/31.**N/C.**
Ghd. 2-10/5/32.**N/C.**
Dar. 29/5-14/7/33.**G.** *West.brake off.*
Dar. 12/11/34-11/1/35.**G.**
Dar. 29/10-17/12/35.**L.**
Dar. 7/4-1/6/37.**G.**
Dar. 2-25/6/37.**N/C.**
Don. 19/8-23/9/38.**G.**
Cow. 27/4/39.**L.**
Cow. 30/9/39.**G.**
Cow. 11/5/40.**L.**
Cow. 23/11/40.**G.**
Cow. 9/5/42.**G.**
Cow. 22/4/44.**G.**
Don. 31/3-5/5/45.**L.**
Cow. 14-21/7/45.**L.**
Cow. 8-15/9/45.**L.**
Cow. 2/4-21/6/46.**G.**
Cow. 14/6-19/7/47.**L.**
Cow. 26/11/47-7/1/48.**G.**
Cow. 29/7-3/9/49.**G.**
Cow. 22/2-12/5/51.**G.**
Cow. 24/11-13/12/52.**H/I.**
Cow. 10/11-12/12/53.**N/C.**
Cow. 19/8-7/10/54.**L/I.**
Cow. 9/4-9/6/56.**G.**
Cow. 16/1-22/2/58.**H/I.**

BOILERS:
8116.
8134 (ex1345) 14/7/33.
D1655 (ex33) 11/1/35.
7D/687 (ex200) 9/5/42.
2848 (ex1394) 21/6/46.
27306 (ex1916) 12/5/51.
27341 (new) 9/6/56.

SHEDS:
Tweedmouth.
St Margarets 19/3/39.
Haymarket 1/10/43.
St Margarets 12/43.

Carlisle 10/45.
St Margarets 21/4/47.

RENUMBERED:
1876 20/6/46.
61876 6/11/48.

CONDEMNED:
17/9/59.
Cut up at Cowlairs.

1367

Doncaster 1718.

To traffic 17/8/29.

REPAIRS:
Ghd. 9-15/4/31.**N/C.**
Dar. 27/5-6/8/31.**G.**
Ghd. 6-14/1/32.**N/C.**
Dar. 24/3-11/5/32.**H.**
Dar. 2/3-12/4/33.**G.** *West.brake off.*
Dar. 2-31/8/34.**L.**
Dar. 6/3-20/4/35.**G.**
Dar. 16/11/36-15/4/37.**G.**
Dar. 3/5-8/7/38.**G.**
Dar. 7/6-18/7/40.**G.**
Don. 15/9-16/10/42.**G.**
Don. 13/10-4/11/44.**G.**
Don. 14/3-3/5/46.**G.**
Don. 10/1-13/2/48.**G.**
Don. 5-29/7/49.**C/H.**
Don. 17/11-2/12/49.**C/L.**
Don. 31/3-11/5/50.**G.**
Don. 27/7-15/8/50.**C/L.**
Don. 16/10-17/11/51.**G.**
Don. 27/10-25/11/53.**G.**
Don. 29/12/53-12/1/54.**N/C.**
Don. 13/10-17/11/55.**G.**
Don. 29/11/57-10/1/58.**G.**
Don. 24/11-18/12/59.**G.**
Don. 19/12/60-3/2/61.**C/L.**

BOILERS:
8117.
D1652 (ex39) 12/4/33.
8123 (ex1391) 20/4/35.
RS4079 (ex1312) 15/4/37.

8120 (ex1364) 18/7/40.
9383 (ex2762) 3/5/46.
10806 (new) 11/5/50.
27199 (ex61927) 17/11/51.
27275 (new) 25/11/53.
24932 (new) 10/1/58.
27254 (ex61822) 18/12/59.

SHEDS:
Tweedmouth.
Colwick 23/11/40.
New England 25/6/45.
Gorton 23/1/49.
London Mid. Reg. 26/6/49.
Gorton 3/7/49.
Norwich 11/3/51.
March 13/5/51.
Lowestoft 7/10/51.
Norwich 23/12/51.
March 31/1/60.
Staveley 7/2/60.
Lincoln 20/3/60.
Immingham 31/7/60.
Colwick 29/10/61.

RENUMBERED:
1877 3/5/46.
E1877 13/2/48.
61877 29/7/49.

CONDEMNED:
24/7/62.
Cut up at Doncaster.

1368

Doncaster 1719.

To traffic 30/8/29.

REPAIRS:
Ghd. 23/2-3/3/31.**N/C.**
Dar. 31/12/31-26/2/32.**G.** *West.brake off.*
Ghd. 28/10/32-11/1/33.**L.**
Dar. 9-21/8/33.**N/C.**
Dar. 26/6-11/8/34.**G.**
Dar. 10/36.**G.**
Dar. 18/8-20/10/37.**H.**

When the valve gear modification was made, an additional Wakefield mechanical lubricator was put on the right hand running plate to serve it. No.159 became a 'one-off' because on valve modification, its additional mechanical was a Silvertown, to which brand the mechanical for the axles was also changed. As BR 61848 it still kept the Silvertown lubricators but no other K3 was so changed. Here in June 1938 at Sheffield (Victoria) it has a Manchester to Nottingham express passenger working. *P.J.Hughes.*

Dar. 11-24/11/38.**G.**
Cow. 12/3/41.**G.**
Cow. 16/1/42.**L.**
Cow. 4/7/42.**G.**
Cow. 12/4/43.**L.**
Cow. 24/12/43.**H.**
Cow. 6/7/44.**L.**
Cow. 6/10/44.**L.**
Cow. 21/4-5/5/45.**L.**
Cow. 5/7-23/8/45.**G.**
Cow. 11-25/5/46.**L.**
Don. 7-21/9/46.**L.**
Don. 18/1-22/2/47.**G.**
Don. 9-30/8/47.**L.**
Don. 1/11-6/12/47.**H.**
Don. 10-22/1/48.**L.**
Ghd. 4-19/10/48.**L.**
Don. 28/1-8/2/49.**C/L.**
Cow. 18/8-7/10/49.**H/I.**
Cow. 21/9-10/11/51.**G.**
Cow. 9-27/6/53.**H/I.**
Cow. 18/10-20/11/54.**L/I.**
Cow. 22/2-5/3/55.**C/L.**
Cow. 16/5-30/6/56.**G.**
Cow. 16/12/57-18/1/58.**L/I.**
Cow. 22/2-22/3/58.**C/L.**
Cow. 11/6-5/7/58.**C/L.**
Cow. 11-28/11/58.**C/L.**

BOILERS:
8119.
8127 *(ex1396)* 11/8/34.
8074 *(ex38)* 10/36.

AW76 *(ex1106)* 24/11/38.
1655 *(ex1365)* 4/7/42.
6D/687 *(ex1121)* 23/8/45.
RS4078 *(ex1322)* 22/2/47.
27322 *(ex1876)* 10/11/51.
27343 *(new)* 30/6/56.

SHEDS:
Tweedmouth.
St Margarets 19/3/39.
Haymarket 8/9/43.
St Margarets 9/44.
Gateshead 13/10/45.
Heaton 6/2/49.
St Margarets 13/2/49.

RENUMBERED:
1878 22/5/46.
E1878 22/1/48.
61878 19/10/48.

CONDEMNED:
6/8/59.
Cut up at Cowlairs.

1386

Doncaster 1720.

To traffic 7/9/29.

REPAIRS:
Dar. 11/11-30/12/31.**G.**

West brake off.
Dar. 22/3-4/5/33.**G.**
Dar. 23/10-4/12/34.**G.**
Dar. 13/8-25/10/35.**H.**
Dar. 14/9-30/10/36.**G.**
Dar. 7-25/11/36.**N/C.**
Don. 12/9-5/10/38.**G.**
Cow. 16/12/39.**G.**
Cow. 27/9/40.**G.**
Cow. 25/10/41.**G.**
Cow. 1/3/43.**L.**
Cow. 11/9/43.**G.**
Cow. 10/2-30/3/46.**G.**
Cow. 13/7-3/8/46.**L.**
Cow. 16/8-18/10/47.**G.**
Cow. 12/1-6/2/48.**G.** *After derailment.*
Cow. 8/6-19/8/50.**G.**
Cow. 14/7-25/8/52.**L/I.**
Cow. 17/12/52-4/2/53.**C/L.**
Cow. 16/2-20/3/54.**H/I.**
Cow. 6/12/55-21/1/56.**G.**
Cow. 26/10-21/11/56.**C/L.**
Cow. 6/7-24/8/57.**H/I.**
Cow. 3-7/9/57.**N/C.**

BOILERS:
8118.
8117 *(ex1367)* 4/5/33.
8073 *(ex39)* 4/12/34.
8131 *(ex1118)* 30/10/36.
3D/687 *(ex2769)* 5/10/38.
8971 *(ex2472)* 11/9/43.

2D/687 *(ex2769)* 30/3/46.
8599 *(ex1855)* 19/8/50.
27319 *(ex61990)* 21/1/56.

SHEDS:
Tweedmouth.
St Margarets 19/3/39.
Haymarket 17/9/43.
St Margarets 9/44.

RENUMBERED:
1879 30/3/46.
61879 19/8/50.

CONDEMNED:
16/6/59.
Cut up at Cowlairs.
Not in use 219 days in 1944.

1387

Doncaster 1721.

To traffic 5/10/29.

REPAIRS:
Ghd. 6-18/2/31.**N/C.**
Dar. 20/1-3/3/52.**G.** *West.brake off.*
Dar. 25/8-7/10/33.**G.**
Dar. 22/3-21/11/35.**G.**
Dar. 2/7-23/9/37.**G.**
Dar. 24/9-6/10/37.**N/C.**

WORKS CODES:- Cow - Cowlairs. Dar - Darlington. Don - Doncaster. Ghd - Gateshead. Gor - Gorton. Inv - Inverurie. Str - Stratford.
REPAIR CODES:- **C/H** - Casual Heavy. **C/L** - Casual Light. **G** - General. **H** - Heavy. **H/I** - Heavy Intermediate. **L** - Light. **L/I** - Light Intermediate. **N/C** - Non-Classified.

Sanding was steam operated to the middle (driving) coupled wheels, but the leading ones had gravity feed. Engines built in 1934 and later had the front sandbox lid set at an angle to help avoid spillage between the frames when replenishing. *W.L.Good.*

What had hitherto been 125 was re-numbered 1836 at its Immingham shed in May 1946, by using 6" stencil figures and local labour. It shows a wartime modification, in that the leading windows of the cab have been replaced by steel plate to reduce risk to the crew should enemy aircraft attack using their machine guns, not unusual around the Humber estuary. *W.L.Good.*

No.32 had a life of 38 years, from 29th August 1924 until 16th September 1962, but it only had a Group Standard tender coupled with it from new to 31st May 1925 so evidence of that coupling is very scarce. It then used a succession of four different GN type tenders for the rest of its life, the first of them already shown on page 23.

Dar. 6/7-24/8/39.**G.**	Don. 12/7-12/8/55.**G.**	D1730 *(ex17)* 21/11/35.	24929 *(ex61831)* 3/12/59.
Don. 15/5-26/6/42.**G.**	Don. 18-26/8/55.**N/C.**	8116 *(ex1331)* 23/9/37.	
Don. 5-18/1/44.**G.**	Don. 27/8-4/10/57.**G.**	8119 *(ex1318)* 24/8/39.	*SHEDS:*
Don. 20/10-23/11/44.**L.**	Don. 5/11-3/12/59.**G.**	9286 *(ex1870)* 16/6/49.	Tweedmouth.
Don. 30/4-16/6/47.**G.**		27158 *(ex61875)* 26/4/51.	York 19/3/39.
Don. 4/5-16/6/49.**G.**	*BOILERS:*	27153 *(ex61945)* 15/5/53.	Sheffield 11/9/40.
Don. 25/3-26/4/51.**G.**	8120.	27277 *(ex61922)* 12/8/55.	New England 25/6/45.
Don. 15/4-15/5/53.**G.**	8116 *(ex1365)* 7/10/33.	27238 *(ex61810)* 4/10/57.	Stratford 14/5/50.

Parkeston 14/12/58.
Cambridge 8/2/59.
March 26/11/61.

RENUMBERED:
1880 29/11/46.
61880 16/6/49.

CONDEMNED:
16/9/62.
*Sold for scrap to Central Wagon Co.
Ince.*

1388

Doncaster 1722.

To traffic 5/10/29.

REPAIRS:
Ghd. 30/7-17/8/31.**N/C.**
Dar. 17/2-6/4/32.**G.** *West.brake off &
cab alt.*
Dar. 15/9-20/10/33.**G.**
Dar. 5/35.**G.**
Dar. 4/37.**G.**
Dar. 9/9-26/10/38.**G.**
Cow. 18/7/39.**G.**
Cow. 29/6/40.**G.**
Cow. 30/1/41.**L.**
Cow. 10/1/42.**G.**
Cow. 26/5/43.**L.**
Cow. 27/11/43.**G.**
Cow. 12/5-2/6/45.**L.**
Cow. 26/9-7/10/45.**L.**
Don. 1/10-9/11/46.**L.**
Don. 15-22/11/46.**N/C.**
Don. 17/5-27/6/47.**G.**
Don. 20/12/47-17/1/48.**L.**
Ghd. 11-19/11/48.**L.**

Cow. 14/3-30/4/49.**G.** *Not repaint-
still LNER.*
Cow. 8/10-20/11/50.**G.**
Cow. 9/1-7/2/52.**L/I.**
Cow. 18/3-18/4/53.**G.**
Cow. 6/12/54-15/1/55.**H/I.**
StM. 24/5-9/6/55.**C/L.**
Cow. 18/8-1/10/55.**C/L.**
Cow. 12/3-21/4/56.**H/I.**
Cow. 2-5/5/56.**N/C.**
Cow. 23/8-13/9/56.**C/L.**
Cow. 23/8-1/10/57.**G.**
Cow. 8-25/1/58.**N/C.**
Cow. 24/3-1/4/58.**N/C.**
Cow. 24/4-14/5/58.**N/C.**
Cow. 26/5-7/6/58.**N/C.**
Cow. 30/7-6/9/58.**C/H.**

BOILERS:
8121.
8120 *(ex1387)* 20/10/33.
AW77 *(ex1101)* 5/35.
8741 *(ex1135)* 27/11/43.
9801 *(new)* 27/6/47.
Renumbered 27331 7/2/52.
27300 *(ex61857)* 18/4/53.
27306 *(ex61876)* 1/10/57.

SHEDS:
Heaton.
Tweedmouth 23/6/31.
St Margarets 19/3/39.
Haymarket 12/43.
St Margarets 9/44.
Gateshead 13/10/45.
Heaton 6/2/49.
St Margarets 13/2/49.

RENUMBERED:
1881 9/11/46.
61881 18/11/48.

CONDEMNED:
21/4/60.
*Cut up at Cowlairs.
Not in use 219 days in 1944.*

1389

Doncaster 1723.

To traffic 12/10/29.

REPAIRS:
Dar. 3-24/3/31.**N/C.**
Dar. 29/7-27/8/31.**L.**
Dar. 3/12/31-5/2/32.**G.** *West.brake
off.*
Don. 25/1-2/3/34.**G.**
Dar. 2/9-25/10/35.**G.**
Dar. 12/7-1/10/37.**G.**
Dar. 6/11-23/12/39.**G.**
Cow. 9/41.**G.**
Cow. 7/43.**H.**
Cow. 9/44.**L.**
Cow. 2/7-5/10/46.**G.**
Cow. 2/8-17/9/48.**G.**
Cow. 1/7-20/8/49.**G.**
Cow. 8/7/50.**L/I.**
Cow. 9/50.**N/C.**
Cow. 8/6-9/7/51.**G.**
Cow. 25/6-18/7/52.**L/I.**
Cow. 27/8-6/10/53.**L/I.**
Cow. 21/5-10/7/54.**C/L.**
Cow. 1/12/54-20/1/55.**G.**
Cow. 4/10-8/11/56.**L/I.**
Cow. 5/9-15/10/58.**H/I.**

BOILERS:
8122.
D1650 *(ex36)* 25/10/35.
8123 *(ex1367)* 1/10/37.

AW78 *(ex1396)* 23/12/39.
27323 *(ex1858)* 9/7/51.
27308 *(ex61855)* 20/1/55.

SHEDS:
Heaton.
Gateshead 19/9/34.
Heaton 1/10/34.
St Margarets 27/2/40.
Carlisle 5/40.
Woodford 11/4/59.

RENUMBERED:
1882 5/10/46.
61882 17/9/48.

CONDEMNED:
28/5/60.
Cut up at Cowlairs.

1391

Doncaster 1724.

To traffic 23/10/29.

REPAIRS:
Dar. 9/10-27/11/31.**G.** *West.brake off.*
Dar. 1-11/4/32.**N/C.**
Ghd. 3-11/8/32.**N/C.**
Dar. 29/6-8/9/33.**G.**
Dar. 4/2-23/3/35.**G.**
Dar. 20/4-11/6/37.**G.**
Dar. 6/12/38-17/1/39.**G.**
Dar. 19/8-5/10/40.**G.**
Dar. 25/4-23/5/41.**N/C.**
Dar. 10/11-9/12/41.**L.**
Dar. 31/3-9/5/42.**L.**
Dar. 28/7-6/9/43.**H.**
Dar. 13/11/44-17/1/45.**G.**

Although the GN tenders used with some of the K3 class were all the 3500 gallon type with coal rails, they were not all alike. This tender with 191 shows one of those built prior to September 1912 because it has open hand grip at the cab entrance. The tender shown with 32 is the modification then made, the opening being discarded on those built later. *J.J.Cunningham.*

Dar. 27/1-22/3/45.**L.**
Don. 12/10-9/11/46.**G.**
Don. 26/8-20/9/47.**L.**
Don. 31/12/48-29/1/49.**G.**
Don. 16/4-11/5/51.**G.**
Don. 3/6-8/7/53.**G.**
Don. 5-13/10/54.**C/L.**
Don. 23/5-8/7/55.**G.**
Don. 27/5-6/7/57.**G.**
Don. 20/8-25/9/59.**G.**

BOILERS:
 8123.
 D1658 *(ex28)* 23/3/35.
 8122 *(ex1392)* 17/1/39.
 RS4078 *(ex1332)* 5/10/40.
 8121 *(ex46)* 6/9/43.
 8874 *(ex1946)* 29/1/49.
 27163 *(ex61965)* 11/5/51.
 27160 *(ex61919)* 8/7/53.
 27176 *(ex61833)* 8/7/55.
 27179 *(ex61893)* 6/7/57.
 27208 *(ex61825)* 25/9/59.

SHEDS:
 Heaton.
 Stockton 1/4/40.
 Darlington 16/7/40.
 Blaydon 14/6/41.
 Heaton 19/6/43.
 Gateshead 8/7/43.
 Neville Hill 23/7/45.
 Hull Dairycoates 5/10/47.

RENUMBERED:
 1883 9/11/46.
 61883 28/1/49.

CONDEMNED:
3/12/62.
Cut up at Doncaster.

1392

Doncaster 1725.

To traffic 2/11/29.

REPAIRS:
Dar. 29/9-19/11/31.**G.** *West.brake off.*
Ghd. 8-15/9/32.**N/C.**
Ghd. 19-22/12/32.**L.**
Don. 20/1-22/2/34.**G.**
Dar. 23/11/35-11/1/36.**G.**
Dar. 27/11/37-22/1/38.**G.**
Dar. 30/7-24/9/38.**L.**
Dar. 2/9-14/10/39.**G.**
Dar. 24/5-5/7/41.**G.**
Dar. 13/2-3/4/43.**G.**
Don. 6/5-10/6/44.**G.**
Don. 15/1-17/2/45.**G.**
Don. 12/10-24/11/45.**L.**
Don. 14/11-7/12/46.**L.**
Don. 5/2-21/3/47.**G.**
Don. 16/7-28/8/47.**H.**
Don. 30/10-8/12/48.**G.**
Don. 28/8-6/10/50.**G.**
Don. 3/6-16/7/52.**G.**
Don. 30/3-30/4/54.**G.**
Don. 8/2-10/3/56.**G.**

Modellers determined on accuracy can take nothing for granted. The batch of ten tenders built for the engines numbered 202 to 231 could reasonably have been expected to be identical, but that was not the case. Nine of them had disc wheels, but 228's had spoked wheels, and it kept that tender throughout its life.

Don. 1/5-11/7/58.**G.**
Don. 4-26/11/58.**C/L.**
Don. 15/6-29/7/60.**G.**
Don. 15/9/61.*Weigh.*
Don. 12/7/62.*Not repaired.*

BOILERS:
 8124.
 8122 *(ex1389)* 11/1/36.
 D1645 *(ex39)* 22/1/38.
 8136A *(ex1304)* 5/7/41.
 8968 *(ex3824)* 3/4/43.
 8737 *(ex111)* 21/3/47.
 27102 *(ex61912)* 6/10/50.
 27243 *(ex61967)* 16/7/52.
 27236 *(ex61839)* 30/4/54.
 27196 *(ex61963)* 10/3/56.
 27280 *(ex61923)* 11/7/58.

SHEDS:
 Heaton.
 March 30/5/48.
 Heaton 10/10/48.
 Hull Dairycoates 10/5/53.
 Heaton 14/9/58.
 Tyne Dock 4/12/60.
 Heaton 25/12/60.
 Tyne Dock 15/1/61.
 Hull Dairycoates 30/7/61.

RENUMBERED:
 1884 27/10/46.
 61884 8/12/48.

CONDEMNED:
23/7/62.
Cut up at Doncaster.

1394

Doncaster 1726.

To traffic 13/11/29.

REPAIRS:
Dar. 23/2-20/3/31.**N/C.**
Ghd. 18/6-3/7/31.**N/C.**
Dar. 8/1-23/2/32.**G.** *West.brake off.*
Dar. 30/4-29/6/34.**G.**
Dar. 19/11/35-17/1/36.**G.**
Dar. 10/11/37-9/2/38.**G.**
Dar. 26/7-23/8/39.**N/C.**
Dar. 10/1-14/2/40.**G.**
Dar. 16/6-21/8/41.**G.**
Cow. 19/11/42.**H.**
Dar. 4-11/1/43.**N/C.**
Cow. 22/10/43.**G.**
Cow. 7-8/9/45.**C/L.**
Cow. 28/2-4/5/46.**G.**
Cow. 24/5-2/7/48.**G.**
Cow. 11-29/1/49.**C/L.**
Cow. 14/11-23/12/50.**L/I.**
Cow. 30/6-8/8/51.**C/L.**
Cow. 18/2-3/5/52.**L/I.**
Cow. 4-27/6/53.**G.**
Cow. 12/4-1/5/54.**C/L.**
Cow. 15/11-18/12/54.**L/I.**
Cow. 8/6-25/8/56.**G.**
Cow. 13/12/56-12/1/57.**C/L.**
Cow. 25/9-9/11/57.**H/I.**
Cow. 3/5-7/6/58.**C/L.**

BOILERS:
 8125.
 8129 *(ex1398)* 29/6/34.
 8132 *(ex1364)* 17/1/36.
 8124 *(ex1325)* 9/2/38.
 8126 *(ex1119)* 14/2/40.
 2848 *(ex46)* 21/8/41.
 8971 *(ex1386)* 4/5/46.
 9284 *(ex1851)* 2/7/48.
 Renumbered 27327 3/5/52.
 27328 *(ex61854)* 27/6/53.
 27345 *(new)* 25/8/56.

SHEDS:
 Heaton.
 Gateshead 19/9/34.
 Heaton 1/10/34.

March 27/10/41.
St Margarets 30/9/42.
Carlisle 11/43.
St Margarets 9/44.

RENUMBERED:
 1885 25/8/46.
 61885 2/7/48.

CONDEMNED:
3/11/59.
Cut up at Cowlairs.
Not in use 217 days in 1944.

1395

Doncaster 1727.

To traffic 18/11/29.

REPAIRS:
Dar. 19/2-8/4/32.**G.** *West.brake off & cab alt.*
Dar. 27/7-4/8/32.**N/C.**
Dar. 4/7-7/9/34.**G.**
Dar. 6/5-21/6/35.**L.**
Dar. 12/10-15/12/36.**G.**
Dar. 16/3-13/6/39.**G.**
Dar. 26/5-9/7/41.**G.**
Don. 7-18/6/42.**L.**
Don. 19/9-22/10/43.**G.**
Don. 23/10-13/12/45.**G.**
Don. 21/8-22/10/47.**G.**
Don. 17/6-14/9/49.**G.**
Don. 26/4-6/6/51.**G.**
Don. 6/2-6/3/53.**G.**
Don. 30/11-31/12/54.**G.**
Don. 8/12/56-16/1/57.**G.**
Don. 11-13/4/57.**C/L.**
Don. 24/9-5/11/58.**G.**
Don. 14/9-13/10/60.**G.**

BOILERS:
 8126.

Two of the original stepped top tenders underwent comprehensive rebuilding at Doncaster after British Railways took over. They were those coupled with 61853 in December 1949 and 61861 in April 1950, which then kept them until their respective withdrawals. They were made flush sided and given high front plate but were the only two to have snap-head rivets. Two more K3's acquired tender with high front plate which were taken from other classes; they were 1811 whose tender came from V2 class 847, and 61873 which came from A2/1 class 510, those transfers taking place in May 1947 and June 1949.

8119 (ex1368) 7/9/34.
8073 (ex1386) 15/12/36.
D1658 (ex1391) 13/6/39.
AW80 (ex1310) 9/7/41.
9285 (ex1954) 14/9/49.
27167 (ex61833) 6/6/51.
27112 (ex61826) 6/3/53.
27292 (new) 31/12/54.
27253 (ex61972) 16/1/57.
27212 (ex61926) 5/11/58.
24908 (ex61821) 13/10/60.

SHEDS:
York.
March 4/9/41.

RENUMBERED:
1886 20/10/46.
61886 14/9/49.

CONDEMNED:
16/9/62.
Sold for scrap to Central Wagon Co. Ince.

1396

Doncaster 1728.

To traffic 29/11/29.

REPAIRS:
Dar. 30/7-15/8/30.**N/C.**
Dar. 18-19/8/30.**N/C.**
Ghd. 10-17/8/31.**N/C.**
Dar. 24/2-21/4/32.**G.** *West.brake off & cab.alt.*
Dar. 9/6-13/8/34.**G.**
Dar. 18/8-15/10/36.**G.**
Dar. 26/11/36-1/3/37.**L.**
Dar. 13/5-14/7/37.**H.**
Dar. 25/5-8/7/39.**G.**

Dar. 10-21/7/39.**N/C.**
Dar. 24-28/7/39.**N/C.**
Dar. 2-25/8/39.**N/C.**
Dar. 1-29/1/41.**L.**
Dar. 1/10-15/11/41.**G.**
Don. 10/10-23/11/43.**G.**
Don. 21/4-8/7/44.**G.**
Don. 13/5-27/6/46.**G.**
Don. 28/7-1/9/48.**G.**
Don. 16/8-22/9/50.**G.**
Don. 26/5-3/7/52.**G.**
Don. 12/4-17/5/54.**G.**
Don. 4/1-11/2/56.**G.**
Don. 16/1-18/2/58.**G.**
Don. 26/2-14/3/59.**C/L.**
Don. 2/3-1/4/60.**G.**

BOILERS:
8127.
AW78 (ex1102) 13/8/34.
8128 (ex1397) 8/7/39.
D1658 (ex1395) 15/11/41.
9384 (new) 23/11/43.
27100 (ex61844) 22/9/50.
27242 (ex61811) 3/7/52.
27259 (new) 17/5/54.
24908 (new) 11/2/56.
27192 (ex61822) 18/2/58.
27290 (ex61956) 1/4/60.

SHEDS:
York.
Gateshead 2/12/29.
March 11/12/41.
Doncaster 16/9/56.

RENUMBERED:
1887 20/10/46.
61887 1/9/48.

CONDEMNED:
2/3/62.
Cut up at Doncaster.

1397

Doncaster 1729.

To traffic 11/12/29.

REPAIRS:
Ghd. 12-30/6/31.**N/C.**
Dar. 13-28/8/31.**N/C.**
Dar. 4/2-24/3/32.**G.** *West.brake off.*
Don. 23/1-23/2/34.**G.**
Dar. 26/8-16/9/35.**N/C.**
Dar. 11/8-26/10/36.**G.**
Dar. 13/1-20/2/39.**G.**
Dar. 11/4-27/5/41.**G.**
Dar. 28/5-11/6/41.**N/C.**
Dar. 5-21/1/42.**L.** *Tender only.*
Dar. 1/9-5/10/42.**L.**
Dar. 21/5-7/7/43.**G.**
Dar. 23/8-9/9/44.**L.**
Don. 26/5-7/7/45.**G.**
Don. 7/8-4/10/47.**G.**
Don. 10/5-16/6/49.**G.**
Don. 3/8-4/9/51.**G.**
Don. 9/1-1/2/52.**C/L.**
Don. 12/6-22/7/53.**G.**
Don. 1-30/3/55.**G.**
Don. 1/6-8/7/55.**C/L.**
Don. 24/1-22/2/57.**G.**
Don. 27/4-28/5/59.**G.**
Don. 28/1-4/2/60.**N/C.**

BOILERS:
8128.
8130 (ex1398) 20/2/39.
2852 (ex3826) 27/5/41.
2941 (ex1339) 7/7/43.
8600 (ex116) 4/10/47.
27187 (ex61934) 4/9/51.
27158 (ex61971) 30/3/55.
24921 (new) 22/2/57.
27126 (ex61866) 28/5/59.

SHEDS:
York.
Neville Hill 20/1/43.
Heaton 28/3/43.
Gateshead 16/7/43.
Neville Hill 23/7/45.
March 23/3/47.
Colwick 16/9/56.

RENUMBERED:
1888 20/10/46.
61888 16/6/49.

CONDEMNED:
25/9/61.
Cut up at Doncaster.

1398

Doncaster 1730.

To traffic 13/12/29.

REPAIRS:
Dar. 10/3-2/5/32.**G.** *West.brake off.*
Dar. 17/4-24/5/34.**G.**
Dar. 9/6-7/8/36.**G.**
Dar. 30/11/37-14/2/38.**G.**
Dar. 21/2-5/4/38.**N/C.**
Dar. 9/3-13/4/40.**G.**
Dar. 18/3-29/4/41.**L.**
Dar. 4/3-11/4/42.**G.**
Dar. 19/5-2/6/42.**N/C.**
Don. 29/1-17/3/45.**G.**
Don. 13/4-4/5/46.**L.**
Don. 6/5-26/6/47.**G.**
Don. 11/9-6/10/48.**L.**
Don. 6/3-11/4/49.**G.**
Don. 31/3-12/5/50.**G.**
Don. 2-15/1/51.**C/L.**
Don. 19/3-23/4/52.**G.**
Don. 12/1-6/2/54.**G.**

Don. 12/6-1/8/56.**G.**
Don. 12-21/3/57.**C/L.**
Don. 15-26/11/57.**C/L.**
Don. 15-31/1/58.**C/L.**
Don. 22/12/58-30/1/59.**G.**
Don. 21/2-29/3/61.**G.**

BOILERS:
8129.
8130 (ex1300) 24/5/34.
RS4080 (ex1307) 7/8/36.
RS4081 (ex1322) 14/2/38.
2859 (ex3829) 13/4/40.
D1730 (ex1307) 11/4/42.
8073 (ex52) 17/3/45.
9994 (new) 11/4/49.
10808 (new) 12/5/50.
27269 (new) 23/4/52.
27169 (ex61906) 6/2/54.
27102 (ex61846) 1/8/56.
24912 (ex61846) 30/1/59.

SHEDS:
York.
Tweedmouth 21/5/42.
Heaton 28/3/43.
Darlington 3/8/43.
Neville Hill 25/6/45.
March 23/3/47.
Norwich 10/10/48.
March 16/12/48.
Gorton 9/1/50.
March 21/1/50.
Lincoln 29/8/54.
Colwick 16/10/60.
Immingham 14/1/62.

RENUMBERED:
1889 14/7/46.
61889 6/10/48.

CONDEMNED:
4/11/62.
Sold for scrap to J.Cashmore, Great
Bridge.

2761

Darlington.

To traffic 19/7/30.

REPAIRS:
Don. 19/9-12/11/31.**G.**
Don. 20/4-9/6/33.**G.**
Don. 19/10-6/12/34.**G.**
Don. 29/12/34-13/2/35.**L.**
Don. 17/9-14/10/36.**G.**
Don. 20/3-2/5/38.**G.**
Don. 13/9-14/10/40.**G.**
Don. 24/1-27/2/41.**L.**
Don. 20/12/42-14/1/43.**G.**
Don. 22/1-21/3/44.**L.**
Don. 13/7-21/9/46.**G.**
Don. 6/10-3/12/48.**G.**
Don. 3/12/50-4/1/51.**G.**
Don. 22/1-17/2/53.**G.**
Don. 28/4-12/5/54.**C/L.**
Don. 24/1-25/2/55.**G.**
Don. 11/1-9/2/57.**G.**
Don. 5/12/58-15/1/59.**G.**
Don. 22/9-20/10/59.**C/L.**
Don. 14/5-9/6/60.**C/L.**
Don. 14/9-21/10/60.**G.**

BOILERS:
1D/687.
8603 (ex1158) 14/10/36.
8966 (ex2453) 14/1/43.
8116 (ex39) 21/9/46.
27131 (ex61816) 4/1/51.
27110 (ex61946) 17/2/53.
27249 (ex61970) 25/2/55.
27291 (ex61989) 9/2/57.
27286 (ex61902) 15/1/59.

SHEDS:
Doncaster.
Kings Cross 31/7/30.
Colwick 14/12/39.
New England 22/4/45.
March 20/9/53.

RENUMBERED:
1890 21/9/46.
61890 3/12/48.

CONDEMNED:
16/9/62.
Sold for scrap to Central Wagon Co.
Ince.

2762

Darlington.

To traffic 29/7/30.

REPAIRS:
Don. 3/5-2/6/32.**G.**
Don. 22/6-25/7/33.**G.**
Don. 23/4-9/6/34.**G.**
Don. 31/7-6/9/35.**G.**
Don. 9/2-6/3/37.**G.**
Don. 26/4-12/5/38.**G.** Front
heat.conn.
Don. 10/2-23/3/40.**G.**
Don. 16/5-13/6/42.**G.**
Don. 25/3-29/4/44.**G.**
Don. 16/3-20/4/46.**G.**
Don. 26/10-4/12/47.**G.**
Don. 25/9-28/10/49.**G.**
Don. 7/10-2/11/51.**G.**
Don. 11-13/2/52.**N/C.**
Don. 14/6-21/7/53.**G.**
Don. 6-12/8/53.**N/C.**
Don. 13/8-25/9/54.**C/L.**
Don. 19/10-17/11/54.**C/L.**
Don. 17/4-20/5/55.**G.**
Don. 27/5-19/7/57.**G.**
Don. 30/6-30/7/59.**G.**
Don. 13-30/1/60.**C/L.**

BOILERS:
2D/687.
D1762 (ex229) 6/3/37.
8595 (ex1158) 12/5/38.
9383 (new) 29/4/44.
8912 (ex2428) 20/4/46.

2859 (ex1860) 28/10/49.
27198 (ex61821) 2/11/51.
27134 (ex61960) 21/7/53.
27260 (ex61805) 20/5/55.
27262 (ex61866) 19/7/57.
27281 (ex spare and 61984) 30/7/59.

SHEDS:
Doncaster.
New England 7/8/30.
March 5/3/36.
Norwich 29/10/38.
Lincoln 19/11/40.
Immingham 20/11/40.
Lincoln 17/6/45.
Immingham 23/9/45.
Lincoln 9/7/61.

RENUMBERED:
1891 17/11/46.
61891 28/10/49.

CONDEMNED:
12/9/61.
Cut up at Doncaster.

2763

Darlington.

To traffic 29/7/30.

REPAIRS:
Don. 29/1-3/3/32.**G.**
Don. 18/5-22/6/33.**G.**
Don. 1-28/11/34.**G.**
Don. 27/1-29/2/36.**G.**
Don. 2-30/11/37.**G.**
Don. 22/7-2/9/39.**G.**
Don. 19-20/1/40.**L.**
Don. 11/10-29/11/41.**G.**
Don. 21/3-22/4/44.**G.**
Don. 7-20/6/44.**L.** Tender only.
Don. 2/2-9/3/46.**L.**
Don. 3/12/46-4/1/47.**G.**
Ghd. 26/4-25/5/48.**L.**

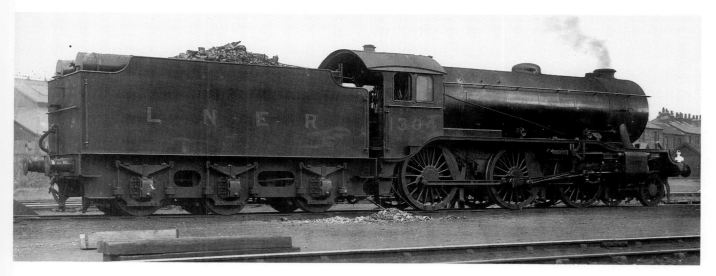

The last 74 of K3 class built in 1934 to 1937 had vacuum brake for engine, tender, and train for which the two vacuum cylinders on the forty built in 1934 and 1935 were 1' 10" diameter and 4' 6" long and were mounted on top of the tender at the rear.

Don. 21/1-5/3/49.**G.**
Don. 30/12/50-24/1/51.**G.**
Don. 3-12/4/51.**N/C.**
Don. 25/3-23/4/53.**G.**
Don. 15/2-17/3/55.**G.**
Don. 9/4-11/5/57.**G.**
Don. 3-8/6/57.**N/C.**
Don. 19-29/10/57.**N/C.**
Don. 29/5-3/7/59.**G.**
Don. 9-14/5/60.**N/C.**
Don. 13/10/61.*Not repaired.*

BOILERS:
7D/687.
D1746 *(ex191)* 29/2/36.
 9280 *(new)* 29/11/41.
 9288 *(ex1914)* 5/3/49.
27139 *(ex61975)* 24/1/51.
27133 *(ex61868)* 23/4/53.
27250 *(ex61941)* 17/3/55.
27274 *(ex61971)* 11/5/57.
27149 *(ex61966)* 3/7/59.

SHEDS:
Doncaster.
New England 5/8/30.
Darlington 29/9/42.
Heaton 28/3/43.
Gateshead 10/7/43.
Neville Hill 23/7/45.
Hull Dairycoates 5/10/47.

RENUMBERED:
 1892 27/10/46.
 61892 25/5/48.

CONDEMNED:
30/10/61.
Cut up at Doncaster.

2764

Darlington.

To traffic 29/7/30.

REPAIRS:
Don. 4/2-12/3/32.**G.**
Don. 6/7-14/8/33.**G.**
Don. 7-30/1/35.**G.**
Don. 22/4-21/5/36.**G.**
Don. 18/8-16/9/36.**L.** *Accident at Postland.*
Don. 26/1-12/2/38.**G.**
Don. 20/2-13/4/40.**G.**
Don. 18/4-23/5/42.**G.**
Don. 16/1-13/2/43.**L.**
Don. 9/9-7/10/44.**G.**
Don. 4-18/11/44.**L.**
Don. 30/4-11/6/47.**G.**
Don. 27/11-22/12/48.**G.**
Don. 18/12/50-12/1/51.**G.**
Don. 30/1-27/2/53.**G.**

Don. 16/12/54-19/1/55.**G.**
Don. 25/3-1/5/57.**G.**
Don. 14/5-11/6/59.**G.**
Don. 30/5-3/6/60.**N/C.**
Don. 25/5-21/7/61.**G.**

BOILERS:
6D/687.
D1664 *(ex167)* 30/1/35.
 9799 *(new)* 11/6/47.
27135 *(ex61970)* 12/1/51.
27125 *(ex61849)* 27/2/53.
27179 *(ex61901)* 19/1/55.
27217 *(ex61910)* 1/5/57.
27295 *(ex61860)* 11/6/59.
24924 *(ex61967)* 21/7/61.

SHEDS:
Doncaster.
March 15/7/38.
Norwich 29/10/38.
March 26/11/41.
Hull Dairycoates 2/9/51.

RENUMBERED:
 1893 6/10/46.
 61893 22/12/48.

CONDEMNED:
17/12/62.
Cut up at Doncaster.

2765

Darlington.

To traffic 29/7/30.

REPAIRS:
Don. 3/2-7/3/32.**G.**
Don. 10/8-21/9/33.**G.**
Don. 24-28/4/34.**L.**
Don. 26/3-26/4/35.**G.**
Don. 14/4-8/5/37.**G.**
Don. 1-20/7/38.**G.**
Gor. 29-30/6/39.**L.** *Front heater conn.*
Don. 12/8-23/9/39.**G.**
Don. 14/2-28/3/42.**G.**
Don. 10/6-15/7/44.**G.**
Don. 7-14/10/44.**L.**
Don. 24/8-17/10/47.**G.**
Don. 10/7-26/8/49.**G.**
Don. 14/10-3/11/50.**C/L.**
Don. 20/11-20/12/51.**G.**
Don. 9-12/3/52.**N/C.**
Don. 24/1-4/2/54.**C/L.**
Don. 2/3-8/4/54.**G.**
Don. 29/7-17/8/55.**C/L.**
Don. 9/5-15/6/56.**G.**
Don. 18/11/58-2/1/59.**G.**
Don. 11-25/1/59.**N/C.**

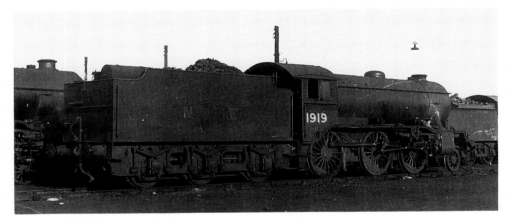

From February 1936 the left hand side vacuum cylinder was dispensed with, and was gradually removed from the forty which had been so fitted. No.1919 here at March shed on 6th April 1946 had been built in 1934 as 1302 and originally had two vacuum cylinders; the date when reduced to one was not recorded, but that engine retained the same tender throughout its life. *H.C.Casserley.*

It was found desirable for the vacuum ejector exhaust pipe to be fitted with a drain pipe to dispose of the condensate, but it seems to have been uncertain whether it should be placed just in front of the cab - as here on E1952 - or at the front where the exhaust pipe entered the smokebox. Numerous photographs can be found for both positions. *J.L.Stevenson.*

BOILERS:
?D/687.
8071 (*ex4009*) 26/4/35.
8601 (*ex1164*) 8/5/37.
?1762 (*ex2762*) 20/7/38.
8134 (*ex1119*) 15/7/44.
8922 (*ex1806*) 17/10/47.
7200 (*ex1860*) 20/12/51.
7273 (*ex61969*) 8/4/54.
7248 (*ex61826*) 15/6/56.
7181 (*ex61904*) 2/1/59.

SHEDS:
Doncaster.
New England 16/10/34.
March 6/3/36.
Stratford 9/5/38.
Gorton 19/9/38.
Annesley 30/10/43.
Woodford 6/1/46.
Annesley 29/6/47.
Colwick 13/7/47.
Lincoln 8/8/48.
Colwick 16/10/60.

RENUMBERED:
1894 18/8/46.
1894 26/8/49.

CONDEMNED:
?0/10/61.
Cut up at Doncaster.

2766

Darlington.

To traffic 30/7/30.

REPAIRS:
Don. 19/11-21/12/31.**G.**
Don. 29/6-2/8/33.**G.**
Don. 30/1-23/2/35.**G.**
Don. 2/7-6/8/36.**G.**
Don. 29/3-29/4/38.**G.**
Gor. 19-21/6/39.**L.** *Front heater*
Donn.
Don. 9-16/12/39.**L.**
Don. 27/1-4/5/40.**G.**
Don. 26/9-31/10/42.**G.**
Don. 24/6-12/8/44.**G.**
Don. 18/5-20/7/46.**G.**
Don. 3/12/48-7/1/49.**G.**
Don. 30/12/49-3/3/50.**G.**
Don. 4/11-7/12/51.**G.**
Don. 29/9-30/10/53.**G.**
Don. 22/7-25/8/55.**G.**
Don. 25/1-9/2/57.**C/L.**
Don. 22/9-2/11/57.**G.**
Don. 5/1-6/2/60.**G.**

BOILERS:
?D/687.
1706 (*ex125*) 23/2/35.
8913 (*ex spare and 2438*) 12/8/44.
?552 (*new*) 20/7/46.
?547 (*ex61863*) 3/3/50.

27274 (*new*) 7/12/51.
27201 (*ex61818*) 30/10/53.
27114 (*ex61852*) 25/8/55.
27297 (*ex61801*) 2/11/57.
27258 (*ex61829*) 6/2/60.

SHEDS:
Doncaster.
Stratford 7/5/38.
Gorton 22/9/38.
Annesley 30/10/43.
Colwick 21/3/48.
March 12/6/49.
Doncaster 16/9/56.

RENUMBERED:
1895 29/9/46.
61895 7/1/49.

CONDEMNED:
18/7/62.
Cut up at Doncaster.

2767

Darlington.

To traffic 2/8/30.

REPAIRS:
Don. 23/3-2/5/32.**G.**
Don. 5/9-22/10/33.**G.**
Don. 20/11/34-10/1/35.**G.**
Cow. 7-15/3/35.**L.**
Don. 22/4-4/6/36.**G.**
Cow. 24/11-7/12/36.**L.**
Don. 18/8-23/9/37.**G.**
Cow. 20-23/12/37.**L.**
Cow. 7-11/1/38.**L.**
Cow. 22-26/1/38.**L.**
Cow. 1-3/2/38.**L.**
Cow. 23-26/3/38.*Spec.*
Cow. 10-13/5/38.**L.**
Cow. 29/4-4/10/38.**L.**
Cow. 23/11-2/12/38.**L.**
Cow. 15/3-4/5/39.**L.**
Cow. 30/5-2/6/39.**L.**
Cow. 20/8-17/9/40.**G.**
Don. 7/1-26/2/42.**G.**
Don. 30/7-2/9/44.**G.**
Don. 26/9-4/10/44.**L.**
Don. 1/1-1/3/47.**G.**
Don. 27/2-4/4/49.**G.**
Don. 12/3-18/4/51.**G.**
Don. 24/2-26/3/53.**G.**
Gor. 20-24/4/54.*Weigh.*
Don. 23/12/54-3/2/55.**G.**
Don. 7/8-18/9/57.**G.**
Don. 2-29/10/59.**G.**
Don. 28/1-5/2/60.**N/C.**

BOILERS:
5D/687.
8596 (*ex1125*) 4/6/36.
8738 (*ex1805*) 1/3/47.
27156 (*ex61848*) 18/4/51.
27171 (*ex61949*) 26/3/53.

27207 (*ex61976*) 3/2/55.
27199 (*ex61906*) 18/9/57.
24930 (*ex61818*) 29/10/59.

SHEDS:
Carlisle.
March 9/6/38.
Carlisle 3/9/38.
Sheffield 23/11/40.
New England 25/6/45.
March 12/6/49.
Norwich 10/10/49.
Gorton 1/1/50.
Colwick 13/6/54.

RENUMBERED:
1896 1/11/46.
61896 4/4/49.

CONDEMNED:
14/5/62.
Cut up at Doncaster.

2768

Darlington.

To traffic 7/8/30.

REPAIRS:
Don. 2/6-1/7/32.**G.**
Don. 7/12/33-10/1/34.**G.**
Don. 26/4-25/5/35.**G.**
Don. 30/9-28/10/36.**G.**
Don. 25/1-19/2/38.**G.**
Cow. 3/5/38.**L.**
Cow. 30/6/39.**H.**
Cow. 22/3/40.**L.**
Cow. 25/1/40.**L.**
Cow. 21/11-19/12/42.**H.**
Cow. 11-30/12/43.**G.**
Cow. 21/9/44.**L.**
Cow. 22/5-14/6/45.**G.**
Don. 12-26/10/46.**L.**
Don. 15-29/3/47.**L.**
Don. 3/1-12/2/48.**G.**
Cow. 16/3-6/5/49.**L/I.**
Cow. 28/12/50-27/1/51.**L/I.**
Cow. 15/8-20/9/52.**G.**
Cow. 28/7-11/9/54.**H/I.**
Cow. 21-23/9/54.**N/C.**
Cow. 14/10-19/11/55.**L/I.**
Cow. 13/9-27/10/56.**G.**
Don. 19/6-5/7/57.**N/C.**
Don. 6/4-8/5/59.**G.**
Don. 9-14/5/60.**N/C.**
Don. 24/3-5/5/61.**G.**
Don. 31/8-3/10/61.**C/L.**

BOILERS:
4D/687 (C1743).
C1744 (*ex1386*) 30/12/43.
8873 (*ex1917*) 12/2/48.
Renumbered 27326 27/1/51.
27330 (*ex61928*) 20/9/52.
27303 (*ex61991*) 27/10/56.
24937 (*new*) 8/5/59.

SHEDS:
St Margarets.
Carlisle 17/5/32.
St Margarets 12/43.
Gateshead 13/10/45.
Heaton 6/2/49.
St Margarets 13/2/49.
Hull Dairycoates 25/2/57.

RENUMBERED:
1897 26/10/46.
E1897 12/2/48.
61897 27/9/48.

CONDEMNED:
17/12/62.
Cut up at Doncaster.

2769

Darlington.

To traffic 8/8/30.

REPAIRS:
Don. 10/11-15/12/32.**G.**
Don. 13/4-12/5/34.**G.**
Don. 26/11-23/12/35.**G.**
Don. 10/5-12/6/37.**G.**
Don. 27/8-18/9/37.**H.**
Cow. 9-2/11/38.**G.**
Cow. 16/12/38.**L.**
Cow. 16/3/40.**G.**
Cow. 9/6/40.**L.**
Cow. 13/12/40.**L.**
Cow. 18/10-22/11/41.**G.**
Cow. 26/10/44.**G.**
Cow. 11/1-16/2/46.**G.**
Cow. 15/4-16/5/47.**H/I.**
Cow. 21/2-16/4/49.**G.**
Cow. 1/9-21/10/50.**G.**
Cow. 23-25/5/51.**C/L.**
Cow. 18/2-25/3/52.**H/I.**
Cow. 6-31/1/53.**H/I.**
Cow. 22/9-1/11/54.**G.**
Cow. 15/3-28/4/56.**H/I.**
Cow. 8/11-14/12/57.**L/I.**

BOILERS:
3D/687(C/1744).
2D/687 (*ex2762*) 18/9/37.
2865 (*ex3831*) 16/2/46.
C1743 (*ex1991*) 21/10/50.
Renumbered 27307 25/3/52.
27326 (*ex61897*) 1/11/54.

SHEDS:
Carlisle.
Eastfield 15/4/32.
Sheffield 15/12/40.
Carlisle 3/5/41.

RENUMBERED:
1898 20/10/46.
61898 19/9/48.

2769 continued over.

WORKS CODES:- Cow - Cowlairs. Dar - Darlington. Don - Doncaster. Ghd - Gateshead. Gor - Gorton. Inv - Inverurie. Str - Stratford.
REPAIR CODES:- **C/H** - Casual Heavy. **C/L** - Casual Light. **G** - General. **H** - Heavy. **H/I** - Heavy Intermediate. **L** - Light. **L/I** - Light Intermediate. **N/C** - Non-Classified.

Until its use ceased from October 1933, engines working on the main lines in N.E.Area required to be fitted with the Raven fog signalling apparatus which was mechanically operated by ramps in the track either making, or avoiding contact with a striker on the engine. On No.28, which Darlington built in 1924 for the N.E.Area, the striker can be discerned at rail level, just to the rear of the middle coupled wheel. Here on 14th September 192? the York based engine has worked to Sheffield (Victoria) and is ready to return. *W.L.Good.*

CONDEMNED:
7/2/59.
Sold for scrap to J.N.Connell, Coatbridge.

1100

A.W. 1111.

To traffic 2/3/31.

REPAIRS:
Dar. 4-18/3/31.**N/C.** *Raven F.S.A.fitted.*
Ghd. 29/5/31.**N/C.** *S'box door stop fitted.*
Dar. 28/9-14/11/32.**G.**
Dar. 31/7-4/8/33.**L.**
Dar. 23/8-26/9/33.**L.**
Dar. 4/12/34-26/1/35.**G.**
Dar. 19/5-11/9/36.**H.**
Dar. 30/11/37-11/2/38.**G.**
Dar. 14-25/2/38.**N/C.**
Dar. 23/1-20/2/40.**G.**
Dar. 10/2-18/3/42.**G.**
Dar. 5-20/6/42.*Tender only.*
Dar. 31/12/42-30/1/43.**L.**
Don. 10/5-24/6/44.**G.**
Don. 5/2-17/3/45.**L.**
Don. 20/7-24/8/46.**G.**
Don. 1-15/2/47.**L.**
Don. 4-27/12/47.**L.**
Ghd. 4-28/4/48.**L.**
Don. 20/7-7/8/48.**G.**
Don. 11/6-13/8/49.**C/L.**
Don. 28/8-7/10/50.**G.**
Don. 29/6-6/7/51.**L.**
Don. 13/11-12/12/52.**G.**
Don. 10/1-11/2/55.**G.**
Don. 5/3-4/4/57.**G.**
Don. 14/1-25/2/59.**G.**
Don. 12-28/8/59.**G.**
Don. 23-26/5/60.**N/C.**
Don. 20/12/61-13/2/62.**G.**
Don. 4-21/7/62.**C/L.**

BOILERS:
AW1111.
8134 *(ex1365)* 26/1/35.
RS4077 *(ex1300)* 11/2/38.
8118 *(ex39)* 20/2/40.
AW81 *(ex1345)* 18/3/42.
27105 *(ex61806)* 7/10/50.
27254 *(ex61940)* 12/12/52.
27222 *(ex61985)* 11/2/55.
24924 *(new)* 4/4/57.
27214 *(ex61956)* 25/2/59.
27294 *(ex61943)* 13/2/62.

SHEDS:
Gateshead.
Heaton 30/9/39.
Darlington 27/7/43.
Hull Dairycoates 23/7/45.
Tweedmouth 7/12/52.
Hull Dairycoates 21/8/55.

RENUMBERED:
1899 27/1/46.
61899 28/4/48.

CONDEMNED:
18/12/62.
Cut up at Doncaster.

1101

A.W. 1112.

To traffic 10/3/31.

REPAIRS:
Dar. 16-20/3/31.**N/C.** *Fog app.fitted.*
Ghd. 28/5/31.**N/C.** *S'box door stop fitted.*
Dar. 27/10-19/12/32.**G.**
Dar. 14/2-6/4/35.**G.**
Dar. 1/5/35.*Weigh.*
Dar. 21/4-29/5/36.**L.**
Dar. 22/3-10/7/37.**G.**
Dar. 13-16/7/37.**N/C.** *Tender only.*

Dar. 20/7-30/8/39.**G.**
Dar. 23/6-23/8/41.**G.**
Cow. 8/10/43.**G.**
Cow. 10/2-26/4/46.**G.**
Cow. 3/12/47-16/1/48.**G.**
Cow. 4/10-15/11/49.**H/I.**
Cow. 4/7-15/9/51.**G.**
Cow. 27/9/51.**N/C.**
Cow. 11/5-6/6/53.**L/I.**
Cow. 28/8-16/9/53.**N/C.**
Cow. 22/3-10/4/54.**N/C.**
Cow. 23/6-14/7/54.**C/L.**
Cow. 15/2-2/4/55.**G.**
Cow. 7-8/4/55.**N/C.**
Cow. 28/2-23/3/57.**H/I.**
Cow. 3-29/11/58.**H/I.**
Cow. 20/1-3/2/60.**N/C.**

BOILERS:
AW1112.
AW83 *(ex1119)* 6/4/35.
RS4076 *(ex46)* 30/8/39.
8130 *(ex1397)* 23/8/41.
8072 *(ex1137)* 26/4/46.
27313 *(ex1990)* 15/9/51.
27315 *(ex61937)* 2/4/55.

SHEDS:
Gateshead.
March 3/9/41.
St Margarets 1/10/42.

RENUMBERED:
1900 10/2/46.
61900 15/11/49.

CONDEMNED:
4/3/60.
Sold for scrap to J.Connell, Coatbridge.
Not in use 218 days in 1944.

1102

A.W. 1113.

To traffic 13/3/31.

REPAIRS:
Dar. 19-26/3/31.**N/C.** *Fog app.fitted.*
Dar. 16/8-28/9/32.**G.**
Dar. 19/9-20/10/33.**L.**
Dar. 4/6-11/7/34.**G.**
Dar. 29/11/35-31/1/36.**G.**
Dar. 13/9-4/11/38.**G.**
Dar. 18/9-3/11/39.**H.**
Dar. 27/8-8/10/40.**G.**
Don. 6-27/6/42.**G.**
Don. 11/11-9/12/44.**G.**
Don. 10/8-7/9/46.**G.**
Don. 15/12/47-17/1/48.**G.**
Don. 3/1-11/2/50.**G.**
Don. 2-26/7/51.**G.**
Don. 11/3-10/4/53.**G.**
Don. 10/12/54-12/1/55.**G.**
Don. 13/11-14/12/56.**G.**
Don. 17/10-28/11/58.**G.**
Don. 2/2-10/3/61.**G.**
Don. 5/12/61.*Not repaired.*

BOILERS:
AW1113.
8125 *(ex1394)* 11/7/34.
8133 *(ex17)* 4/11/38.
8129 *(ex3824)* 8/10/40.
D1709 *(ex3818)* 27/6/42.
2838 *(ex1917)* 11/2/50.
27179 *(ex61985)* 26/7/51.
27164 *(ex61800)* 12/1/55.
27285 *(ex61903)* 14/12/56.
24916 *(ex61970)* 28/11/58.

SHEDS:
Gateshead.
Colwick 23/11/40.
Heaton 29/9/42.
Tweedmouth 6/1/52.
Hull Dairycoates 20/11/60.

RENUMBERED:
1901 20/1/46.
61901 9/2/50.

CONDEMNED:
27/12/61.
Cut up at Doncaster.

1106

A.W. 1114.

To traffic 18/3/31.

REPAIRS:
Dar. 24-27/3/31.**N/C.** *Fog app. fitted.*
Ghd. 22-29/1/32.**N/C.**
Dar. 19/10-7/12/32.**G.**
Dar. 15/11/33-25/1/34.**L.**
Dar. 5/12/34-22/2/35.**G.**
Dar. 28/4-27/6/36.**G.**
Dar. 31/3-28/6/37.**H.**
Dar. 8/2-30/3/38.**G.**
Dar. 31/3-3/5/38.**N/C.**
Dar. 4-19/10/39.**N/C.**
Dar. 19/12/39-23/1/40.**G.**
Dar. 27/10-12/12/41.**G.**
Don. 4/12/43-8/1/44.**G.**
Don. 19/1-23/2/46.**G.**
Don. 10/7-17/8/46.**L.**
Don. 9-16/11/46.**L.**
Don. 5/10-6/11/48.**G.**
Don. 11/9-7/10/50.**G.**
Don. 8/7-14/8/52.**G.**
Don. 10/6-22/7/54.**G.**
Don. 26/10-6/11/54.**C/L.**
Don. 24/7-1/9/56.**G.**
Don. 15/11-20/12/58.**G.**
Don. 30/5-3/6/60.**N/C.**

BOILERS:
AW1114.
AW76 *(ex1100)* 22/2/35.
2941 *(new)* 30/3/38.
AW82 *(ex33)* 23/1/40.
8125 *(ex1318)* 12/12/41.
8870 *(ex1903)* 6/11/48.

27104 *(ex1884)* 7/10/50.
27102 *(ex61884)* 14/8/52.
27181 *(ex61979)* 22/7/54.
27286 *(ex61875)* 1/9/56.
27246 *(ex61972)* 20/12/58.

SHEDS:
Gateshead.
Heaton 30/3/31.
Darlington 3/8/43.
Hull Dairycoates 23/7/45.

RENUMBERED:
1902 16/2/46.
61902 5/11/48.

CONDEMNED:
3/7/61.
Cut up at Doncaster.

1108

A.W. 1115.

To traffic 1/4/31.

REPAIRS:
Dar. 14-18/4/31.**N/C.** *Fog app.fitted.*
Dar. 4/7-29/8/32.**G.**
Dar. 7/7/33.*Weigh.*
Dar. 19/6-28/8/34.**G.**
Dar. 25/8-18/9/36.**N/C.**
Dar. 22/3-2/8/37.**G.**
Dar. 3/8-29/9/37.**N/C.**
Dar. 26/2-28/3/40.**G.**
Dar. 11/3-18/4/42.**G.**
Don. 26/4-27/5/44.**G.**
Dar. 5/7-10/8/45.**L.**
Don. 6/7-10/8/46.**G.**
Don. 5-31/7/48.**G.**
Don. 24/9-2/10/48.**L.**
Don. 26/8-8/10/49.**C/H.**
Don. 21/11-19/12/50.**G.**
Don. 26/9-24/10/52.**G.**
Don. 3-7/11/52.**N/C.**
Don. 25/8-30/9/54.**G.**
Don. 22/10-24/11/56.**G.**

Don. 16/6-5/7/58.**C/L.**
Don. 27/7-21/8/59.**G.**
Don. 2-6/5/60.**N/C.**

BOILERS:
AW1115.
Renumbered 80 28/8/34.
D1646 *(ex33)* 2/8/37.
RS4077 *(ex1100)* 28/3/40.
8870 *(ex1364)* 18/4/42.
10505 *(new)* 31/7/48.
27261 *(new)* 19/12/50.
27119 *(ex61925)* 24/10/52.
27285 *(new)* 30/9/54.
24917 *(new)* 24/11/56.
27236 *(ex61861)* 21/8/59.

SHEDS:
Hull Dairycoates.
Hull Botanic Gardens 21/4/31.
Gateshead 23/6/31.
Heaton 28/3/43.
Hull Dairycoates 5/10/47.

RENUMBERED:
1903 27/1/46.
61903 30/7/48.

CONDEMNED:
23/11/61.
Cut up at Doncaster.

1117

A.W. 1116.

To traffic 27/3/31.

REPAIRS:
Dar. 8-16/4/31.**N/C.** *Fog app.fitted.*
Ghd. 8-17/8/32.**N/C.**
Dar. 9/11/32-4/1/33.**G.**
Dar. 29/10-28/12/34.**G.**
Dar. 1/37.**G.**
Dar. 18/11/38-5/1/39.**G.**
Dar. 22-30/4/40. **N/C.**
Dar. 25/10-2/12/40.**G.**

Dar. 30/1-11/3/41.**H.**
Dar. 3/43.**G.**
Don. 10/3-21/4/45.**G.**
Don. 9-25/5/46.**L.**
Don. 31/12/46-1/2/47.**G.**
Don. 7-23/7/48.**L.**
Don. 23/12/48-28/1/49.**G.**
Don. 22/1-15/2/51.**G.**
Don. 29/10-26/11/52.**G.**
Don. 23/9-22/10/54.**G.**
Don. 4-21/1/55.**C/L.**
Don. 18/8-6/10/56.**G.**
Don. 13/10-22/11/58.**G.**
Don. 7-14/6/60.**N/C.**
Don. 19/5/61.*Not repaired.*

BOILERS:
AW1116.
8117 *(ex1386)* 28/12/34.
8135A *(ex1362)* 1/37.
AW79 *(ex1118)* 5/1/39.
8122 *(ex1391)* 2/12/40.
8074 *(ex1324)* 3/43.
8920 *(ex1959)* 28/1/49.
27142 *(ex1893)* 15/2/51.
27106 *(ex61834)* 26/11/52.
27119 *(ex61903)* 22/10/54.
27181 *(ex61902)* 6/10/56.
27247 *(ex61875)* 22/11/58.

SHEDS:
Heaton.
Stockton 23/10/39.
Darlington 30/12/40.
Blaydon 14/6/41.
Heaton 21/6/43.
Gateshead 10/7/43.
March 30/5/48.
Heaton 31/10/48.
Hull Dairycoates 25/9/55.

RENUMBERED:
1904 20/1/46.
61904 5/5/48.

CONDEMNED:
5/6/61.
Cut up at Doncaster.

Two features qualify 61981 for inclusion. Like E1952 it was always maintained by Doncaster works, but on this one they fitted the ejector exhaust drain pipe at the front end. Scant evidence is to be seen of its other feature - that it had been fitted with a hopper ashpan. Here it is at Doncaster shed on 30th March 1960. Nos.61981 and 61923 were so fitted, and also with a rocking grate, in January 1954, and by September 1955 ten more, 61930/8/42/50/69/71/5/7/80/6, had also been equipped similarly. It was reported that their grates were easy to clean and distortion was minimal, so others may have been fitted later but not recorded.
J.R.Goult.

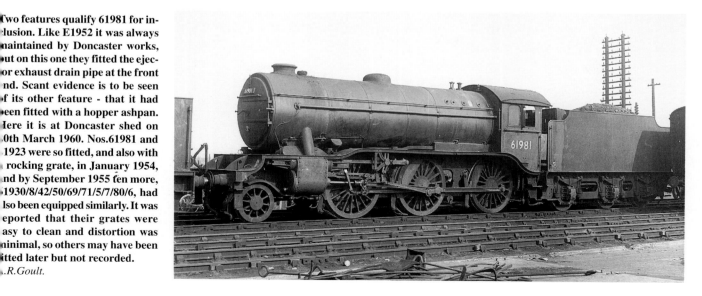

61989 leaving Scarborough on 25th June 1960 would be on a return working to somewhere in the Sheffield area, its 41H shed plate indicating allocation to Staveley, and it worked "under the wires" around there, as shown by it having electrification warning signs. It is however included to show that at least some K3's were fully fitted with Automatic Warning System, the detector for which was given protection from damage by the screw coupling having a plate behind it. *N.Skinner.*

1118

A.W. 1117.

To traffic 31/3/31.

REPAIRS:
Dar. 13-17/4/41.**N/C.** *Fog app.fitted.*
Dar. 1/11-22/12/32.**G.**
Ghd shed. 7-20/4/33.**L.**
Dar. 30/8-11/9/33.**L.**
Dar. 28/8-6/10/34.**G.**
Dar. 8-19/10/34.**N/C.**
Dar. 11/8-3/10/36.**G.**
Dar. 26/5-28/7/38.**G.**
Dar. 16-21/9/39.**N/C.**
Dar. 27/8-7/10/40.**G.**
Don. 27/8-30/10/42.**G.**
Don. 19/3-15/4/44.**G.**
Don. 21/6-21/7/45.**L.**
Don. 23/4-2/7/46.**G.**
Don. 9/1-15/2/47.**L.**
Don. 20/2-3/4/48.**G.**
Don. 21-22/4/49.*Weigh.*
Don. 11/5-28/7/49.**G.**
Don. 4/12/51-11/1/52.**G.**
Don. 26/7-26/8/53.**G.**
Don. 9/1-4/2/55.**G.**
Don. 18-26/8/55.**N/C.**
Don. 16/10-17/11/56.**G.**
Don. 7/7-14/8/58.**G.**
Don. 15-29/1/59.**N/C.**
Don. 21/12/60-31/1/61.**G.**
Don. 23-28/2/61.**N/C.**

BOILERS:
AW1117.
8131 *(ex1312)* 6/10/34.
AW79 *(ex1119)* 3/10/36.
8140A *(ex1306)* 28/7/38.

RS4080 *(ex36)* 7/10/40.
8131 *(ex141)* 30/10/42.
8802 *(ex2451)* 2/7/46.
27204 *(ex61962)* 11/1/52.
27155 *(ex61935)* 26/8/53.
27131 *(ex61949)* 4/2/55.
27290 *(ex61800)* 17/11/56.
27232 *(ex61912)* 14/8/58.
27203 *(ex61942)* 31/1/61.

SHEDS:
Heaton.
Stockton 28/10/39.
Darlington 7/10/40.
Colwick 23/11/40.
Immingham 8/8/48.
Colwick 14/1/62.
Lincoln 1/7/62.

RENUMBERED:
1905 20/1/46.
61905 3/4/48.

CONDEMNED:
4/11/62.
Sold for scrap to Cox & Danks, Wadsley Bridge.

1119

A.W. 1118.

To traffic 14/4/31.

REPAIRS:
Dar. 21-24/4/31.**N/C.** *Fog app.fitted.*
Dar. 19-28/10/32.**N/C.**
Dar. 27/1-16/3/33.**G.**
Dar. 5-14/7/33.**N/C.**

Dar. 31/7-4/8/33.**N/C.**
Dar. 1/2-16/3/35.**G.**
Dar. 26/8-25/10/35.**L.**
Dar. 14/7-9/9/36.**G.**
Dar. 22/3-13/5/38.**G.**
Dar. 18/12/39-27/1/40.**G.**
Dar. 7-21/2/40.**N/C.**
Dar. 16-22/5/41.*Tender.*
Dar. 26/5-2/7/42.**G.**
Dar. 3-19/2/43.**L.**
Don. 9-13/3/44.**G.**
Don. 2-16/9/44.**L.**
Don. 2/2-16/3/46.**G.**
Don. 29/11/47-10/1/48.**G.**
Don. 25/8-4/9/48.**L.**
Don. 20/9-5/11/49.**G.**
Don. 15/5-13/6/51.**G.**
Don. 28/3-12/5/52.**G.**
Don. 25/11-30/12/53.**G.**
Don. 5/10-9/11/55.**G.**
Don. 13/6-20/7/57.**G.**
Don. 2/5-4/6/59.**G.**
Don. 8/6-15/7/61.**G.**

BOILERS:
AW1118.
AW79 *(ex1106)* 16/3/35.
8126 *(ex1312)* 9/9/36.
8127 *(ex1362)* 27/1/40.
8134 *(ex1308)* 2/7/42.
8139A *(ex1325)* 13/3/44.
2941 *(ex1397)* 10/1/48.
10534 *(new)* 5/11/49.
27169 *(ex61803)* 13/6/51.
27199 *(ex61877)* 30/12/53.
27261 *(ex61950)* 20/7/57.
27243 *(ex61939)* 4/6/59.
27199 *(ex61896)* 15/7/61.

SHEDS:
Hull Dairycoates.
Hull Botanic Gardens 21/4/31.
Heaton 23/6/31.
Tyne Dock 15/1/61.
Hull Dairycoates 16/7/61.

RENUMBERED:
1906 27/1/46.
61906 2/9/48.

CONDEMNED:
17/12/62.
Cut up at Doncaster.

1121

A.W. 1119.

To traffic 17/4/31.

REPAIRS:
Don. 25/8-5/10/32.**G.**
Don. 18/1-22/2/34.**G.**
Don. 20/10-23/11/35.**G.**
Don. 12/10-14/11/36.**G.**
Don. 26/5-16/6/38.**G.**
Don. 2/12/39-6/1/40.**G.**
Don. 17/1-28/2/42.**G.**
Cow. 14/1-12/2/44.**G.**
Cow. 10/4-5/5/45.**G.**

Don. 8-15/12/45.**L.**
Don. 5/3-22/4/47.**G.**
Don. 15/10-1/12/48.**G.**
Don. 21/1-19/2/51.**G.**
Don. 22-26/2/51.**N/C.**
Don. 13/4-14/5/53.**G.**
Don. 28/1-1/3/55.**G.**
Don. 22/8-10/10/57.**G.**
Don. 14/7-19/8/60.**G.**

BOILERS:
8595.
6D/687 *(ex2764)* 23/11/35.
AW77 *(ex1388)* 5/5/45.
27143 *(ex61820)* 19/2/51.
27175 *(ex61939)* 14/5/53.
27167 *(ex61866)* 1/3/55.
27107 *(ex61824)* 10/10/57.

SHEDS:
Doncaster.
Gorton 15/5/34.
Doncaster 8/9/34.
St Margarets 30/9/42.
Aberdeen 6/8/45.
Doncaster 13/10/45.
March 27/9/53.
Sheffield 16/9/56.
Colwick 6/12/59.

RENUMBERED:
1907 20/1/46.
61907 1/12/48.

CONDEMNED:
16/9/62.
Sold for scrap to Albert Looms, Spondon.

1125

A.W. 1120.

To traffic 23/4/31.

REPAIRS:
Don. 30/4-24/6/32.**G.**
Don. 11/12/33-9/2/34.**G.**
Don. 4/10-19/11/35.**G.**
Don. 19/3-28/10/37.**G.**
Don. 2/12/39-13/1/40.**G.**
Don. 22/8-3/10/42.**G.**
Don. 6/1-24/2/45.**G.**
Don. 26/1-19/2/46.**L.**
Don. 13/10-21/11/47.**G.**
Don. 13/12/49-27/1/50.**G.**
Don. 23/10-9/11/50.**C/L.**
Don. 11/6-18/7/52.**G.**
Don. 26/3-29/4/54.**G.**
Don. 2/3-24/4/56.**G.**
Don. 1/5-3/6/58.**G.**
Don. 11-14/11/58.**N/C.**

BOILERS:
8596.
9D/687 *(ex2765)* 19/11/35.
8129 *(ex1102)* 3/10/42.
8118 *(ex3824)* 24/2/45.
9281 *(ex1962)* 27/1/50.
27244 *(ex61942)* 18/7/52.

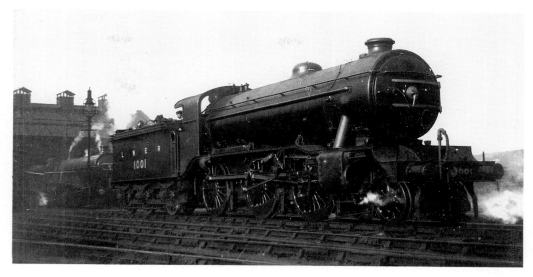

After Grouping, the ten then forming the K3 class changed to black instead of green painting, the three done in March and May 1923 getting tender lettered L & N E R, but the ampersand was then discarded. The next two 1001 and 1006 done in July had simply L N E R as seen on 1001 at King's Cross shed 6th November 1923 when it was still fitted with pyrometer connection to the cab from the superheater header.

The LNER soon realised that it was not enough to identify the K3 only as 1007, because they also had a J27, a J11, and an N7 all carrying that number. The first attempt to resolve the duplication was to add an Area suffix (N for Great Northern) which 1004/7/9 acquired.

27103 (ex61986) 29/4/54.
27101 (ex61806) 24/4/56.
27178 (ex61841) 3/6/58.

SHEDS:
Doncaster.
Gorton 22/3/34.
Doncaster 8/9/34.
March 19/11/35.
New England 5/3/36.
Gorton 21/9/38.
Woodford 24/10/43.
Gorton 26/6/49.
Norwich 11/3/51.
March 13/5/51.
Lowestoft 7/10/51.
Norwich 9/12/51.
March 31/1/60.
Staveley 14/2/60.
Mexborough 18/6/61.

RENUMBERED:
 1908 20/1/46.
61908 27/1/50.

CONDEMNED:
19/1/62.
Cut up at Doncaster.

1133

A.W. 1121.

To traffic 27/4/31.

REPAIRS:
Don. 1/12/32-9/1/33.**G.**
Don. 14/11-15/12/34.**G.**
Don. 27/4-23/5/36.**G.**
Don. 13/12/37-8/1/38.**G.**
Don. 2-30/9/39.**G.**
Don. 19/7-6/9/41.**G.**
Don. 15/8-19/9/42.**G.**
Cow. 14/8/43.**G.**
Cow. 4/9/43.**L.**
Cow. 18/7-30/8/46.**G.**
Cow. 17/6-7/8/48.**G.**
Cow. 23/11/49-7/1/50.**H/I.**
Cow. 18/9-3/11/51.**G.**
Cow. 9/7-23/8/52.**C/L.**
Cow. 18/9-11/10/52.**C/L.**

Cow. 11/5-6/6/53.**L/I.**
Cow. 1/3-16/4/55.**G.**
Cow. 16-19/5/55.**N/C.**
Cow. 1/11-17/12/55.**C/L.**
Stm. 23/4-28/6/56.**C/L.**
Cow. 21/1-23/2/57.**L/I.**
Cow. 25/8-27/9/58.**L/I.**
Cow. 14/9-8/10/59.**C/L.**
Cow. 17/11/59-9/1/60.**C/L.**

BOILERS:
 8597.
 8800 (ex2934) 8/1/38.
D1746 (ex2763) 19/9/42.
 8604 (ex1306) 30/8/46.
27332 (new) 3/11/51.
27307 (ex61898) 16/4/55.

SHEDS:
Doncaster.
March 4/1/42.
St Margarets 29/9/42.

RENUMBERED:
 1909 13/1/46.
61909 7/8/48.

CONDEMNED:
1/4/60.
Cut up at Cowlairs.
Not in use 222 days in 1944.

1135

A.W. 1122.

To traffic 30/4/31.

REPAIRS:
Don. 15/12/32-26/1/33.**G.**
Don. 11/10-9/11/34.**G.**
Don. 8/4-15/5/36.**G.**
Don. 28/12/37-15/1/38.**G.**
Don. 16/9-21/10/39.**G.**

WORKS CODES:- Cow - Cowlairs. Dar - Darlington. Don - Doncaster. Ghd - Gateshead. Gor - Gorton. Inv - Inverurie. Str - Stratford.
REPAIR CODES:- **C/H** - Casual Heavy. **C/L** - Casual Light. **G** - General. **H** - Heavy. **H/I** - Heavy Intermediate. **L** - Light. **L/I** - Light Intermediate. **N/C** - Non-Classified.

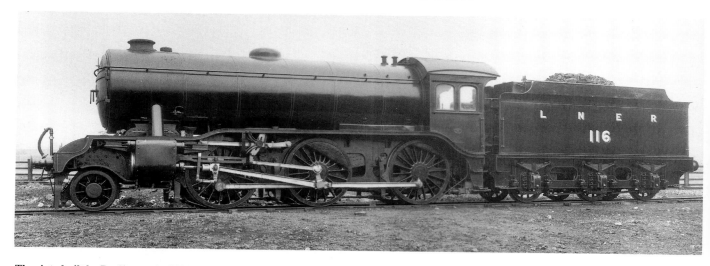

The sixty built by Darlington in 1924/5, and numbered in the 17 to 231 range were in black with single red lining, and initially had lining on their cylinder casings. When 116 was repaired by Doncaster in April 1929 it could have been expected to have had its number transferred from tender to cab, but Doncaster found that the C.M.E.'s records did not have a photograph of the Darlington built K3's, so 116 remedied that deficiency. *L.N.E.R.*

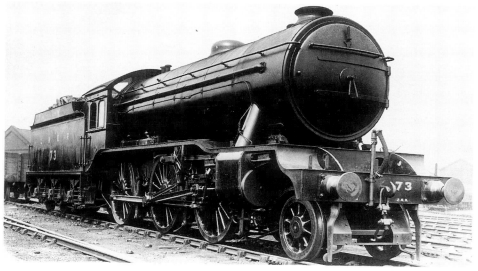

Until March 1938, Darlington (and Gateshead) were the only works which put the class of an engine on the front buffer beam, and for those built in 1924/5, 2.6.0. was used. Although the complete LNER classification became effective towards the end of 1923, Darlington obstinately continued to use the old N.E.R. classification until the second week of January 1931, both in their written works records, and on the engines.

Don. 30/8-11/10/41.**G.**
Cow. 7/9-9/10/43.**G.**
Cow. 29/12/43-1/12/44.**L.**
Cow. 19/2-17/3/45.**G.**
Cow. 13/4-11/5/45.**L.**
Don. 23/5-27/6/47.**G.**
Don. 4/11-21/12/49.**G.**
Don. 29/2-4/4/52.**G.**
Don. 16/3-9/4/54.**G.**
Don. 12/3-11/4/57.**G.**
Don. 4/7-3/8/60.**G.**

BOILERS:
 8598.
 8741 *(new)* 15/5/36.
 9376 *(new)* 9/10/43.
 8924 *(ex1986)* 21/12/49.
 27223 *(ex61982)* 4/4/52.
 27217 *(ex61871)* 9/4/54.
 27157 *(ex61956)* 11/4/57.
 27109 *(ex61864)* 3/8/60.

SHEDS:
Doncaster.
March 3/3/42.
St Margarets 30/9/42.
Aberdeen 6/8/45.
Doncaster 13/10/45.
Gorton 14/5/50.
Woodford 2/4/60.

RENUMBERED:
 1910 27/1/46.
61910 21/12/49.

CONDEMNED:
17/7/62.
Cut up at Doncaster.

1137

A.W. 1123.

To traffic 5/5/31.

REPAIRS:
Don. 8/12/32-13/1/33.**G.**
Don. 7/5-9/6/34.**G.**
Don. 25/11/35-3/1/36.**G.**
Don. 22/9-20/10/37.**G.**
Don. 15/7-26/8/39.**G.**
Don. 23/8-27/9/41.**G.**
Cow. 9/9/43.**G.**
Cow. 27/1-2/3/46.**H/I.**
Cow. 10/2-20/3/48.**G.**
Cow. 24/5-1/7/50.**G.**
Cow. 25-27/12/50.**N/C.**
Cow. 12/4-5/5/51.**C/L.**
Cow. 11/3-19/4/52.**H/I.**
Cow. 7/1-13/2/54.**L/I.**
Cow. 20/5-9/7/55.**G.**
Cow. 21/7-27/8/55.**C/H.**
Cow. 26/6-12/7/56.**N/C.**
Cow. 4/12/56-12/1/57.**H/I.**
Cow. 15-17/1/57.**N/C.**
Cow. 12/2-15/3/58.**H/I.**

BOILERS:
 8599.
 8072 *(ex113)* 3/1/36.
 8124 *(ex1333)* 2/3/46.
 8605 *(ex1936)* 1/7/50.
 Renumbered 27312 19/4/52.
 27313 *(ex61900)* 9/7/55.

SHEDS:
Doncaster.
March 9/10/41.
St Margarets 3/10/42.

RENUMBERED:
 1911 2/3/46.
61911 20/3/48.

CONDEMNED:
30/11/59.
Cut up at Cowlairs.
Not in use 222 days in 1944.

Equally it took until March 1938 before there was recognition that it was helpful to show the class at the front end, and not have to climb into the cab to find it. Then the C.M.E.'s office issued instructions to all workshops for it to be added, as seen on 167 outside the Weigh House at Doncaster on 17th September 1938 following a general repair.

After putting only N E on tender from 1942, it was possible to restore L N E R in January 1946 and K3 class 3825 ex Doncaster works on the 26th was one of the first to benefit. Concurrently, the Thompson general re-numbering scheme was beginning to be effective, and as part of it, 3825 was changed to 1985 on 17th November 1946.

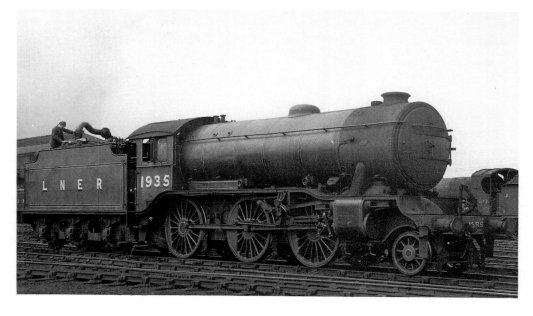

In 1946 also, the LNER announced an intention that all except the streamlined A4 class were to be painted green, lined out in black and white. However laudable that was, it did not prove feasible, and in K3 class it resulted in only a single example. Doncaster turned out 1935 in that livery on 9th November 1946, and this shows how attractive it would have been. It also overtook it, and when it next went for repair, Doncaster removed both the green painting and its L N E R lettering. *R.H.G.Simpson.*

1141

A.W. 1124.

To traffic 7/5/31.

REPAIRS:
Don. 5/10-7/11/32.**G.**
Don. 15/2-22/3/34.**G.**
Don. 11/11-18/12/35.**G.**
Don. 5-30/1/37.**G.**
Don. 27/6-21/7/38.**G.**
Don. 30/3-27/4/40.**G.**
Don. 12/9-24/10/42.**G.**
Don. 5/8-9/9/44.**G.**
Don. 25/5-6/7/46.**G.**
Don. 11/1-25/3/48.**G.**
Don. 11/6-14/7/50.**G.**
Don. 17-19/10/51.**N/C.**
Don. 19/3-24/4/52.**G.**
Don. 5/5-1/7/53.**G.**
Don. 25/3-11/5/54.**C/L.**
Don. 6/3-13/4/55.**G.**
Don. 8/8-8/9/56.**G.**
Don. 12/6-24/7/58.**G.**
Don. 23/1-5/2/59.**N/C.**
Don. 5/1-14/2/61.**G.**

BOILERS:
8600.
D1647 *(ex32)* 18/12/35.
8597 *(ex1133)* 21/7/38.
2808 *(ex1345)* 25/3/48.
9994 *(ex61889)* 14/7/50.
27225 *(ex61947)* 24/4/52.
27191 *(ex61872)* 1/7/53.

27113 *(ex61973)* 13/4/55.
27232 *(ex61982)* 8/9/56.
27118 *(ex61826)* 24/7/58.
27193 *(ex61848)* 14/2/61.
Renumbered S.B.4521.

SHEDS:
Doncaster.
Stratford 16/5/40.
Immingham 23/11/40.
Lincoln 1/8/43.
Immingham 14/10/45.
Lincoln 22/10/61.
Kings Cross 15/4/62.

RENUMBERED:
1912 17/2/46.
61912 25/3/48.

CONDEMNED:
16/9/62.
To Stationary Boiler Stock.
3/65 Withdrawn from service.
*Sold for scrap to J.Cashmore, Great
Bridge.*

1154

A.W. 1125.

To traffic 12/5/31.

REPAIRS:
Don. 7-31/10/32.**G.**
Don. 12/10-10/11/34.**G.**

Don. 24/9-19/10/35.**L.**
Don. 5-21/8/36.**G.**
Don. 9/2-4/3/38.**G.**
Gor. 15-18/6/38.**L.** *Front heat.conn.*
Don. 2/12/39-27/1/40.**G.**
Don. 14/3-18/4/42.**G.**
Don. 30/9-28/10/44.**G.**
Don. 6-20/1/45.**L.**
Don. 16/6-27/8/47.**G.**
Don. 13/10-12/11/48.**G.**
Don. 23/1-23/3/50.**G.**
Don. 8/1-8/2/52.**G.**
Don. 18/5-18/6/54.**G.**
Don. 30/8-10/10/57.**G.**
Don. 24/2-4/3/60.**N/C.**
Don. 20/1-8/3/61.**G.**

BOILERS:
8601.
D1772 *(ex146)* 21/8/36.
8872 *(new)* 4/3/38.
2852 *(ex2427)* 12/11/48.
8118 *(ex1968)* 23/3/50.
27213 *(ex61905)* 8/2/52.
27224 *(ex61822)* 18/6/54.
27269 *(ex61811)* 10/10/57.
27114 *(ex61807)* 8/3/61.

SHEDS:
Doncaster.
Gorton 19/10/35.
Woodford 30/10/43.
Gorton 26/6/49.
Woodford 18/7/59.

RENUMBERED:
1913 27/1/46.
61913 12/11/48.

CONDEMNED:
12/2/62.
Cut up at Doncaster.

1156

A.W. 1126.

To traffic 14/5/31.

REPAIRS:
Don. 27/9-27/10/32.**G.**
Don. 5/5-20/6/34.**G.**
Don. 13/3-24/4/36.**G.**
Don. 16/2-12/3/38.**G.**
Don. 18/11-16/12/39.**G.**
Don. 7/12/40-11/1/41.**G.**
Don. 21/11/42-2/1/43.**G.**
Don. 17/7-7/8/43.**L.**
Don. 18/11/44-10/2/45.**G.**
Don. 2-30/11/46.**L.**
Don. 11/1-3/2/48.**L.**
Don. 22/12/48-4/2/49.**G.**
Don. 8/1-12/2/51.**G.**
Don. 5/5-4/6/53.**G.**
Don. 25/7-25/8/55.**G.**
Don. 10/1-8/2/58.**G.**
Don. 8-17/7/58.**C/L.**
Don. 2/2-4/3/60.**G.**

BOILERS:
8602.
8070 *(ex134)* 24/4/36.
9288 *(new)* 2/1/43.
3222 *(ex2440)* 4/2/49.
27141 *(ex1888)* 12/2/51.
27154 *(ex61813)* 25/8/55.
27177 *(ex61815)* 8/2/58.
27188 *(ex61807)* 4/3/60.

SHEDS:
Doncaster.
March 27/12/39.
Gorton 10/1/50.
Colwick 13/6/54.
Immingham 31/7/60.
Colwick 17/9/61.

RENUMBERED:
1914 28/1/46.
E1914 3/2/48.
61914 4/2/49.

CONDEMNED:
23/8/62.
Cut up at Doncaster.

1158

A.W. 1127.

To traffic 18/5/31.

REPAIRS:
Don. 2/7-25/8/32.**G.**

After nationalisation on 1st January 1948, the first steps at showing new ownership were very tentative.
E1897 at Darlington shed on 6th March 1948 carries BRITISH RAILWAYS in only 7" unshaded letters. As
happened in 1923, again there was more than one engine carrying the same number. The Southern Region's
1897 curiously also happened to be a 3-cylinder 2-6-0; the Western Region's example was an 0-6-0 pannier
tank, and on London Midland Region it was vacant through withdrawal of a Midland 0-6-0 tank engine.
1923's futile attempt at a letter differentiation was probably unknown to the generation now responsible for
making a decision, but they quickly learned that history *could* repeat itself. Only twelve K3 class received the
E prefix, the first eight having it placed in front of the figures, and the other four got it above them, as seen
here, combined with 7" lettering on the tender. Another thirteen K3's got E prefix above the number but
their tenders had BRITISH RAILWAYS in 8" lettering. Use of the letter differentiation was abandoned as
early as 12th March 1948, and Cowlairs never got around to using it.

Don. 9/1-9/3/34.**G.**
Don. 24/12/35-1/2/36.**G.**
Don. 21/3-11/5/37.**G.**
Don. 12/11-10/12/38.**G.**
Don. 6/7-3/8/40.**G.**
Don. 12/9-17/10/42.**G.**
Don. 27/11-25/12/43.**G.**
Don. 8/12/45-5/1/46.**G.**
Don. 26/9-3/11/47.**G.**
Don. 10/10-17/11/49.**G.**
Don. 16/8-21/9/51.**G.**
Don. 19-27/11/51.**N/C.**
Don. 9/11-10/12/53.**G.**
Don. 17/8-24/9/55.**G.**
Don. 29/9-1/10/55.**N/C.**
Don. 4/7-9/8/57.**G.**
Don. 18-23/8/57.**N/C.**
Don. 30/11-5/12/57.**G.**
Don. 20-25/9/58.**C/L.**
Don. 13/5-11/6/59.**G.**
Don. 12-15/6/59.**N/C.**
Don. 14-26/5/60.**C/L.**
Don. 29/3-17/5/61.**G.**

BOILERS:
8603.
8595 *(ex1121)* 1/2/36.
1727 *(ex141)* 11/5/37.
8601 *(ex109)* 17/10/42.
9375 *(new)* 25/12/43.
2830 *(ex1339)* 17/11/49.
27189 *(ex61954)* 21/9/51.
27278 *(new)* 10/12/53.
27147 *(ex61953)* 24/9/55.
27120 *(ex61873)* 9/8/57.
27112 *(ex61816)* 11/6/59.

SHEDS:
Doncaster.
Copley Hill 21/8/44.
New England 26/11/44.
Doncaster 17/2/52.
March 27/9/53.

RENUMBERED:
1915 10/2/46.
61915 17/11/49.

CONDEMNED:
26/9/62.
*Sold for scrap to Central Wagon Co.
Ince.*

1162

A.W. 1128.

To traffic 21/5/31.

REPAIRS:
Don. 15/12/32-25/1/33.**G.**
Don. 21/12/34-25/1/35.**G.**
Don. 27/4-29/5/36.**G.**
Don. 26/1-12/2/38.**G.**
Don. 16/9-21/10/39.**G.**
Don. 2/8-6/9/41.**G.**
Cow. 27/3-17/4/43.**G.**

Cow. 13/3/43.**L.**
Cow. 13/1-3/2/45.**G.**
Cow. 1/5-6/7/46.**G.**
Cow. 3/6-8/7/48.**G.**
Cow. 25/9-9/2/51.**G.**
Cow. 4/10-3/11/51.**C/H.**
Cow. 4-29/8/52.**L/I.**
Cow. 8/9-12/10/53.**L/I.**
Cow. 17/9-20/11/54.**C/H.**
Cow. 16/6-10/8/55.**G.**
Cow. 10/8-6/9/57.**L/I.**
Cow. 27/9-5/10/57.**N/C.**
Cow. 10/10-14/11/58.**H/I.**

BOILERS:
8604.
8071 *(ex spare and 2765)* 21/10/39.
7D/687 *(ex1365)* 6/7/46.
27263 *(new)* 9/2/51.
27324 *(ex61983)* 10/8/55.

SHEDS:
Doncaster.
March 12/11/41.
St Margarets 29/9/42.
Carlisle 8/7/51.

RENUMBERED:
1916 27/1/46.
61916 8/7/48.

CONDEMNED:
31/12/60.
Cut up at Cowlairs.

1164

A.W. 1129.

To traffic 29/5/31.

REPAIRS:
Don. 3/1-6/2/33.**G.**
Don. 14/11-15/12/34.**G.**
Don. 13/5-12/6/36.**G.**
Don. 4-26/3/38.**G.**
Don. 23/9-11/11/39.**G.**
Don. 22/11/41-3/1/42.**G.**
Don. 29/1-26/2/44.**G.**
Don. 4-25/3/44.**L.**
Don. 29/9-27/10/45.**G.**
Don. 26/10-9/11/46.**L.**
Don. 1-15/3/47.**L.**
Don. 15/9-15/11/47.**G.**
Don. 7-24/1/48.**L.**
Ghd. 30/12/48-18/1/49.**L.**
Cow. 26/3/49.**C/L.**
Don. 7/12/49-14/1/50.**G.**
Don. 28/8-10/10/51.**G.**
Don. 19/10-19/11/53.**G.**
Don. 24/10-19/11/55.**G.**
Don. 28/1-21/2/58.**G.**
Don. 12/4-14/5/60.**G.**

BOILERS:
8605.
8873 *(new)* 26/3/38.
2838 *(ex32)* 15/11/47.
10539 *(new)* 14/1/50.
Renumbered 27193 10/10/51.
27201 *(ex61829)* 21/2/58.

SHEDS:
Doncaster.
Heaton 29/9/42.
Tweedmouth 6/1/52.
Ardsley 10/9/61.

RENUMBERED:
1917 27/1/46.
E1917 24/1/48.
61917 18/1/49.

CONDEMNED:
26/11/62.
Cut up at Doncaster.

1166

A.W. 1130.

To traffic 10/6/31.

REPAIRS:
Don. 24/10-16/12/32.**G.**
Don. 10/4-16/6/34.**G.**
Don. 12/11-21/12/35.**G.**
Don. 9/1-23/2/37.**G.**
Don. 24/7-26/8/38.**G.**
Don. 17/2-30/3/40.**G.**
Don. 30/1-6/3/43.**G.**
Don. 24/2-14/4/45.**G.**
Don. 10/3-3/5/47.**G.**
Don. 2/6-20/7/49.**G.**
Don. 15/10-9/11/51.**G.**
Don. 24/8-2/10/53.**G.**
Don. 29/7-2/9/55.**G.**
Don. 10/12/57-22/1/58.**G.**
Don. 29/10-28/11/59.**G.**

BOILERS:
8606.
8740 *(new)* 23/2/37.
8603 *(ex2761)* 6/3/43.
RS4076 *(ex spare and 1322)* 14/4/45.
9795 *(new)* 3/5/47.
27270 *(new)* 9/11/51.
27266 *(ex61927)* 2/10/53.
27270 *(ex61818)* 22/1/58.
27176 *(ex61824)* 28/11/59.

SHEDS:
Doncaster.

In July 1948 British Railways announced their standard livery intentions, and, as mixed traffic engines, K3 class were entitled to red, cream, and grey lining on their black paint. It took a while for that to be implemented by the workshops. At Eastfield shed in mid-August, 61909 had just left Cowlairs after general repair, still unlined, with number in 12" figures, and without cast numberplate on smokebox door. Note that both the 6 and 9 were in the mistaken version of Gill Sans which Doncaster had sent out, in that they had curled tails.

WORKS CODES:- Cow - Cowlairs. Dar - Darlington. Don - Doncaster. Ghd - Gateshead. Gor - Gorton. Inv - Inverurie. Str - Stratford.
REPAIR CODES:- **C/H** - Casual Heavy. **C/L** - Casual Light. **G** - General. **H** - Heavy. **H/I** - Heavy Intermediate. **L** - Light. **L/I** - Light Intermediate. **N/C** - Non-Classified.

For a year there was considerable variation in appearance as engines came out of works. The five-figure numbering was first used on 61848 by Doncaster on 17th March 1948, but it was almost the end of April before they began to fit smokebox numberplates. From Cowlairs on 24th April came 61992 with that still applied in shaded transfers, and matching L N E R on its tender, no smokebox plate being fitted. From June 1949 BRITISH RAILWAYS on tender was discarded in favour of an emblem, but transfers for it were somewhat delayed and 61870 was among the K3's sent out with plain tender, as here at Doncaster on 12th June 1949. Note it is fully lined, and correct Gill Sans 6 appears both on cab and on number plate. *J.P.Wilson.*

Mexborough 1/3/41.
Doncaster 25/8/46.
Norwich 18/10/53.
Lowestoft 6/11/55.
Norwich 26/2/56.
Lowestoft 25/3/56.
Norwich 13/5/56.
March 12/6/60.

RENUMBERED:
 1918 7/2/46.
61918 20/7/49.

CONDEMNED:
28/3/62.
Cut up at Doncaster.

1302

A.W. 1156.

To traffic 21/7/34.

REPAIRS:
Dar. 16-30/11/34.**N/C.**
Dar. 16/1-19/2/35.**L.**
Dar. 23/9-23/11/36.**G.**
Dar. 26/11-23/12/36.**N/C.**
Dar. 8/12/38-6/4/39.**L.**
Dar. 18/10-22/11/39.**G.**
Dar. 6/1-6/2/42.**G.**
Don. 19/12/43-22/1/44.**G.**
Don. 22/11/45-11/1/46.**G.**
Don. 12-30/12/46.**L.**
Don. 27/2-10/5/47.**G.**
Don. 27/6-13/7/47.**L.**
Don. 15/2-18/3/49.**G.**
Don. 1/4-3/5/51.**G.**
Don. 18/5-19/6/53.**G.**

Don. 13/10-17/11/55.**G.**
Don. 17/6-12/7/57.**C/L.**
Don. 11/4-13/5/58.**G.**
Don. 1-9/4/59.**N/C.**

BOILERS:
8135A.
 8127 *(ex1368)* 23/11/36.
 8117 *(ex1331)* 22/11/39.
 8128 *(ex1396)* 6/2/42.
 8872 *(ex1913)* 18/3/49.
 27160 *(ex1892)* 3/5/51.
 27170 *(ex61866)* 19/6/53.
 27128 *(ex61977)* 13/5/58.

SHEDS:
Heaton.
Gateshead 1/10/34.
March 14/2/42.
Gorton 10/1/50.
Lincoln 13/6/54.

RENUMBERED:
 1919 31/3/46.
61919 18/3/49.

CONDEMNED:
29/6/61.
Cut up at Doncaster.

1304

A.W. 1157.

To traffic 25/7/34.

REPAIRS:
Don. 18/2-14/3/35.**L.**
Dar. 31/8-21/10/36.**G.**

Don. 31/1-25/2/39.**G.**
Dar. 24/3-1/5/41.**G.**
Dar. 29/4-14/5/42.**L.**
Don. 4/2-4/3/44.**G.**
Don. 30/1-24/2/45.**L.**
Don. 6/10-10/11/45.**G.**
Don. 28/9-5/10/46.**L.**
Don. 3-28/2/48.**G.**
Don. 27/9-22/10/49.**C/L.**
Don. 11/7-12/8/50.**G.**
Don. 28/8-2/10/52.**G.**
Don. 1-30/7/54.**G.**
Don. 5-13/3/56.**C/L.**
Don. 14/1-14/2/57.**G.**
Don. 24/2-4/4/59.**G.**
Don. 12/9/61.*Not repaired.*

BOILERS:
8136A.
AW79 *(ex1117)* 1/5/41.
 8803 *(ex1943)* 12/8/50.
 27129 *(ex61970)* 2/10/52.
 27243 *(ex61884)* 30/7/54.
 27292 *(ex61886)* 14/2/57.
 24936 *(new)* 4/4/59.

SHEDS:
Heaton.
Gateshead 1/10/34.
Stockton 16/10/39.
Darlington 16/7/40.
Blaydon 14/6/41.
Heaton 19/6/43.
Darlington 3/8/43.
Hull Dairycoates 23/7/45.

RENUMBERED:
 1920 31/3/46.
 E1920 28/2/48.
61920 17/10/49.

CONDEMNED:
18/9/61.
Cut up at Doncaster.

1308

A.W. 1158.

To traffic 30/7/34.

REPAIRS:
Dar. 10/12/35-4/2/36.**G.**
Dar. 25/2-4/5/38.**G.**
Dar. 7/2-15/3/40.**G.**
Dar. 19/1-21/2/42.**G.**
Don. 19/12/43-27/1/44.**G.**
Don. 3/3-12/4/46.**G.**
Don. 24/1-14/3/47.**L.**
Don. 11/4-28/5/48.**G.**
Don. 1/1-6/2/50.**G.**
Don. 28/11-28/12/51.**G.**
Don. 30/12/53-26/1/54.**G.**
Don. 27/6-11/7/55.**C/L.**
Don. 31/5-14/7/56.**G.**
Don. 31/8-27/9/56.**C/L.**
Don. 7/4-9/5/59.**G.**

BOILERS:
8137A.
 8129 *(ex1394)* 4/2/36.
 8138A *(ex1399)* 4/5/38.
 8134 *(ex1333)* 15/3/40.
 AW82 *(ex1106)* 21/2/42.
 8606 *(ex69)* 28/5/48.
 1D/687 *(ex1981)* 6/2/50.
 27202 *(ex61877)* 28/12/51.
 27214 *(ex61923)* 26/1/54.
 27273 *(ex61894)* 14/7/56.
 27169 *(ex61978)* 9/5/59.

SHEDS:
Heaton.
Tweedmouth 16/10/34.
Heaton 19/3/39.
Tweedmouth 5/6/39.
Heaton 8/4/40.
March 21/3/42.
Norwich 17/10/47.
Yarmouth 3/10/48.
Norwich 12/12/48.
March 24/6/51.
Lincoln 22/6/52.
Stratford 5/10/52.
Parkeston 16/3/58.
March 12/6/60.

RENUMBERED:
 1921 12/4/46.
61921 28/5/48.

CONDEMNED:
25/7/61.
Cut up at Doncaster.

1310

A.W. 1159.

To traffic 2/8/34.

GRESLEY K3

61936 was ex Cowlairs on 19th August 1949 fully lined and with transfer emblem applied, cab figures being the standard 10" adopted to fit inside the panel of lining. Paint shop were still using the wrong 6 and 9, but on the smokebox plate they had been corrected. *A.G.Ellis.*

REPAIRS:
Dar. 5/3-4/5/36.**G.**
Dar. 31/7-24/9/37.**G.**
Don. 8/3-6/4/39.**G.**
Dar. 31/8-2/9/39.**N/C.**
Dar. 17/12/40-24/1/41.**G.**
Dar. 9/9-13/10/41.**L.**
Dar. 26/8-24/9/43.**G.**
Dar. 19/9-9/10/44.**L.**
Don. 17/11-29/12/45.**G.**
Dar. 20/11-27/12/46.**L.**
Don. 20/4-22/5/48.**G.**
Don. 13/10-19/11/49.**G.**
Don. 3-30/1/52.**G.**
Don. 3/11-3/12/53.**G.**
Don. 4/7-9/8/55.**G.**
Don. 11/12/59-14/1/60.**G.**
Don. 19-25/3/60.**N/C.**
Don. 2/5/62.*Not repaired.*

BOILERS:
8138A.
8137A *(ex1308)* 4/5/36.
AW80 *(ex1108)* 24/9/37.
8132 *(ex17)* 24/1/41.
8965 *(ex2936)* 24/9/43.
8597 *(ex1141)* 22/5/48.
9D/687 *(ex61953)* 19/11/49.
27209 *(ex61961)* 30/1/52.
27277 *(new)* 3/12/53.
24900 *(new)* 9/8/55.
24932 *(ex61877)* 14/1/60.

SHEDS:
Heaton.
Tweedmouth 16/10/34.
Heaton 19/3/39.
Gateshead 24/1/40.
Heaton 28/3/43.
Hull Dairycoates 12/5/46.

RENUMBERED:
 1922 22/3/46.
61922 22/5/48.

CONDEMNED:
7/5/62.
Cut up at Doncaster.

1324

A.W. 1160.

To traffic 10/8/34.

REPAIRS:
Dar. 8-29/3/35.**L.**
Dar. 19/11/35-24/1/36.**G.**
Dar. 7/9-22/10/37.**G.**
Dar. 26/5-7/7/39.**G.**
Don. 30/10-18/11/40.**G.**
Dar. 23/12/42-9/2/43.**G.**
Don. 21/7-1/9/45.**G.**
Don. 19/2-27/3/48.**G.**
Don. 24/11-4/12/48.**L.**
Don. 19-29/1/49.**C/L.**
Don. 5/10-10/12/49.**G.**
Don. 3-20/7/51.**G.**
Don. 15/1-14/2/52.**G.**
Don. 1/12/53-7/1/54.**G.**
Don. 24/10-24/11/55.**G.**
Don. 20/3-25/4/58.**G.**
Don. 24/11-19/12/59.**G.**
Don. 29/3-2/4/60.**N/C.**
Don. 25/4/62.*Not repaired.*

BOILERS:
8139A.
D1730 *(ex1387)* 22/10/37.
 8074 *(ex1368)* 7/7/39.
D1654 *(ex1332)* 9/2/43.
 8912 *(ex1891)* 10/12/49.
27214 *(ex61984)* 14/2/52.
27280 *(new)* 7/1/54.
27186 *(ex61869)* 25/4/58.
27168 *(ex61984)* 19/12/59.

SHEDS:
Heaton.
Tweedmouth 16/10/34.
Heaton 19/3/39.
Gateshead 24/1/40.
Blaydon 28/3/43.
Heaton 23/6/43.
Darlington 16/7/43.
Hull Dairycoates 23/7/45.
Heaton 14/9/58.
Hull Dairycoates 17/1/60.

RENUMBERED:
 1923 23/3/46.
61923 25/3/48.

CONDEMNED:
30/4/62.
Cut up at Doncaster.

1306

A.W. 1161.

To traffic 5/9/34.

REPAIRS:
Dar. 22/6-8/8/36.**G.**
Dar. 12/5-4/7/38.**G.**
Cow. 8/7/39.**G.**
Cow. 23/1/40.**L.**
Cow. 8/6/40.**L.**
Cow. 5/4/41.**G.**
Cow. 12/7/41.**L.**
Cow. 21/2-4/4/42.**H.**
Cow. 1/1/43.**L.**
Cow. 3/9/43.**G.**
Cow. 9/5-5/7/46.**G.**
Cow. 19/4-3/5/47.**L.**
Cow. 10/11/47-22/1/48.**G.**
Cow. 15/8-24/9/49.**L/I.**
Cow. 17/11/50-20/4/51.**G.**
Cow. 12/12/51-5/1/52.**C/L.**
Cow. 8/4-14/5/53.**H/I.**
Cow. 18-22/5/54.**N/C.**
Cow. 28/4-25/6/55.**G.**
Cow. 8-30/3/57.**L/I.**
Cow. 18/8-19/9/58.**H/I.**
Cow. 18/12/58.**N/C.**
Cow. 11/4-4/5/59.**C/L.**

BOILERS:
8140A.
 8115 *(ex1333)* 4/7/38.
 8604 *(exDon and 1162)* 4/4/42.
 2867 *(ex3832)* 5/7/46.
27340 *(exDon new)* 20/4/51.
27211 *(exDon & 61835)* 25/6/55.

SHEDS:
Heaton.
Tweedmouth 16/10/34.
St Margarets 19/3/39.
Haymarket 1/10/43.
St Margarets 9/44.

RENUMBERED:
 1924 17/3/46.
61924 9/4/49.

CONDEMNED:
20/12/60.
Cut up at Cowlairs.
Not in use 220 days in 1944.

2934

A.W. 1152.

To traffic 13/9/34.

REPAIRS:
Don. 3/12/35-9/1/36.**G.**
Don. 3-31/3/37.**G.**
Don. 8-29/6/37.**H.** *Boiler change due to shortage of water.*
Don. 11/2-11/3/39.**G.**
Don. 27/1-24/2/40.**G.**
Don. 20/6-25/7/42.**G.**
Don. 26/8-30/9/44.**G.**
Don. 9/3-6/4/46.**G.**
Don. 11/1-13/2/48.**G.**
Don. 23/4-25/5/50.**G.**
Don. 3/10-1/11/50.**C/L.**
Don. 5/8-4/9/52.**G.**
Don. 13/10-12/11/53.**C/L.**
Don. 24/5-18/6/54.**C/L.**
Don. 12/7-14/9/54.**G.**
Don. 22/1-21/2/57.**G.**
Don. 2/12/58-8/1/59.**G.**

BOILERS:
 8800.
1D/687 *(ex2761)* 29/6/37.
 8801 *(ex2935)* 30/9/44.
 2852 *(ex1913)* 25/5/50.
Renumbered 27119 1/11/50.
27123 *(ex61948)* 4/9/52.
27320 *(ex61968)* 14/9/54.
27294 *(ex61985)* 21/2/57.
24906 *(ex61847)* 8/1/59.

SHEDS:
Doncaster.
Gorton 19/7/43.
Annesley 30/10/43.
Woodford 6/1/46.
Lincoln 29/6/47.
Doncaster 10/11/57.

RENUMBERED:
 1925 6/4/46.
E1925 13/2/48.
61925 25/5/50.

CONDEMNED:
24/7/61.
Cut up at Doncaster.

61932 shows Doncaster's official photograph for recording the current standard livery for K3 class, but it was only taken on 19th October 1949, and from 1st September, nine others, 61838/41/60/72/75/86, 61929/54/62, had left works in that style. *British Railways.*

2935

A.W. 1153.

To traffic 21/9/34.

REPAIRS:
Don. 4/2-7/3/36.**G.**
Don. 22/4-14/5/37.**G.**
Don. 25/3-14/4/38.**L.**
Don. 30/11/38-6/1/39.**G.**
Don. 15/2-15/3/41.**G.**
Don. 25/4/41.**L.** *Front heater conn.*
Don. 24/7-21/8/43.**G.**
Don. 6/1-10/2/45.**G.**
Don. 8/9-27/10/45.**G.**
Don. 2/6-23/7/47.**G.**
Don. 9/6-21/7/49.**G.**
Don. 4/3-3/4/52.**G.**
Don. 24/6-17/7/53.**N/C.**
Don. 18/7-3/9/54.**G.**
Don. 25/3-3/5/56.**G.**
Don. 21/7-22/8/58.**G.**
Don. 16/2-3/3/61.**C/L.**

BOILERS:
8801.
8963 *(ex2429)* 21/8/43.
8914 *(ex140)* 27/10/45.
2825 *(ex1926)* 21/7/49.
27220 *(ex61922)* 3/4/52.
27241 *(ex61940)* 3/9/54.
27212 *(ex61969)* 3/5/56.
27197 *(ex61959)* 22/8/58.

SHEDS:
Doncaster.
Norwich 8/5/39.
March 24/11/41.
Lowestoft 13/10/47.
Norwich 15/11/59.
March 31/1/60.
Staveley 21/2/60.
Lincoln 20/3/60.

RENUMBERED:
1926 12/1/47.
61926 21/7/49.

CONDEMNED:
10/4/62.
Cut up at Doncaster.

2936

A.W. 1154.

To traffic 1/1/35.

REPAIRS:
Don. 3/4-6/5/36.**G.**
Don. 31/12/37-19/1/38.**G.**
Don. 2/9-21/10/39.**G.**
Don. 10/1-21/2/42.**G.**
Dar. 1/6-13/7/43.**G.**
Dar. 30/12/43-12/4/44.**L.**
Don. 24/2-17/3/45.**G.**
Don. 9/2-9/3/46.**L.**
Don. 23/6-2/8/47.**G.**
Ghd. 14/12/48-7/1/49.**L.**
Don. 14/11-24/12/49.**G.**
Don. 14-30/3/51.**L.**
Don. 8-31/10/51.**G.**
Don. 14/8-23/9/53.**G.**
Don. 13/9-7/10/54.**C/L.**
Don. 31/8-7/10/55.**G.**
Don. 30/7-29/8/57.**G.**
Don. 29/7-27/8/59.**G.**
Don. 25/4-2/5/60.**N/C.**
Don. 13-29/4/61.**N/C.**

Don. 6/7/61.*Not repaired.*

BOILERS:
8802.
8965 *(ex2446)* 21/2/42.
8140A *(ex38)* 13/7/43.
6D/687 *(ex1878)* 2/8/47.
10538 *(new)* 24/12/49.
27266 *(new)* 31/10/51.
27173 *(ex61963)* 23/9/53.
27137 *(ex61807)* 7/10/55.
27122 *(ex61809)* 29/8/57.
27222 *(ex61980)* 27/8/59.

SHEDS:
Doncaster.
Blaydon 30/9/42.
Heaton 19/6/43.
Gateshead 8/7/43.
Neville Hill 23/7/45.
Hull Dairycoates 5/10/47.
Heaton 14/9/52.
Hull Dairycoates 17/1/60.

RENUMBERED:
1927 24/11/46.
61927 7/1/49.

Ever prone to exceptions, Cowlairs works sent out 61992 on 4th January 1952 repainted but entirely devoid of lining, almost three years after that had been made standard, although they had used correct 6 and 9. Note the curious flat top dome cover which it had acquired at its April 1948 repair, and it seems to have been the only K3 so fitted. *A.G.Ellis.*

CONDEMNED:
17/7/61.
Cut up at Doncaster.

2937

A.W. 1155.

To traffic 1/1/35.

REPAIRS:
Don. 12/7-1/8/35.**L.**
Don. 7/5-6/6/36.**G.**
Don. 4-23/2/38.**G.**
Don. 21/10-18/11/39.**G.**
Don. 27/9-25/10/41.**G.**
Don. 8/4-6/5/44.**G.**
Don. 1/6-3/8/46.**G.**
Don. 8/2-8/3/47.**L.**
Don. 15/4-14/5/48.**G.**
Cow. 25/7-9/9/50.**G.**
Cow. 5/6-7/7/52.**G.**
Cow. 24/6-21/8/54.**H/I.**
Cow. 23/8-11/9/54.**C/L.**
Cow. 5/4-16/6/56.**H/I.**
Cow. 9/12/57-18/1/58.**G.**
Cow. 5-8/2/58.**N/C.**
Cow. 20/2-22/3/58.**C/L.**

BOILERS:
8803.
8964 *(ex2445)* 6/5/44.
9553 *(new)* 3/8/46.
27314 *(ex61878)* 7/7/52.
27322 *(ex61878)* 18/1/58.

SHEDS:
Doncaster.
Blaydon 30/9/42.
Gateshead 26/6/43.
Heaton 6/2/49.
St Margarets 13/2/49.

RENUMBERED:
1928 20/10/46.
61928 14/5/48.

CONDEMNED:
6/2/60.
Cut up at Cowlairs.

2325

R.S.H. 4075.

To traffic 17/8/34.

REPAIRS:
Dar. 4/12/35-31/1/36.**G.**
Dar. 25/8-19/10/37.**G.**
Don. 2-30/11/38.**G.**
Dar. 1-15/8/39.**N/C.**
Dar. 11/10-15/11/40.**G.**
Don. 8/3-18/4/43.**G.**
Don. 1/5-9/6/45.**G.**
Don. 29/6-12/8/47.**G.**
Don. 22/8-7/10/49.**G.**
Don. 25/12/51-25/1/52.**G.**
Don. 27-28/3/52.**N/C.**
Don. 23/3-22/4/54.**G.**

Don. 14/12/55-18/1/56.**G.**
Don. 23/5-1/6/56.**C/L.**
Don. 29/3-1/5/58.**G.**
Don. 22-27/1/59.**C/L.**
Don. 12/1-10/2/60.**G.**

BOILERS:
RS4075.
8124 *(ex1392)* 31/1/36.
8137A *(ex1310)* 19/10/37.
8139A *(ex1300)* 15/11/40.
8909 *(ex2468)* 18/4/43.
10531 *(new)* 7/10/49.
27208 *(ex61952)* 25/1/52.
27197 *(ex61930)* 22/4/54.
24907 *(new)* 18/1/56.
27188 *(ex61930)* 1/5/58.
27105 *(ex61853)* 10/2/60.

SHEDS:
Darlington.
Heaton 16/10/34.
Gateshead 22/1/40.
Colwick 23/11/40.
New England 25/6/45.
March 16/6/46.
New England 30/10/46.
March 20/9/53.

RENUMBERED:
1929 17/3/46.
61929 7/10/49.

CONDEMNED:
4/7/62.
Cut up at Doncaster.

1332

R.S.H. 4076.

To traffic 1/9/34.

REPAIRS:
Dar. 18/2-7/4/36.**G.**
Dar. 9/6-16/7/37.**L.**

Dar. 19/5-25/7/38.**G.**
Dar. 26/3-26/4/40.**G.**
Dar. 24/8-30/9/42.**G.**
Dar. 23/4-28/6/45.**G.**
Dar. 5-12/7/45.**N/C.**
Don. 1/2-1/3/47.**G.**
Don. 21/8-6/9/47.**L.**
Ghd. 21/9-13/10/47.**N/C.**
Don. 12/12/47-7/2/48.**G.**
Don. 21/11-21/12/49.**G.**
Don. 26/9-24/10/51.**G.**
Don. 20-30/4/53.**C/L.**
Don. 27/5-10/6/53.**G.**
Don. 9/3-2/4/54.**G.**
Don. 22/11-31/12/55.**G.**
Don. 6/3-10/4/58.**G.**
Don. 19/7-24/8/60.**G.**

BOILERS:
RS4076.
D1654 *(ex53)* 26/4/40.
8123 *(ex33)* 30/9/42.
8137A *(ex3825)* 28/6/45.
2799 *(ex3822)* 7/2/48.
3216 *(ex2455)* 21/12/49.
27197 *(ex61959)* 24/10/51.
27188 *(ex61873)* 2/4/54.
24911 *(ex61844)* 10/4/58.
27180 *(ex61952)* 24/8/60.

SHEDS:
Darlington.
Heaton 16/10/34.
Gateshead 24/1/40.
Blaydon 28/3/43.
Gateshead 26/6/43.
Heaton 6/2/49.
Tweedmouth 6/1/52.
Tyne Dock 8/10/61.
Hull Dairycoates 14/1/62.

RENUMBERED:
1930 7/4/46.
E1930 7/2/48.
61930 21/12/49.

CONDEMNED:
17/12/62.
Cut up at Doncaster.

1333

R.S.H. 4077.

To traffic 7/9/34.

REPAIRS:
Dar. 26/11/34-23/1/35.**L.**
Dar. 30/8-31/10/35.**L.**
Dar. 28/4-18/6/36.**G.**
Dar. 16/2-11/5/38.**G.**
Dar. 23/1-29/2/40.**G.**
Cow. 10/41.**G.**
Cow. 7/43.**G.**
Cow. 23/10-24/11/45.**G.**
Cow. 20-27/4/46.**L.**
Cow. 3/10-22/11/47.**G.**
Cow. 5/7-26/8/50.**G.**
Cow. 8-12/9/50.**N/C.**
Cow. 26/1-24/2/51.**C/L.**
Cow. 4-6/12/51.**C/L.**
Cow. 22/9-18/10/52.**H/I.**
Cow. 24/11-17/12/53.**C/L.**
Cow. 22/3-1/5/54.**G.**
Cow. 27/3-12/5/56.**H/I.**
Cow. 25/12/57-8/2/58.**G.**
Cow. 20/11-24/12/58.**C/L.**

BOILERS:
RS4077.
8115 *(ex1300)* 18/6/36.
8134 *(ex1100)* 11/5/38.
8124 *(ex1394)* 29/2/40.
8115 *(ex1306)* 24/11/45.
8124 *(ex1911)* 26/8/50.
Renumbered 27304 24/2/51.
27337 *(new)* 1/5/54.
27333 *(ex61857)* 8/2/58.

SHEDS:
Darlington.
Heaton 16/10/34.

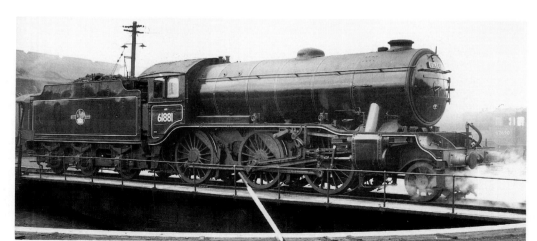

Change from emblem to BR crest was effective from mid-June 1957 at Cowlairs, but the first K3 to get it there was 61879 ex works 24th August, and from then to 7th February 1959 on 61968, Cowlairs had applied it to twenty two of the class. On the right hand side, all had the lion facing the wrong way and none survived to have it corrected. Note the very close spacing which that works used for the figures on the cab side.

For so large a class, and in use for more than forty years, K3 was remarkably fortunate in escaping with only one drastic accident. In September 1956 No.61846 was working empty coaches from Bridlington to Filey Holiday Camp station, and the brake connection between tender and train had not been made properly. Down the hill from Speeton control was lost, so 61846 hit and demolished the station's concrete buffer stops. Even so, a casual/light repair at Doncaster, 21st September to October 19th, was all that it needed. *Ken Hoole.*

On Saturday 15th June 1935 at Welwyn Garden City 4009 was on a down express parcels when it ran into the back of the 10.53 p.m. passenger train from King's Cross to Newcastle, due to a signalman's error of judgement, which caused 14 deaths. This shows 4009 on 30th June at Doncaster works awaiting a general repair. That explains why another general was needed only four months after its previous one. As a result of this accident the universally known "Welwyn control" was introduced, and still applies.

St Margarets 11/3/40.
Haymarket 10/43.
St Margarets 9/44.

RENUMBERED:
 1931 7/4/46.
61931 26/8/50.

CONDEMNED:
24/7/59.
Into Cowlairs for cut up 26/10/59.
Not in use 220 days in 1944.

1339

R.S.H. 4078.

To traffic 15/9/34.

REPAIRS:
Dar. 18/12/35-21/2/36.**G.**
Dar. 3/2-25/3/38.**G.**
Dar. 3/1-9/2/40.**G.**
Dar. 21/2-2/3/40.**N/C.**
Dar. 22/6-6/8/42.**G.**

Don. 2/10-25/11/44.**G.**
Don. 23/4-31/5/47.**G.**
Ghd. 8-24/11/48.**L.**
Don. 12/9-22/10/49.**G.**
Don. 1-27/11/51.**G.**
Don. 6-28/8/53.**G.**
Don. 1-31/3/55.**G.**
Don. 4-30/3/57.**G.**
Don. 21/5-18/6/59.**G.**
Don. 16-20/5/60.**N/C.**
Don. 29/1/62.*Not repaired.*

BOILERS:
RS4078.
RS4075 *(ex1325)* 21/2/36.
 2941 *(ex1106)* 9/2/40.
RS4077 *(ex1108)* 6/8/42.
 2830 *(ex3820)* 25/11/44.
 2796 *(ex1819)* 22/10/49.
 27272 *(new)* 27/11/51.
 24923 *(new)* 30/3/57.
 27249 *(ex61961)* 18/6/59.

The gremlins were even-handed in their treatment of K3 class, Filey was North Eastern, Welwyn was Great Northern, and the other reportable accident was Great Central at Liverpool on 4th October 1937 when Gorton's 3817 hauling seven coaches on the boat train which had left Harwich at 7.25 a.m. was running too quickly into the sharply curved No.1 platform of Central Station at about 2.41 p.m., two minutes before it was due. It struck the platform coping and was derailed. This is how Doncaster received it, and took its picture on 29th October. *L.N.E.R.*

SHEDS:
Darlington.
Heaton 18/10/34.
Tweedmouth 8/4/40.
Heaton 28/3/43.
Darlington 10/8/43.
Hull Dairycoates 23/7/45.
Heaton 14/9/52.
Tweedmouth 30/11/52.
Heaton 27/12/53.
Hull Dairycoates 25/9/55.

RENUMBERED:
1932 31/3/46.
61932 24/11/48.

CONDEMNED:
12/2/62.
Cut up at Doncaster.

1399

R.S.H. 4079.

To traffic 29/9/34.

REPAIRS:
Dar. 2/8-10/9/35.**L.**
Dar. 25/3-15/5/36.**G.**
Dar. 27/1-11/3/38.**G.**
Dar. 14/3-16/4/40.**G.**
Cow. 10/41.**G.**
Cow. 18/12/43-8/1/44.**G.**
Cow. 1/10-7/11/45.**G.**
Cow. 21/10-28/11/46.**G.**
Cow. 29/3-7/6/47.**L.**
Cow. 1/2-19/3/49.**L/I.**
Cow. 19/3-30/6/51.**G.**
Cow. 19/1-7/2/53.**L/I.**

Cow. 7/1-20/3/54.**C/L.**
Cow. 12/8-17/9/55.**G.**
Cow. 8/3-7/4/56.**C/L.**
Cow. 12-27/3/57.**H/I.**
Cow. 21/6-10/8/57.**C/L.**
Cow. 26/11-20/12/58.**L/I.**
Cow. 25/4-5/5/59.**N/C.**

BOILERS:
RS4079.
8138A *(ex1310)* 15/5/36.
  2909 *(new)* 11/3/38.
8138A *(ex1308)* 16/4/40.
D1746 *(ex1909)* 28/11/46.
Renumbered 27301 30/6/51.
27263 *(ex61916)* 17/9/55.

SHEDS:
Darlington.
York 10/11/34.
St Margarets 25/4/40.
Carlisle 1/10/43.
St Margarets 5/3/45.

RENUMBERED:
1933 17/11/46.
61933 19/3/49.

CONDEMNED:
16/9/60.
Cut up at Cowlairs.

1307

R.S.H. 4081.

To traffic 29/11/34.

REPAIRS:
Dar. 24/4-11/6/36.**G.**
Dar. 25/1-11/3/38.**G.**
Dar. 2/8-13/9/39.**G.**
Dar. 9/8-10/9/40.**H.**
Dar. 15/12/41-20/1/42.**G.**
Dar. 21/2-3/3/42.**N/C.**
Dar. 24/11-23/12/43.**G.**
Dar. 29/8-4/10/44.**L.**
Don. 8/1-15/2/47.**G.**
Don. 5/7-13/8/49.**G.**
Don. 12/7-10/8/51.**G.**
Don. 6/7-7/8/53.**G.**
Don. 4/7-9/8/55.**G.**
Dar. 19/12/57-8/2/58.**G.**
Don. 22/4-1/6/60.**G.**

BOILERS:
RS4080.
D1649 *(ex46)* 11/6/36.
D1730 *(ex1324)* 13/9/39.
  8126 *(ex1394)* 20/1/42.
  8132 *(ex1310)* 23/12/43.
  8914 *(ex1926)* 13/8/49.
27182 *(ex61874)* 10/8/51.
27165 *(ex61808)* 7/8/53.
27168 *(ex61977)* 9/8/55.
24901 *(ex61874)* 8/2/58.

SHEDS:
To Stock Gateshead.
Heaton 1/1/35.
Tweedmouth 10/3/36.
York 19/3/39.
Blaydon 1/6/40.
Heaton 19/6/43.
Darlington 27/7/43.
Hull Dairycoates 23/7/45.
Tweedmouth 8/6/58.
Ardsley 10/9/61.

RENUMBERED:
1934 12/5/46.
61934 11/8/49.

CONDEMNED:
26/11/62.
Cut up at Doncaster.

1322

R.S.H. 4080.

To traffic 6/12/34.

REPAIRS:
Dar. 3-21/5/35.**N/C.**
Dar. 20/3-15/5/36.**G.**
Dar. 1/11/37-4/1/38.**G.**
Dar. 31/8-7/10/39.**G.**
Dar. 10/1-27/2/41.**L.** *Tender only.*
Dar. 17/11-27/12/41.**G.**
Dar. 5/1-19/2/44.**G.**
Dar. 26/10-30/11/44.**L.**
Don. 28/9-9/11/46.**G.**
Don. 25/1-8/2/47.**L.**
Dar. 5/3-2/4/48.**L.**
Don. 11/4-14/5/49.**G.**
Don. 20/3-13/4/51.**G.**
Don. 27/8-5/9/52.**G.**
Don. 20/7-19/8/53.**G.**
Don. 7/6-15/7/55.**G.**
Dar. 10/10-16/11/57.**G.**
Don. 15/12/59-21/1/60.**G.**
Don. 21-25/3/60.**N/C.**
Don. 10/7/62.*Not repaired.*

BOILERS:
RS4081.
D1650 *(ex1389)* 4/1/38.

WORKS CODES:- Cow - Cowlairs. Dar - Darlington. Don - Doncaster. Ghd - Gateshead. Gor - Gorton. Inv - Inverurie. Str - Stratford.
REPAIR CODES:- **C/H** - Casual Heavy. **C/L** - Casual Light. **G** - General. **H** - Heavy. **H/I** - Heavy Intermediate. **L** - Light. **L/I** - Light Intermediate. **N/C** - Non-Classified.

65

AW83 (ex1101) 7/10/39.
RS4076 (ex1101) 27/12/41.
RS4078 (ex1391) 19/2/44.
    8964 (ex2937) 9/11/46.
27155 (ex61849) 13/4/51.
27234 (ex61800) 19/8/53.
27160 (ex61883) 15/7/55.
27284 (ex61965) 16/11/57.
24900 (ex61922) 21/1/60.

SHEDS:
To stock Gateshead Works.
Heaton 1/1/35.
Gateshead 22/1/40.
Blaydon 28/3/43.
Heaton 23/6/43.
Darlington 16/7/43.
Hull Dairycoates 23/7/45.

RENUMBERED:
1935 12/5/46.
61935 2/4/48.

CONDEMNED:
23/7/62.
Cut up at Doncaster.

2938

R.S.H. 4082.

To traffic 15/1/35.

REPAIRS:
Don. 10/3-7/4/36.**G.**
Don. 23/6-16/7/37.**G.**
Cow. 19/2/38.**L.**
Cow. 8-22/4/39.**L.**
Cow. 16/8/39.**G.**
Cow. 26/11-18/12/40.**G.**

Cow. 23/1-27/2/43.**G.**
Cow. 17/5/44.**G.**
Cow. 28/8-22/9/45.**G.**
Cow. 17/9-31/10/47.**G.**
Cow. 12/7-22/8/48.**L.**
Cow. 30/6-19/8/49.**G.**
Cow. 1-26/5/51.**L/I.**
Cow. 2/9-4/10/52.**G.**
Cow. 20/12/53-25/1/54.**H/I.**
Cow. 28/10-26/11/54.**L/I.**
Cow. 14/12/55-24/1/56.**G.**
Cow. 6/2-3/3/56.**C/L.**
Cow. 21/8-27/9/57.**L/I.**
Cow. 24/11-19/12/58.**H/I.**
Cow. 9/10-20/11/59.**C/L.**

BOILERS:
(C1822)/RS4082.
    8605 (ex32) 22/9/45.
    9373 (ex1968) 19/8/49.
Renumbered 27329 26/5/51.
27316 (ex61851) 4/10/52.
27340 (ex61924) 24/1/56.

SHED:
Carlisle.

RENUMBERED:
1936 7/7/46.
61936 21/8/48.

CONDEMNED:
22/11/61.
Cut up at Cowlairs.

2939

R.S.H. 4083.

To traffic 11/1/35.

REPAIRS:
Don. 7/5-18/6/36.**G.**
Don. 12/8-1/9/37.**G.**
Cow. 9/11/38.**L.**
Cow. 6/5-3/6/39.**G.**
Cow. 15/9/39.**L.**
Cow. 23/3/40.**L.**
Cow. 26/7-30/8/41.**G.**
Cow. 17/10/42.**L.**
Cow. 17/2-10/3/45.**G.**
Cow. 15/9-6/10/45.**L.**
Cow. 11/12/46-14/3/47.**G.**
Cow. 10-17/5/47.**L.**
Cow. 10/11-24/12/48.**G.**
Cow. 12/4-6/5/51.**G.**
Cow. 22/1-25/2/52.**L/I.**
Cow. 4-28/8/53.**L/I.**
Cow. 10/9-25/10/54.**G.**
Cow. 15/6-3/8/56.**L/I.**
Cow. 13-18/8/56.**N/C.**
Cow. 20/3-28/4/58.**G.**

BOILERS:
(C1823)/RS4083.
    8917 (ex1955) 14/3/47.
Renumbered 27315 6/5/51.
27338 (new) 25/10/54.
27328 (ex spare and 61885) 28/4/58.

SHEDS:
Carlisle.
March 28/6/59.
Carlisle 14/2/60.

RENUMBERED:
1937 13/10/46.
61937 19/9/48.

CONDEMNED:
12/3/60.
Cut up at Cowlairs.

2940

R.S.H.4084.

To traffic 11/1/35.

REPAIRS:
Don. 26/2-9/4/36.**G.**
Don. 27/4-4/6/37.**G.**
Cow. 17/8-14/11/38.**G.**
Cow. 27/7-8/9/39.**G.**
Cow. 11/6-6/7/40.**G.**
Cow. 16-20/7/40.**N/C.**
Don. 6/3-15/4/41.**G.**
Don. 31/3-29/4/44.**G.**
Don. 13/4-31/5/46.**G.**
Don. 27/1-22/4/48.**G.**
Don. 11/4-25/5/50.**G.**
Don. 16/1-18/2/52.**G.**
Don. 15/10-13/11/53.**G.**
Don. 2-22/7/54.**C/L.**
Don. 23/8-30/9/55.**G.**
Don. 2-30/11/57.**G.**
Don. 23/9-10/10/58.**C/L.**

BOILERS:
(C1824)/RS4084.
5D/687 (ex92) 29/4/44.
RS4081 (ex61956) 25/5/50.
27215 (ex61976) 18/2/52.
27149 (ex61958) 13/11/53.
27278 (ex61915) 30/9/55.
27240 (ex61949) 30/11/57.

SHEDS:
Carlisle.
Sheffield 23/11/40.
New England 25/6/45.
March 12/6/49.
Sheffield 16/9/56.

4004 here in June 1938 is running through Doncaster station on the Up main and working empty coaching stock, the first vehicle being a 12 wheeled Restaurant Car. Note that it now has its classification on front buffer beam, and cab has had sight screen fitted.

(*above*) **4005** leaving York could well have been deputising for a Pacific, because it has an Edinburgh to King's Cross express passenger train, which it had just taken over, and would probably work no further south than Doncaster, where it was then shedded. *Real Photos.*

(*right*) In August 1945, and clearly showing the almost total lack of exterior maintenance due to the war, No.39 has a Class 3 goods at Woodhead which it is taking to Woodford from Manchester. The gantries were part of the Manchester to Sheffield electrification installation, progress on which had been suspended during the war.

RENUMBERED:
1938 30/5/46.
1938 22/4/48.

CONDEMNED:
9/12/61.
Cut up at Doncaster.

425

N.B.L. 24225.

To traffic 20/8/35.

REPAIRS:
Don. 10/12/36-23/1/37.**G.**
Don. 1-30/7/38.**G.**
Don. 24/8-28/9/40.**G.**
Don. 9/1-13/2/43.**G.**
Don. 17/6-26/8/44.**G.**
Don. 4/8-1/9/45.**G.**
Don. 21/5-8/7/47.**G.**

Don. 24/4-3/6/49.**G.**
Don. 7/6-10/7/51.**G.**
Don. 9/4-8/5/53.**G.**
Don. 30/1-2/3/55.**G.**
Don. 8/5-15/6/57.**G.**
Don. 11/3-22/4/59.**G.**
Don. 8/3-14/4/61.**G.**
Don. 3-10/11/61.**N/C.**

BOILERS:
8909.
8925 (*ex2463*) 30/7/38.
RS4079 (*ex1300*) 13/2/43.
2803 (*ex2499*) 26/8/44.
8603 (*ex1166*) 1/9/45.
27175 (*ex61949*) 10/7/51.
27190 (*ex61824*) 8/5/53.
27243 (*ex61926*) 15/6/57.
24922 (*ex61954*) 22/4/59.

SHEDS:
Doncaster.

Kings Cross 17/9/35.
Colwick 14/12/39.
New England 25/6/45.
March 16/2/47.
Norwich 14/10/47.
Lowestoft 3/10/48.
Norwich 27/2/49.
Lowestoft 19/10/49.
Norwich 1/1/50.
Lincoln 4/12/60.
Colwick 11/12/60.
Immingham 14/1/62.

RENUMBERED:
1939 28/10/46.
61939 3/6/49.

CONDEMNED:
4/11/62.
Sold for scrap to J.Cashmore, Great Bridge.

2426

N.B.L. 24226.

To traffic 22/8/35.

REPAIRS:
Don. 18/2-24/3/37.**G.**
Don. 24/8-22/9/38.**G.**
Don. 10/8-14/9/40.**G.**
Don. 17/10-14/11/42.**G.**
Don. 14/10-11/11/44.**G.**
Don. 4/8/45.**L.**
Don. 19/10-14/11/46.**G.**
Don. 25/2-23/4/47.**G.**
Don. 15/9-6/11/47.**G.**
Don. 22/9-12/11/48.**G.**
Don. 20/6-20/7/50.**G.**
Don. 23/5-19/6/52.**G.**
Don. 1/3-1/4/54.**G.**
Don. 7/12/55-12/1/56.**G.**
Don. 29/12/57-30/1/58.**G.**

Working from Heaton shed, No.46 shows the kind of jobs on which the North Eastern Area engines were first employed, this No.2 express goods from Newcastle to Edinburgh being at Goswick in Northumberland. Loaded trains of 40 wagons, such as this one were well within their capability. Although a mid-1920's scene, containers were already in use.

Don. 7/3-7/4/60.**G.**

BOILERS:
 8910.
 8D/687 *(ex121)* 14/11/42.
 9989 *(new)* 12/11/48.
 9551 *(ex61947)* 20/7/50.
 27241 *(ex61802)* 19/6/52.
 27219 *(ex61867)* 1/4/54.
 27105 *(ex61829)* 12/1/56.
 27266 *(ex61918)* 30/1/58.
 27192 *(ex61887)* 7/4/60.

SHEDS:
Doncaster.
Kings Cross 7/10/35.
Stratford 28/2/39.
March 3/12/41.
Doncaster 16/9/56.

RENUMBERED:
 1940 18/8/46.
 61940 12/11/48.

CONDEMNED:
4/5/62.
Cut up at Doncaster.

2427

N.B.L. 24227.

To traffic 26/8/35.

REPAIRS:
Don. 3-31/12/36.**G.**

Don. 12/8-2/9/38.**G.**
Don. 25/3-13/5/39.**L.**
Don. 5/4-10/5/41.**G.**
Dar. 15/4-12/5/43.**L.**
Dar. 31/8-28/9/43.**G.**
Don. 1/6-13/7/46.**G.**
Don. 8/7-14/8/48.**G.**
Don. 18-24/8/48.**N/C.**
Don. 3-25/1/51.**G.**
Don. 18/9-17/10/52.**G.**
Don. 11/10-11/11/54.**G.**
Don. 1-31/10/56.**G.**
Don. 11/2-24/3/59.**G.**
Don. 16-21/5/60.**N/C.**
Don. 21/7/61.*Not repaired.*

BOILERS:
 8911.
 8928 *(ex2468)* 2/9/38.
 2852 *(ex1397)* 28/9/43.
 9555 *(ex61828)* 14/8/48.
 27138 *(ex61814)* 25/1/51.
 27250 *(ex61977)* 17/10/52.
 27106 *(ex61904)* 11/11/54.
 27119 *(ex61904)* 31/10/56.
 27113 *(ex61943)* 24/3/59.

SHEDS:
Doncaster.
Kings Cross 30/9/35.
Colwick 14/12/39.
Heaton 29/9/42.
Darlington 10/8/43.
Hull Dairycoates 23/7/45.

RENUMBERED:
 1941 10/11/46.

61941 12/8/48.

CONDEMNED:
31/7/61.
Cut up at Doncaster.

2428

N.B.L. 24228.

To traffic 28/8/35.

REPAIRS:
Don. 2/10-7/11/36.**G.**
Don. 21/2-7/4/37.**G.**
Don. 19/11-10/12/38.**G.**
Don. 31/8-12/10/40.**G.**
Don. 17/7-21/8/43.**G.**
Don. 22/9-20/10/45.**G.**
Don. 28/10-10/12/47.**G.**
Don. 10/7-22/8/49.**G.**
Don. 8/10-6/11/51.**G.**
Don. 3/2-7/3/53.**L.**
Don. 2-30/3/54.**G.**
Don. 20/6-2/8/56.**G.**
Don. 10/10-20/11/58.**G.**
Don. 22/12/60-8/2/61.**G.**

BOILERS:
 8912.
 8926 *(ex2438)* 20/10/45.
 27265 *(new)* 6/11/51.
 27210 *(ex61984)* 30/3/54.
 24914 *(new)* 2/8/56.
 27203 *(ex61845)* 20/11/58.
 27133 *(ex61859)* 8/2/61.

SHEDS:
Doncaster.
Kings Cross 2/10/35.
Stratford 9/5/39.
March 15/9/41.
Norwich 14/10/47.
Yarmouth 12/10/49.
Norwich 1/1/50.
March 24/6/51.
Lincoln 29/6/52.
Stratford 5/10/52.
Parkeston 9/3/58.
March 12/6/60.

RENUMBERED:
 1942 28/10/46.
 61942 20/8/49.

CONDEMNED:
16/9/62.
*Sold for scrap to Central Wagon Co,
Ince.*

2438

N.B.L. 24229.

To traffic 30/8/35.

REPAIRS:
Don. 20/9-9/10/37.**G.**
Gor. 4-5/3/38.**L.** *Front heater conn.*
Gor. 15/7/38.**N/C.** *Heat detector
fitted.*
Don. 15/4-20/5/39.**G.**
Don. 16/3-13/4/40.**G.**

Don. 22/8-19/9/42.**G.**
Don. 10/3-5/5/45.**G.**
Don. 9/2-2/3/46.**L.**
Don. 16/6-2/9/47.**G.**
Don. 6/12/49-12/1/50.**G.**
Don. 15/5-12/6/52.**G.**
Don. 16/8-24/9/54.**G.**
Don. 16/12/54-6/1/55.**N/C.**
Don. 30/8-11/10/56.**G.**
Don. 21/1-26/2/59.**G.**
Don. 5/6-8/7/61.**G.**

BOILERS:
 8913.
 8926 *(ex2466)* 19/9/42.
 8803 *(ex2937)* 5/5/45.
 8596 *(ex1853)* 12/1/50.
 27238 *(ex61974)* 12/6/52.
 27132 *(ex61837)* 24/9/54.
 27113 *(ex61912)* 11/10/56.
 27294 *(ex61925)* 26/2/59.
 27223 *(ex61954)* 8/7/61.
Renumbered S.B.4522.

SHEDS:
Doncaster.
Gorton 10/10/35.
Woodford 30/10/43.
Annesley 12/9/48.
March 20/9/53.
Boston 17/7/55.
Sheffield 17/11/57.
Colwick 6/12/59.

RENUMBERED:
1943 29/9/46.
61943 12/1/50.

CONDEMNED:
10/65.
Sold for scrap to Geo.Cohen, Ickles.

The engines allocated to Scottish Area were most frequently to be seen on the Waverley route and here 191 has a Class B goods about to pass through the station at Galashiels, and going to Carlisle, whose Canal shed was its home base for its first 14 years, and again for another three during the 1939-45 war.

(middle) **On 15th September 1945 coming in to Guide Bridge station, 202 is working from Manchester (Central) to Sheffield (Victoria) on this express passenger train. Until it went for repair in February 1939, the front buffer beam carried no more than No.202. It now tells those concerned that it is a K3, its shed is DONC, and that it is L 6 in the Southern Area Freight Train Load Classification.**
H.C.Casserley.

(right) **2426 passing through Sandy in the 1937 summer has the goods train equivalent of the passenger** *FLYING SCOTSMAN.* **The 3.40 p.m. No.1 express goods from King's Cross to Glasgow well merited its widely known sobriquet of just the "Scotch goods", and was treated with much the same respect as the streamlined trains. It was primarily for that train that the V2 class - the celebrated 'Green Arrows' were introduced.**

The flow of coal to the London area was colossal and continuous, and K3 class shared with the mineral engines in hauling it, and in returning the empty wagons as 112 is doing whilst picking up water from Langley troughs in 1932.

In the up direction the express meat trains from Northern Scotland, and the fish trains from Hull to London ran with lamps indicating their importance. Doncaster shedded 2443 in Doncaster station is switching from Up main to Up goods line on one such train. The long lattice bridge was the main access to the Plant from the town.

2439

N.B.L. 24230.

To traffic 3/9/35.

REPAIRS:
Don. 8-30/10/37.**G.**
Gor. 14-15/7/38.**N/C.** *Heat detector fitted.*
Gor. 18-21/7/38.**L.** *Front heater conn.*
Don. 22/7-26/8/39.**G.**
Don. 10-24/8/40.**L.**
Don. 10/10-7/11/42.**G.**
Don. 12-26/2/44.**G.**
Don. 15/9-13/10/45.**G.**
Don. 13/7-3/8/46.**L.**
Don. 22/2-24/3/48.**G.**
Don. 4/8-1/9/50.**G.**
Don. 28/11-19/12/52.**G.**
Don. 16/6-22/7/55.**G.**
Don. 11/12/57-18/1/58.**G.**
Don. 16-22/12/59.**N/C.**
Don. 17/8-28/9/60.**G.**

BOILERS:
8914.
9287 *(new)* 7/11/42.
9989 *(61940)* 1/9/50.
27140 *(ex61972)* 19/12/52.
27283 *(ex61839)* 22/7/55.
24902 *(ex61849)* 18/1/58.
27183 *(ex61972)* 28/9/60.

SHEDS:
Doncaster.
Gorton 24/9/35.
Woodford 24/10/43.
Lincoln 29/6/47.
Immingham 18/12/60.
Colwick 14/1/62.

RENUMBERED:
1944 20/1/46.
61944 24/3/48.

CONDEMNED:
16/9/62.
Sold for scrap to Albert Looms, Spondon.

2440

N.B.L. 24231.

To traffic 5/9/35.

REPAIRS:
Don. 23/10-16/11/37.**G.**
Gor. 11-15/3/38.**L.** *Front heater conn.*
Gor. 24/6/38.**N/C.** *Heat detector fitted.*
Don. 2/9-7/10/39.**G.**
Don. 3/1-14/3/42.**G.**
Don. 25/4-27/5/44.**G.**
Don. 13/7-10/8/46.**G.**

Don. 9/12/48-15/1/49.**G.**
Don. 27/2-30/3/51.**G.**
Don. 21/4-22/5/53.**G.**
Don. 20/8-17/9/54.**C/H.**
Don. 15/8-23/9/55.**G.**
Dar. 25/11/57-11/1/58.**G.**
Don. 30/10-2/12/59.**G.**
Don. 4-8/4/60.**N/C.**
Don. 15/2/62.*Not repaired.*

BOILERS:
8915.
3222 *(new)* 14/3/42.
9992 *(new)* 15/1/49.
27153 *(ex61862)* 30/3/51.
27166 *(ex61803)* 22/5/53.
27160 *(ex61935)* 11/1/58.
27147 *(ex61852)* 2/12/59.

SHEDS:
Doncaster.
Gorton 9/10/35.
Colwick 24/6/38.
Heaton 29/9/42.
Gateshead 8/7/43.
Neville Hill 23/7/45.
Hull Dairycoates 5/10/47.

RENUMBERED:
1945 1/12/46.
61945 14/1/49.

CONDEMNED:
26/2/62.
Cut up at Doncaster.

2442

N.B.L. 24232.

To traffic 10/9/35.

REPAIRS:
Don. 2/10-26/11/36.**G.**
Don. 30/4-14/6/38.**G.**
Don. 10/2-16/3/40.**G.**
Don. 8/3-5/4/41.**G.**
Don. 1/8-5/9/42.**G.**
Don. 8/4-10/6/44.**G.**
Don. 6/7-3/8/46.**G.**
Don. 9/10-10/11/47.**L.**
Don. 21/7-3/9/48.**G.**
Don. 20/9-20/10/50.**G.**
Don. 14/12/50-18/1/51.**C/L.**
Don. 31/12/52-28/1/53.**G.**
Don. 4/11-3/12/54.**G.**
Don. 19/9-13/10/56.**G.**
Don. 5/7-6/8/58.**G.**
Don. 7-23/10/59.**C/L.**
Don. 26/3-25/5/60.**G.**
Don. 21/1-7/2/61.**C/L.**

BOILERS:
8916.
8875 *(new)* 14/6/38.

2801 *(ex1958)* 3/9/48.
27110 *(ex1952)* 20/10/50.
27115 *(ex61805)* 28/1/53.
27108 *(ex61845)* 3/12/54.
27233 *(ex61804)* 13/10/56.
27153 *(ex61963)* 6/8/58.
24913 *(ex61838)* 25/5/60.

SHEDS:
Doncaster.
New England 2/10/35.
March 18/6/40.
Sheffield 19/11/40.
Colwick 30/9/44.
New England 22/4/45.
March 31/1/49.
Doncaster 30/8/53.
March 27/9/53.

RENUMBERED:
1946 31/3/46.
61946 3/9/48.

CONDEMNED:
14/6/62.
Cut up at Doncaster.

2443

N.B.L. 24233.

To traffic 13/9/35.

REPAIRS:
Don. 10/12/36-9/1/37.**G.**
Don. 14/6-6/7/38.**G.**
Don. 20/1-24/2/40.**G.**
Don. 9/3-13/4/40.**L.**
Don. 25/4-30/5/42.**G.**
Don. 11/12/43-29/1/44.**G.**
Don. 27/4-1/6/46.**G.**
Don. 21/2-1/4/48.**G.**
Don. 7/2-14/4/50.**G.**
Don. 9/1-8/2/52.**G.**
Don. 15/12/53-14/1/54.**G.**
Don. 22/9-21/10/55.**G.**
Don. 12/11-20/12/57.**G.**
Don. 22-25/12/57.**N/C.**
Don. 9/11-10/12/59.**G.**

BOILERS:
8917.
8916 *(ex2442)* 6/7/38.
9551 *(new)* 1/6/46.
10803 *(new)* 14/4/50.
27212 *(ex61947)* 8/2/52.
27282 *(new)* 14/1/54.
24928 *(new)* 20/12/57.
27100 *(ex spare and 61836)* 10/12/59.

SHEDS:
Doncaster.
Norwich 26/5/40.
March 28/11/41.
Norwich 17/10/47.
Lowestoft 8/8/48.

Norwich 5/9/48.
Yarmouth 6/10/48.
Norwich 12/12/48.
March 24/6/51.
Colwick 16/9/56.

RENUMBERED:
1947 1/6/46.
61947 1/4/48.

CONDEMNED:
1/8/62.
Cut up at Doncaster.

2447

N.B.L. 24234.

To traffic 18/9/35.

REPAIRS:
Don. 13/11-12/12/36.**G.**
Don. 28/2-2/4/38.**G.**
Don. 10/2-9/3/40.**G.**
Don. 14/3-25/4/42.**G.**
Don. 25/3-22/4/44.**G.**
Don. 13/4-18/5/46.**G.**
Don. 28/3-2/4/47.**N/C.**
Don. 16/3-3/5/48.**G.**
Don. 2/12/49-6/1/50.**C/L.**
Don. 26/10-30/11/50.**G.**
Don. 14/7-14/8/52.**G.**
Don. 6/5-8/6/54.**G.**
Don. 17/4-18/5/56.**G.**
Don. 3/3-1/4/58.**G.**
Don. 15/12/59-22/1/60.**G.**

BOILERS:
8918.
2790 *(ex2498)* 18/5/46.
27123 *(ex61946)* 30/11/50.
27248 *(ex61908)* 14/8/52.
27247 *(ex61869)* 8/6/54.
24913 *(new)* 18/5/56.
27298 *(ex61817)* 1/4/58.
27166 *(ex61874)* 22/1/60.

SHEDS:
Doncaster.
New England 10/10/35.
March 11/3/40.

RENUMBERED:
1948 8/12/46.
61948 1/5/48.

CONDEMNED:
28/3/62.
Cut up at Doncaster.

2448

N.B.L. 24235.

To traffic 21/9/35.

REPAIRS:
Don. 13/1-5/3/37.**G.**
Don. 28/1-25/3/38.**L.**
Don. 29/10-26/11/38.**G.**
Don. 10/8-14/9/40.**G.**
Don. 6/3-10/4/43.**G.**
Don. 17/2-24/3/45.**G.**
Don. 8-29/9/45.**L.**
Don. 20/4-5/6/47.**G.**
Don. 11/1-16/2/49.**G.**
Don. 21/5-20/6/51.**G.**
Don. 11/2-12/3/53.**G.**
Don. 22/12/54-28/1/55.**G.**
Don. 29/7-3/9/57.**G.**
Don. 26/11-23/12/59.**G.**

BOILERS:
8919.
9798 *(new)* 5/6/47.
27171 *(ex61904)* 20/6/51.
27131 *(ex61890)* 12/3/53.
27240 *(ex61964)* 28/1/55.
27156 *(ex61980)* 3/9/57.
27227 *(ex61844)* 23/12/59.

SHEDS:
Doncaster.
New England 13/10/35.
Stratford 15/12/38.
March 15/9/41.
Lowestoft 14/10/47.
Norwich 4/1/59.
Lincoln 4/12/60.
Colwick 11/12/60.
New England 17/9/61.
Doncaster 17/9/61.

RENUMBERED:
1949 17/3/46.
61949 16/2/49.

CONDEMNED:
10/4/62.
Cut up at Doncaster.

2449

N.B.L. 24236.

To traffic 26/9/35.

REPAIRS:
Don. 3-25/2/37.**G.**
Don. 11/8-13/9/38.**G.**
Don. 4/5-8/6/40.**G.**
Don. 13/2-13/3/43.**G.**
Don. 3/3-14/4/45.**G.**
Don. 29/12/46-8/2/47.**G.**
Don. 13/1-18/2/49.**G.**
Don. 5-28/2/51.**G.**
Don. 8-13/3/51.**N/C.**
Gor. 31/1-1/2/52.**N/C.**
Gor. 20-23/7/52.**N/C.**
Don. 23/3-2/5/53.**G.**
Don. 14/7-18/8/54.**C/L.**
Don. 12/7-16/8/55.**G.**
Don. 14/4-25/5/57.**G.**

Don. 4/3-11/4/59.**G.**
Don. 28/4-12/5/60.**C/L.**
Don. 15/2-21/3/61.**G.**
Don. 7-11/4/61.**N/C.**

BOILERS:
8920.
2793 *(ex3813)* 8/2/47.
27146 *(ex61941)* 28/2/51.
27261 *(ex61815)* 16/8/55.
27131 *(ex61905)* 25/5/57.
27241 *(ex61967)* 11/4/59.

SHEDS:
Doncaster.
New England 11/10/35.
March 12/6/49.
Lowestoft 10/10/49.
Gorton 1/1/50.
Sheffield 13/6/54.
Lincoln 26/9/54.
Immingham 8/5/55.
Colwick 18/12/60.
Immingham 9/7/61.
Lincoln 14/1/62.
Doncaster 16/9/62.

RENUMBERED:
1950 17/3/46.
61950 18/2/49.

CONDEMNED:
4/11/62.
Sold for scrap to Cox & Danks,
Wadsley Bridge.

2450

N.B.L. 24237.

To traffic 1/10/35.

REPAIRS:
Don. 4/9-8/10/36.**G.**
Don. 8/1-2/2/38.**G.**
Don. 28/10-25/11/39.**G.**
Don. 21/3-2/5/42.**G.**
Don. 10/3-19/5/45.**G.**
Don. 4/3-23/4/47.**G.**
Don. 9/5-17/6/49.**G.**
Don. 23/7-23/8/51.**G.**
Don. 5/10-13/11/53.**G.**
Don. 10/5-2/6/54.**C/L.**
Don. 22/4-1/6/56.**G.**
Don. 22/7-22/8/58.**G.**
Str. 18/12/59-8/1/60.**C/L.**
Str. 7/3-2/4/60.**C/L.**
Don. 9/8-16/9/60.**G.**
Don. 13/9/61.*Weigh.*

BOILERS:
8921.
8915 *(ex2440)* 2/5/42.
2825 *(ex3815)* 19/5/45.
9796 *(ex1989)* 17/6/49.
27184 *(ex61962)* 23/8/51.
27225 *(ex61912)* 13/11/53.

WORKS CODES:- Cow - Cowlairs. Dar - Darlington. Don - Doncaster. Ghd - Gateshead. Gor - Gorton. Inv - Inverurie. Str - Stratford.
REPAIR CODES:- **C/H** - Casual Heavy. **C/L** - Casual Light. **G** - General. **H** - Heavy. **H/I** - Heavy Intermediate. **L** - Light. **L/I** - Light Intermediate. **N/C** - Non-Classified.

The first engine of the class, built in March 1920 as GNR 1000, became LNER 4000 and then 1800 followed by British Railways making it 61800. When withdrawn on 13th July 1962 it was the longest serving K3, but here at Stoke tunnel on 16th October 1959, and working from Doncaster it was still being rostered to work Class A main line goods trains. Like the axe at the Tower of London, it was still regarded as the original, although then carrying its twelfth boiler (and still to be worth fitting with yet another one in 1960), and coupled to its third tender. It would be fascinating to learn just how much (little?) of the 1920 engine was in this picture. *L.Perrin.*

Running under the wires of another electrification scheme (fortunately completed in this case) on 14th June 1958, Stratford based 61840 is near Shenfield with a local passenger train. The use of a white disc in place of a lamp is worth noting. *A.R.Goult.*

2459

N.B.L. 24239.

To traffic 9/10/35.

REPAIRS:
Don. 26/10-14/11/35.**L.**
Don. 22/2-15/4/37.**G.**
Don. 5-26/11/38.**G.**
Don. 2/3-13/4/40.**G.**
Don. 9/11-28/12/40.**G.**
Don. 7/6-2/8/41.**L.**
Don. 5/6-10/7/43.**G.**
Don. 30/6-4/8/45.**G.**
Don. 15/8-29/9/47.**G.**
Don. 26/11-18/12/47.**L.**
Don. 25/12/47-14/1/48.**L.**
Don. 25/9-28/10/49.**G.**
Don. 7-21/12/50.**C/L.**
Don. 19/6-25/7/51.**G.**
Don. 19/7-20/8/53.**G.**
Don. 16/11-23/12/53.**N/C.**
Don. 8/8-22/9/55.**G.**
Don. 12/12/55-10/1/56.**C/L.**
Don. 15/9-23/10/57.**G.**
Don. 19/10-18/11/59.**G.**
Don. 2-4/5/60.**N/C.**

BOILERS:
8923.
9D/687 *(ex3821)* 4/8/45.
10535 *(new)* 28/10/49.

27223 *(ex61869)* 1/6/56.
27229 *(ex61819)* 22/8/58.
27146 *(ex61951)* 16/9/60.

SHEDS:
Doncaster.
New England 13/10/35.
Doncaster 24/1/40.
March 20/2/40.
Sheffield 19/11/40.
Colwick 4/10/44.
New England 25/6/45.
Stratford 12/10/52.
Parkeston 16/3/58.
Lincoln 4/12/60.
Colwick 11/12/60.
Doncaster 13/8/61.

RENUMBERED:
1951 24/3/46.
61951 17/6/49.

CONDEMNED:
4/11/62.
Cut up at Doncaster.

2451

N.B.L. 24238.

To traffic 4/10/35.

REPAIRS:
Don. 2-23/12/36.**G.**
Don. 9-30/4/38.**G.**
Don. 30/12/39-27/1/40.**G.**
Don. 31/1-14/3/42.**G.**
Dar. 10/7-3/8/43.**L.**
Don. 22/4-17/5/44.**G.**
Don. 4-11/11/44.**L.**
Don. 29/12/45-16/2/46.**G.**
Don. 30/1-28/2/48.**G.**
Don. 10/1-18/2/50.**G.**
Don. 7-10/6/50.**C/L.**
Don. 17/12/51-17/1/52.**G.**
Don. 31/5-2/7/54.**G.**
Don. 19/12/55-27/1/56.**G.**
Don. 8/4-9/5/58.**G.**
Don. 12/7-17/8/60.**G.**

BOILERS:
8922.
8911 *(ex2427)* 27/1/40.

8802 *(ex2936)* 14/3/42.
8915 *(ex2450)* 16/2/46.
9376 *(ex61910)* 18/2/50.
27268 *(new)* 17/1/52.
27180 *(ex61871)* 9/5/58.
27175 *(ex61974)* 17/8/60.

SHEDS:
Doncaster.
New England 3/11/35.
Darlington 3/10/42.
Heaton 28/3/43.
Tweedmouth 30/11/52.
Hull Dairycoates 10/9/61.

RENUMBERED:
1952 15/9/46.
E1952 28/2/48.
61952 17/2/50.

CONDEMNED:
6/12/62.
Cut up at Doncaster.

27180 *(ex61869)* 25/7/51.
27147 *(ex61852)* 20/8/53.
27141 *(ex61914)* 22/9/55.
27207 *(ex61896)* 23/10/57.
27299 *(ex61987)* 18/11/59.

SHEDS:
Doncaster.
New England 21/11/35.
March 18/4/40.
Norwich 17/10/47.
Lowestoft 22/8/48.
Norwich 19/12/48.
Lowestoft 7/10/43.
Norwich 27/12/53.
Colwick 11/12/60.
New England 17/9/61.
Doncaster 17/9/61.

RENUMBERED:
1953 15/9/46.
61953 28/10/49.

CONDEMNED:
14/3/62.
Cut up at Doncaster.

2461

N.B.L. 24240.

To traffic 15/10/35.

REPAIRS:
Don. 26/2-1/4/37.**G.**
Don. 26/11-24/12/38.**G.**
Don. 8-29/6/40.**G.**
Don. 26/9-24/10/42.**G.**
Don. 24/2-31/3/45.**G.**

Don. 22/5-28/6/47.**G.**
Don. 19/7-1/9/49.**G.**
Don. 31/7-31/8/51.**G.**
Don. 15/9-17/10/53.**G.**
Don. 23/7-25/8/54.**C/L.**
Don. 27/9-26/10/55.**G.**
Don. 14/8-25/9/58.**G.**
Don. 12/1-25/2/61.**G.**

BOILERS:
8924.
9285 *(new)* 24/10/42.
2845 *(ex1838)* 1/9/49.
27186 *(ex61971)* 31/8/51.
27195 *(ex61961)* 17/10/53.
27163 *(ex61960)* 26/10/55.
27223 *(ex61951)* 25/9/58.
27118 *(ex61912)* 25/2/61.

SHEDS:
Doncaster.
March 31/10/35.
New England 6/3/36.
March 26/5/48.
New England 4/10/48.
March 20/9/53.
Sheffield 16/9/56.
March 15/3/59.
Norwich 28/6/59.
March 26/7/59.

RENUMBERED:
1954 23/9/46.
61954 1/9/49.

CONDEMNED:
16/9/62.
Sold for scrap to Central Wagon Co, Ince.

2463

N.B.L. 24241.

To traffic 22/10/35.

REPAIRS:
Don. 6/2-6/3/37.**G.**
Don. 24/6-11/7/38.**G.**
Don. 9/12/39-13/1/40.**G.**
Don. 17/1-21/2/42.**G.**
Cow. 21/12/43.**G.**
Cow. 22/7-13/9/46.**G.**
Cow. 16/11-31/12/48.**G.**
Cow. 5/10-11/11/50.**G.**
Cow. 27/1-21/2/53.**G.**
Cow. 14/7-4/9/54.**H/I.**
Cow. 11/4-14/5/55.**C/L.**
Cow. 1/8-8/9/56.**G.**
Cow. 30/5-20/6/58.**L/I.**

BOILERS:
8925.
8917 *(ex2443)* 11/7/38.
8071 *(ex1916)* 13/9/46.
8971 *(ex1885)* 31/12/48.
27318 *(ex61823)* 21/2/53.
27316 *(ex61936)* 8/9/56.

SHEDS:
Doncaster.
St Margarets 5/9/42.
Carlisle 17/9/43.
St Margarets 9/44.

RENUMBERED:
1955 12/4/46.
61955 31/12/48.

CONDEMNED:
27/5/60.
Cut up at Cowlairs.
Not in use 222 days in 1944.

2466

N.B.L. 24242.

To traffic 30/10/35.

REPAIRS:
Don. 3-26/3/38.**G.** *Front heat conn.*
Don. 6/1-10/2/40.**G.**
Don. 1/8-5/9/42.**G.**
Don. 24/3-26/5/45.**G.**
Don. 12/9-24/10/47.**G.**
Gor. 8/12/49.*Weigh.*
Don. 16/1-8/3/50.**G.**
Don. 18-20/10/50.**C/L.**
Don. 12-29/3/51.**C/L.**
Don. 6/3-7/4/52.**G.**
Don. 11/2-9/4/53.**G.**
Don. 3/12/54-4/1/55.**G.**
Don. 4/10-8/11/56.**G.**
Don. 25/7-19/8/57.**C/L.**
Don. 18/9-28/10/58.**G.**
Don. 16/12/58-1/1/59.**N/C.**
Don. 13/2-24/3/60.**G.**

BOILERS:
8926.
8921 *(ex2450)* 5/9/42.
RS4081 *(ex28)* 26/5/45.
10802 *(new)* 8/3/50.
27222 *(ex61871)* 7/4/52.
27258 *(ex61979)* 9/4/53.
27157 *(ex61989)* 4/1/55.
27214 *(ex61921)* 8/11/56.

It was not until 1938 that the Great Eastern lines had been made capable of taking the weight of K3 class, but from then, the class did a considerable amount of very varied work on them. After serving its first 27 years at New England shed, 61850 then had spells at March, Mexborough, and Doncaster, and here on 3rd August 1959 is starting its homeward journey working the 1.05 p.m. train from Cambridge to Peterborough (North). Note that it has been fitted with the full Automatic Warning System. *T.J.Edgington*

After being shedded at Hull Dairycoates for five years from September 1951, No.61869 was transferred to Heaton, and from that shed, worked this No.2 express goods which is crossing the viaduct at Durham. It has been fitted with the mechanical portion for the A.W.S. but appears to be still awaiting the receiver, and electrical parts which was the experience of quite a number of the class. *I.S.Carr.*

27290 *(ex61905)* 28/10/58.
24927 *(ex61817)* 24/3/60.

SHEDS:
Doncaster.
Gorton 26/11/35.
Woodford 30/10/43.
Gorton 26/6/49.
Immingham 27/5/51.

RENUMBERED:
 1956 17/2/46.
61956 8/12/49.

CONDEMNED:
16/9/62.
Cut up at Doncaster.

2467

N.B.L. 24243.

To traffic 7/11/35.

REPAIRS:
Don. 1/3-4/4/38.**G.** *Front heat.conn.*
Don. 20/1-2/3/40.**G.**
Don. 2-30/1/43.**G.**
Don. 7/8-4/9/43.**L.**
Don. 20/10-24/11/45.**G.**
Don. 17/12/46-18/1/47.**L.**
Don. 16/12/47-28/1/48.**G.**
Don. 15/2-22/3/49.**C/L.**
Don. 2/4-15/5/50.**G.**
Don. 8/4-14/5/52.**G.**
Don. 7/2-10/3/54.**G.**
Don. 19/11-21/12/55.**G.**
Don. 7/5-12/6/58.**G.**
Don. 26/4-2/6/60.**G.**

BOILERS:
 8927.
 2829 *(ex3818)* 2/3/40.
8135A *(ex Cowlairs and spare from Oct. 1942)* 24/11/45.
10805 *(new)* 15/5/50.
27232 *(ex61912)* 14/5/52.
27202 *(ex61921)* 10/3/54.

27276 *(ex61958)* 21/12/55.
27264 *(ex61981)* 12/6/58.
27153 *(ex61946)* 2/6/60.

SHEDS:
Doncaster.
Gorton 30/11/35.
Stratford 23/9/38.
March 28/11/41.
Norwich 16/10/47.
Yarmouth 6/1/57.
Norwich 10/2/57.
Lowestoft 26/5/57.
Norwich 17/11/57.
Colwick 11/12/60.

RENUMBERED:
 1957 6/10/46.
E1957 28/1/48.
61957 22/3/49.

CONDEMNED:
16/9/62.
Sold for scrap to Albert Looms.

2468

N.B.L. 24244.

To traffic 25/11/35.

REPAIRS:
Don. 21/2-9/4/37.**G.**
Don. 12/7-16/8/38.**G.**
Don. 20/1-9/3/40.**G.**
Don. 18/7-15/8/42.**G.**
Don. 11-25/11/44.**G.**
Don. 13-20/1/45.**L.**
Don. 7/12/46-31/1/47.**G.**
Don. 18/7-26/8/48.**G.**
Don. 12/2-17/3/51.**G.**
Don. 1/10-5/11/53.**G.**
Don. 6/11-8/12/55.**G.**
Don. 21/5-8/7/58.**G.**

BOILERS:
 8928.
 8909 *(ex2425)* 16/8/38.
 8911 *(ex2451)* 15/8/42.

2801 *(ex3819)* 31/1/47.
8965 *(ex1922)* 26/8/48.
27149 *(ex61972)* 17/3/51.
27276 *(new)* 5/11/53.
24905 *(new)* 8/12/55.
27276 *(ex61957)* 8/7/58.

SHEDS:
Doncaster.
March 29/3/40.
Yarmouth 14/10/47.
Lowestoft 19/11/47.
Staveley 6/3/60.
Langwith 18/6/61.
Mexborough 10/9/61.

RENUMBERED:
1958 29/9/46.
61958 26/8/48.

CONDEMNED:
1/5/62.
Cut up at Doncaster.

2417

A.W. 1270.

To traffic 16/5/36.

REPAIRS:
Dar. 3/12/36-12/3/37.**L.**
Don. 19/6-5/8/38.**G.** *Front heat.conn.*
Don. 19/2-8/4/40.**G.**
Don. 27/9-21/11/42.**G.**
Don. 18/2-7/4/45.**G.**
Don. 28/2-18/5/47.**G.**
Don. 20/11/48-10/1/49.**G.**
Don. 5/9-19/10/51.**G.**
Don. 3/12/53-7/1/54.**G.**
Don. 25/12/55-7/2/56.**G.**
Don. 15/6-25/7/57.**C/H.**
Don. 6/6-22/7/58.**G.**

BOILERS:
8962.
8924 *(ex2461)* 21/11/42.
8920 *(ex1949)* 18/5/47.
2909 *(ex3824)* 10/1/49.
7264 *(new)* 19/10/51.
7183 *(ex61962)* 7/1/54.
7197 *(ex61929)* 7/2/56.
7271 *(ex61969)* 22/7/58.

SHEDS:
Gorton.
Stratford 19/9/38.
March 12/12/40.
Lowestoft 14/10/47.
Norwich 10/10/48.
Lowestoft 19/1/49.
Staveley 28/2/60.
Mexborough 12/6/60.
Millhouses 23/7/61.
Staveley 10/9/61.

RENUMBERED:
1959 18/8/46.
61959 8/1/49.

61886 had only two sheds, York until 4th September 1941 and then March, from where in 1953 it is seen on a Lincoln-March passenger train at Gosberton near Spalding. This top view of a low-front straight sided tender will be appreciated by modellers. *L.Perrin.*

CONDEMNED:
13/11/61.
Cut up at Doncaster.

2429

A.W. 1271.

To traffic 21/5/36.

REPAIRS:
Don. 14/7-10/8/38.**G.** *Front heat.conn.*
Don. 27/7-24/8/40.**G.**
Don. 27/2-27/3/43.**G.**
Don. 8-22/1/44.**G.**
Don. 22/4-6/5/44.**L.**
Don. 13/7-17/8/46.**G.**
Don. 31/10-3/12/48.**G.**
Don. 19/12/50-19/1/51.**G.**
Don. 8/6-17/7/53.**G.**
Don. 18/9-19/10/55.**G.**
Don. 13/1-20/2/56.**C/L.**
Don. 9/5-14/6/58.**G.**
Don. 7-12/3/59.**N/C.**
Don. 13/12/60-24/1/61.**G.**

BOILERS:
8963.
2909 *(ex17)* 27/3/43.
9381 *(new)* 22/1/44.
8125 *(ex1902)* 3/12/48.
27134 *(ex61817)* 19/1/51.
27163 *(ex61883)* 17/7/53.
27173 *(ex61927)* 19/10/55.
27255 *(ex61838)* 14/6/58.
27232 *(ex61905)* 24/1/61.

SHEDS:
Gorton.
Walton 28/8/38.
Gorton 10/6/39.
Woodford 30/10/43.

Lincoln 29/6/47.
Immingham 9/7/61.

RENUMBERED:
1960 29/9/46.
61960 3/12/48.

CONDEMNED:
16/9/62.
Sold for scrap to J.Cashmore, Great Bridge.

2445

A.W. 1272.

To traffic 27/5/36.

REPAIRS:
Don. 15/11-11/12/37.**G.**
Don. 13/5-1/7/39.**G.**
Don. 22/2-22/3/41.**G.**
Don. 12/2-11/4/42.**L.** *After collision.*
Don. 14/8-11/9/43.**G.**
Don. 16/6-14/7/45.**G.**
Don. 17/3-10/5/47.**G.**
Don. 30/3-29/4/49.**G.**
Don. 2/9-10/10/51.**G.**
Don. 17/8-9/10/53.**G.**
Don. 27/6-28/7/55.**G.**
Don. 8/2-14/3/57.**G.**
Don. 20/4-16/5/59.**G.**

BOILERS:
8964.
9377 *(new)* 11/9/43.
27195 *(ex61872)* 10/10/51.
27177 *(ex61837)* 9/10/53.
27234 *(ex61935)* 28/7/55.
27249 *(ex61890)* 14/3/57.
27259 *(ex61808)* 16/5/59.

SHEDS:
Doncaster.
Copley Hill 28/8/44.
New England 16/7/45.
March 16/6/46.
New England 27/11/46.
March 11/6/50.
Lowestoft 8/10/50.
March 10/12/50.
Doncaster 16/9/56.

RENUMBERED:
1961 15/9/46.
61961 29/4/49.

CONDEMNED:
2/10/61.
Cut up at Doncaster.

2446

A.W. 1273.

To traffic 28/5/36.

REPAIRS:
Don. 8-11/7/36.**L.**
Don. 7-31/12/37.**G.**
Don. 8/7-12/8/39.**G.**
Don. 18/10-22/11/41.**G.**
Don. 5-26/2/44.**G.**
Don. 13/1-17/2/45.**G.**
Don. 29/12/45-26/1/46.**L.**
Don. 15/9-17/10/47.**G.**
Don. 29/8-14/10/49.**G.**
Don. 18/7-16/8/51.**G.**
Don. 17/11-17/12/53.**G.**
Don. 2/12/55-12/1/56.**G.**
Don. 22/2-26/3/58.**G.**
Don. 25/3-7/5/60.**G.**

BOILERS:
8965.

9281 *(new)* 22/11/41.
10532 *(new)* 14/10/49.
27183 *(ex61953)* 16/8/51.
27267 *(ex61987)* 17/12/53.
27287 *(ex61974)* 26/3/58.

SHEDS:
Doncaster.
New England 26/8/39.
Darlington 30/9/42.
Heaton 28/3/43.
March 30/5/48.
Heaton 31/10/48.
Tweedmouth 6/1/52.
Heaton 14/9/58.
Tweedmouth 11/9/60.
Tyne Dock 8/10/61.
Hull Dairycoates 14/1/62.

RENUMBERED:
1962 15/9/46.
61962 14/10/49.

CONDEMNED:
18/12/62.
Cut up at Doncaster.

2453

A.W. 1274.

To traffic 4/6/36.

REPAIRS:
Don. 27/11-22/12/37.**G.**
Don. 6/1-17/2/40.**G.**
Don. 24/10-28/11/42.**G.**
Don. 20/1-3/3/45.**G.**
Don. 25/5-12/7/47.**G.**
Don. 6/7-18/8/49.**G.**

Don. 11/5-1/6/50.**C/L.**
Don. 28/5-26/7/51.**G.**
Don. 7/8-3/9/53.**G.**
Don. 24/12/54-21/1/55.**C/L.**
Don. 23/12/55-2/2/56.**G.**
Don. 19/5-1/7/58.**G.**
Don. 24/10-13/12/60.**G.**

BOILERS:
8966.
8910 *(ex2426)* 28/11/42.
8601 *(ex1158)* 3/3/45.
27173 *(ex1919)* 26/7/51.
27196 *(ex61821)* 3/9/53.
27153 *(ex61880)* 2/2/56.
27225 *(ex61827)* 1/7/58.
27228 *(ex61873)* 13/12/60.

SHEDS:
Doncaster.
March 9/7/38.
Norwich 28/10/38.
Immingham 19/11/40.
Lincoln 22/6/52.
Stratford 5/10/52.
Parkeston 14/12/58.
March 12/6/60.

RENUMBERED:
1963 18/8/46.
61963 18/8/49.

CONDEMNED:
16/9/62.
Sold for scrap to Central Wagon Co, Ince.

2455

A.W. 1275.

To traffic 9/6/36.

REPAIRS:
Don. 7-30/12/37.**G.**
Don. 25/5-22/6/40.**G.**
Don. 13/12/41-24/1/42.**G.**
Don. 21/10-11/11/44.**G.**
Don. 10-24/11/45.**L.**
Don. 16/4-24/5/47.**G.**
Don. 3/11-9/12/49.**G.**
Don. 6-20/7/51.**C/L.**
Don. 20/5-20/6/52.**G.**
Don. 14/12/54-14/1/55.**G.**
Don. 1-23/3/55.**N/C.**
Don. 25/2-4/4/57.**G.**
Don. 23-25/5/57.**N/C.**
Don. 14/2-20/3/59.**G.**
Don. 24/8-19/10/60.**C/H.**

BOILERS:
8967.
3216 *(new)* 24/1/42.
10536 *(new)* 9/12/49.
27240 *(ex61918)* 20/6/52.
27112 *(ex61886)* 14/1/55.
24922 *(new)* 4/4/57.
24939 *(new)* 20/3/59.

SHEDS:
Doncaster.
Kings Cross 17/9/36.
Colwick 14/12/39.
Annesley 17/7/41.
Gorton 3/5/43.
Woodford 24/10/43.
Lincoln 24/6/47.
Doncaster 10/11/57.

RENUMBERED:
1964 15/9/46.
61964 9/12/49.

CONDEMNED:
7/7/61.
Cut up at Doncaster.

2458

A.W. 1276.

To traffic 12/6/36.

REPAIRS:
Dar. 10-31/12/36.**N/C.**
Dar. 27/1-12/2/37.**N/C.**
Dar. 8/6-17/9/37.**H.**
Dar. 18/7-5/10/38.**G.**
Dar. 5-9/2/40.**N/C.**
Dar. 1-27/6/40.**G.**
Dar. 16/6-18/8/41.**L.**
Dar. 16/3-15/4/43.**G.**
Don. 9/8-2/9/44.**G.**
Don. 12/10-9/11/46.**G.**
Ghd. 8/3-3/4/48.**L.**
Don. 20/8-4/9/48.**L.**
Don. 13/6-30/7/49.**G.**
Don. 12-20/8/49.**L.**
Don. 17/2-21/3/51.**G.**
Don. 4-8/5/51.**N/C.**
Don. 28/5-9/6/52.**L.**
Don. 5/5-5/6/53.**G.**
Don. 28/4-27/5/55.**G.**
Dar. 2/9-16/10/57.**G.**
Don. 12/11-11/12/59.**G.**
Don. 15/1-11/2/60.**C/L.**
Don. 4-9/4/60.**N/C.**

BOILERS:
8968.
RS4075 *(ex1339)* 27/6/40.
D1650 *(ex3829)* 15/4/43.
8918 *(ex1829)* 30/7/49.
27150 *(ex61907)* 21/3/51.
27174 *(ex61971)* 5/6/53.
27284 *(ex61825)* 27/5/55.
27265 *(ex61986)* 16/10/57.
24928 *(ex61947)* 11/12/59.

SHEDS:
Gateshead.
York 31/5/39.
Neville Hill 27/1/43.
Heaton 28/3/43.
Hull Dairycoates 5/10/47.

RENUMBERED:
1965 27/1/46.
61965 3/4/48.

CONDEMNED:
3/12/62.
Cut up at Doncaster.

Passing through Wilbraham Road station in the southern suburbs of Manchester in June 1954, Gorton based 61910 is taking the Liverpool (Central) to Harwich (Parkeston Quay) boat train as far as Guide Bridge where electric haulage would replace it. Although only hauling the train over the 11 miles from Manchester (Central) to Guide Bridge, the K3 has an arduous journey ahead of it.

2465

A.W. 1277.

To traffic 16/6/36.

REPAIRS:
Dar. 13/1-4/2/37.**N/C.**
Dar. 15/2-4/3/37.**N/C.**
Dar. 15/6-25/8/38.**G.**
Dar. 1/8-7/9/40.**G.**
Don. 14/2-8/3/41.**G.**
Don. 26/6-7/8/43.**G.**
Don. 15/12/45-28/2/46.**G.**
Don. 19/1-19/2/48.**G.**
Don. 16/10-16/11/50.**G.**
Don. 20/5-9/7/53.**G.**
Don. 24/2-29/3/56.**G.**
Don. 18/3-29/4/59.**G.**

BOILERS:
8969.
D1646 (ex1108) 7/9/40.
8969 (ex3822) 7/8/43.
8963 (ex2935) 28/2/46.
27120 (ex61887) 16/11/50.
27185 (ex61860) 9/7/53.
27149 (ex61938) 29/3/56.
27292 (ex61920) 29/4/59.

SHEDS:
Gateshead.
York 29/5/39.
Colwick 23/11/40.
New England 25/6/45.
Lincoln 11/8/46.
Gorton 10/2/52.
Woodford 17/11/57.
Immingham 5/1/58.
Colwick 9/7/61.

RENUMBERED:
1966 1/12/46.
E1966 19/2/48.
61966 16/11/50.

CONDEMNED:
19/2/62.
Cut up at Doncaster.

2471

A.W. 1278.

To traffic 7/7/36.

REPAIRS:
Cow. 6-14/10/36.**L.**
Cow. 9-10/11/36.**N/C.**
Don. 31/5-21/7/37.**G.**
Cow. 7-10/9/37.**N/C.** Experimental
fire door.
Cow. 18-21/2/38.**N/C.** Experimental
door removed.
Cow. 5-8/4/38.**N/C.**
Cow. 28/10-21/11/38.**L.**

Cow. 28/2-31/3/39.**G.**
Cow. 10/7-7/8/40.**G.**
Don. 25/1-28/3/42.**G.**
Don. 20/8-23/9/44.**G.**
Don. 13/6-6/9/46.**G.**
Don. 27/4-2/6/48.**G.**
Don. 13/5-12/6/50.**G.**
Don. 5/5-6/6/52.**G.**
Don. 30/5-6/7/54.**G.**
Don. 8/4-17/5/56.**G.**
Don. 4/2-14/3/59.**G.**
Don. 29/3-3/4/61.Not repaired.

BOILERS:
8970.
2805 (ex2470) 6/9/46.
9550 (ex61969) 12/6/50.
27237 (ex61939) 6/6/52.
27126 (ex61826) 6/7/54.
27241 (ex61926) 17/5/56.
24924 (ex61899) 14/3/59.

SHEDS:
St Margarets.
Carlisle 29/1/37.
St Margarets 16/2/37.
Carlisle 15/3/39.
Sheffield 23/11/40.
New England 25/6/45.
March 20/9/53.
Sheffield 16/9/56.

RENUMBERED:
1967 1/11/46.
61967 2/6/48.

CONDEMNED:
3/4/61.
Cut up at Doncaster.

2472

A.W. 1279.

To traffic 6/8/36.

REPAIRS:
Don. 18/1-16/2/38.**G.**
Cow. 31/8/39.**G.**
Cow. 21/12/40.**G.**
Dar. 3-28/11/42.**L.**
Cow. 17/7-21/8/43.**H.**
Cow. 21/10/44.**N/C.**
Cow. 1/10-27/12/46.**G.**
Cow. 19/8-24/9/48.**G.**
Cow. 8/9-9/11/50.**L/I.**
Cow. 15-29/3/51.**C/L.**
Cow. 2/7-19/8/52.**H/I.**
Cow. 15/1-27/2/54.**G.**
Cow. 16/11-10/12/55.**H/I.**
Cow. 22-26/12/55.**N/C.**
Cow. 23/4-1/6/57.**L/I.**
Cow. 7/1-7/2/59.**G.**

BOILERS:
8971.
9373 (new ex Don) 21/8/43.

2836 (ex1983) 24/9/48.
27321 (ex61955) 27/2/54.
27330 (ex61897) 7/2/59.

SHEDS:
St Margarets.
Carlisle 29/1/37.
St Margarets 16/2/37.
Carlisle 15/3/39.
St Margarets 9/44.

RENUMBERED:
1968 17/3/46.
61968 24/9/48.

CONDEMNED:
23/10/61.
Cut up at Inverurie.
Not in use 224 days in 1944.

2470

Darlington.

To traffic 13/10/36.

REPAIRS:
Don. 11/4-7/5/38.**G.** Heat detector
fitted.
Don. 21/10-2/12/39.**G.**
Don. 20/12/41-24/1/42.**G.**
Dar. 15/10-27/11/43.**L.**
Don. 5/5-10/6/44.**G.**
Don. 6/4-11/5/46.**G.**
Don. 10/3-17/4/48.**G.**
Don. 28/3-13/5/50.**G.**
Don. 14/11-11/12/51.**G.**
Don. 12-20/11/52.**L.**
Don. 2-20/1/53.**G.**
Don. 15/1-12/2/54.**G.**
Don. 21/2-28/3/56.**G.**
Don. 19/4-22/5/58.**G.**
Don. 8/11/60-10/1/61.**G.**
Don. 2-16/2/61.**C/L.**

BOILERS:
2805.
9550 (new) 11/5/46.
10501 (ex61984) 13/5/50.
27273 (new) 11/12/51.
27212 (ex61947) 12/2/54.
27271 (ex61871) 28/3/56.
27130 (ex61840) 22/5/58.
27212 (ex61886) 10/1/61.

SHEDS:
Doncaster.
Heaton 30/9/42.
Tweedmouth 30/11/52.
Tyne Dock 8/10/61.
Hull Dairycoates 14/1/62.

RENUMBERED:
1969 15/9/46.
61969 14/4/48.

CONDEMNED:
17/12/62.
Cut up at Doncaster.

2473

Darlington.

To traffic 21/10/36.

REPAIRS:
Don. 28/4-18/5/38.**G.** Heat detector
fitted.
Don. 18/11-23/12/39.**G.**
Don. 11/7-1/8/42.**G.**
Don. 22/7-12/8/44.**G.**
Don. 10/12/46-22/1/47.**G.**
Don. 9/1-25/2/49.**G.**
Don. 29/11-28/12/50.**G.**
Don. 19/7-19/8/52.**G.**
Don. 17/10-17/11/54.**G.**
Don. 13/11-22/12/56.**G.**
Don. 30/9-10/11/58.**G.**
Don. 6/10-10/11/60.**G.**

BOILERS:
2814.
8070 (ex1156) 12/8/44.
9993 (new) 25/2/49.
27129 (ex61829) 28/12/50.
27249 (ex61827) 19/8/52.
27288 (new) 17/11/54.
24916 (new) 22/12/56.
27209 (ex61843) 10/11/58.
27162 (ex61830) 10/11/60.

SHEDS:
Doncaster.
Norwich 26/1/40.
March 30/11/41.
Lowestoft 14/10/47.
Norwich 28/12/47.
Yarmouth 13/5/56.
Norwich 15/7/56.
Yarmouth 13/1/57.
Norwich 17/2/57.
Lowestoft 18/5/58.
Norwich 14/9/58.
Colwick 1/1/61.
Doncaster 13/8/61.

RENUMBERED:
1970 3/11/46.
61970 25/2/49.

CONDEMNED:
4/11/62.
Sold for scrap to Cox & Danks,
Wadsley Bridge.

2498

Darlington.

To traffic 23/10/36.

REPAIRS:
Don. 2-26/5/38.**G.**
Don. 28/10-2/12/39.**G.**
Don. 20/9-25/10/41.**G.**
Don. 13/11-11/12/43.**G.**
Don. 15/12/45-12/1/46.**G.**
Don. 1/2-18/3/48.**G.**.
Don. 12/6-12/8/49.**G**
Don. 19/8-1/9/49.**C/L.**
Don. 31/5-6/7/51.**G.**
Don. 24/4-28/5/53.**G.**
Don. 23/9-19/10/54.**C/L.**
Don. 24/2-29/3/55.**G.**
Don. 16/3-17/4/57.**G.**
Don. 17/12/58-23/1/59.**G.**
Don. 14/3/61.*Not repaired.*

BOILERS:
2790.
2803 *(ex2425)* 12/1/46.
27174 *(ex61896)* 6/7/51.
27158 *(ex61880)* 28/5/53.
27274 *(ex61802)* 29/3/55.
27272 *(ex61932)* 17/4/57.
24918 *(ex61989)* 23/1/59.

SHEDS:
Doncaster.
March 11/4/42.
Lowestoft 16/10/47.
Yarmouth 19/11/47.
Norwich 28/12/47.
Lowestoft 12/10/49.
Norwich 1/1/50.
Yarmouth 29/10/50.
Norwich 3/12/50.
Colwick 1/1/61.

RENUMBERED:
1971 22/9/46.
61971 18/3/48.

CONDEMNED:
20/3/61.
Cut up at Doncaster.

2499

Darlington.

To traffic 30/10/36.

REPAIRS:
Don. 20/4-14/5/38.**G.** *Heat detector fitted.*
Don. 18/11/39-13/1/40.**G.**
Don. 23/5-20/6/42.**G.**
Don. 15/7-19/8/44.**G.**
Don. 26/10-22/11/46.**G.**
Don. 29/12/47-4/2/48.**L.**
Don. 12/11-17/12/48.**G.**
Don. 16/5-8/6/49.**C/L.**
Don. 7/1-2/2/51.**G.**
Don. 31/10-28/11/52.**G.**
Don. 31/10-1/12/54.**G.**
Don. 16/11-20/12/56.**G.**
Don. 1/9-16/10/58.**G.**
Don. 11/8-16/9/60.**G.**

BOILERS:
2803.
RS4080 *(ex1118)* 19/8/44.
9381 *(ex1960)* 17/12/48.
27140 *(ex61973)* 2/2/51.
27109 *(ex61842)* 28/11/52.
27253 *(ex61978)* 1/12/54.
27246 *(ex61976)* 20/12/56.
27183 *(ex61982)* 16/10/58.
27229 *(ex61951)* 16/9/60.

SHEDS:
Doncaster.
Gorton 19/7/43.
Annesley 24/10/43.
New England 18/11/45.
March 20/9/53.
Colwick 8/1/61.
Doncaster 13/8/61.

RENUMBERED:
1972 22/11/46.
E1972 4/2/48.
61972 17/12/48.

CONDEMNED:
16/9/62.
Cut up at Doncaster.

3813

Darlington.

To traffic 4/11/36.

REPAIRS:
Don. 7-28/5/38.**G.**
Don. 30/12/39-3/2/40.**G.**
Don. 22/2-15/3/41.**L.**
Don. 21/2-4/4/42.**G.**
Don. 29/4-3/6/44.**G.**
Don. 21-28/4/45.**N/C.** *For inspection by CGM.*
Don. 26/10-22/11/46.**G.**
Don. 15/8-24/9/48.**G.**
Don. 10/12/50-12/1/51.**G.**
Don. 25/2-26/3/53.**G.**
Don. 20/3-22/4/55.**G.**
Don. 5/10-8/11/57.**G.**
Don. 3-12/6/58.**N/C.**
Don. 14-25/3/59.**C/L.**
Don. 29/6-30/7/60.**G.**

BOILERS:
2793.
8739 *(ex1842)* 22/11/46.
27132 *(ex61903)* 12/1/51.
27113 *(ex61870)* 26/3/53.
27258 *(ex61956)* 22/4/55.
24926 *(new)* 8/11/57.

SHEDS:
Doncaster.
Mexborough 7/5/39.
Doncaster 9/7/39.
March 25/5/47.
Norwich 15/10/47.
Lowestoft 19/11/47.
Norwich 7/12/47.
Lowestoft 6/10/48.

Norwich 4/1/59.
Staveley 10/4/60.
Colwick 3/6/62.
Lincoln 17/6/62.
Doncaster 16/9/62.

RENUMBERED:
1973 22/11/46.
61973 24/9/48.

CONDEMNED:
4/11/62.
Cut up at Doncaster.

3814

Darlington.

To traffic 11/11/36.

REPAIRS:
Gor. 22-25/6/38.**L.** *Front heater conn.*
Don. 17/9-8/10/38.**G.**
Don. 3/8-7/9/40.**G.**
Don. 26/12/42-23/1/43.**G.**
Don. 24/2-7/4/45.**G.**
Don. 17/1-3/4/47.**G.**
Don. 13/6-5/8/49.**G.**
Don. 21/4-19/5/52.**G.**
Don. 3/10-9/11/54.**G.**
Don. 7-29/3/55.**N/C.**
Don. 19/3-18/4/56.**C/L.**
Don. 2-14/5/56.**N/C.**
Don. 21/5-15/6/56.**C/L.**
Don. 8/1-6/2/58.**G.**
Don. 1-5/2/60.**N/C.**
Don. 8/7-11/8/60.**G.**

BOILERS:
2799.
8962 *(ex2417)* 23/1/43.
9792 *(new)* 3/4/47.
27127 *(ex61816)* 19/5/52.
27287 *(new)* 9/11/54.
27175 *(ex61830)* 6/2/58.
27279 *(ex61815)* 11/8/60.

SHEDS:
Doncaster.
Gorton 23/1/37.
Annesley 30/10/43.
Colwick 30/1/55.
Immingham 18/12/60.

RENUMBERED:
1974 17/11/46.
61974 5/8/49.

CONDEMNED:
2/7/62.
Cut up at Doncaster.

3815

Darlington.

To traffic 17/11/36.

REPAIRS:
Gor. 28/5-4/6/38.**L.** *Front heater conn.*
Don. 17/9-8/10/38.**G.**
Don. 17/8-28/9/40.**G.**
Don. 16/1-6/2/43.**G.**
Don. 20/1-3/3/45.**G.**
Don. 13/12/46-1/2/47.**G.**
Don. 16/3-18/4/47.**H.**
Don. 28/3-28/4/49.**G.**
Don. 20/6/49.*Not repaired. Sent to works in error.*
Don. 2/9-12/10/50.**G.**
Don. 18/3-16/4/53.**G.**
Don. 25/3-27/4/55.**G.**
Don. 14/3-12/4/57.**G.**
Don. 26/1-11/3/60.**G.**
Don. 31/10-8/11/60.**N/C.**
Don. 21/8/61.*Not repaired.*

BOILERS:
2825.
RS4077 *(ex1339)* 3/3/45.
27107 *(ex61895)* 12/10/50.
27159 *(ex61813)* 16/4/53.
27210 *(ex61942)* 12/4/57.
24904 *(ex61827)* 11/3/60.

SHEDS:
Doncaster.
Gorton 21/1/37.
Annesley 30/10/43.
Colwick 16/9/56.
Annesley 18/11/56.
Ardsley 17/5/59.
Low Moor 11/6/61.

RENUMBERED:
1975 14/7/46.
61975 28/4/49.

CONDEMNED:
4/9/61.
Cut up at Doncaster.

3816

Darlington.

To traffic 20/11/36.

REPAIRS:
Gor. 26-30/7/38.**L.**
Don. 17/9-8/10/38.**G.**
Gor. 13-17/12/38.**L.** *Front heater conn.*
Don. 13/7-24/8/40.**G.**
Don. 28/11-19/12/42.**G.**
Don. 8/4-15/5/44.**L.**
Don. 26/5-23/6/45.**G.**
Don. 3/11-10/1/47.**G.**
Don. 13/3-2/5/48.**G.**
Don. 20/6-9/8/49.**G.**
Don. 20/12/51-25/1/52.**G.**
Don. 9/4-6/5/53.**G.**
Don. 28/11-24/12/54.**G.**
Don. 9-29/2/56.**C/L.**
Don. 12/10-15/11/56.**G.**
Don. 27/11-7/12/56.**N/C.**
Don. 23/10-28/11/58.**G.**

Still absolutely incredible for my generation to believe, there hasn't even been a railway at this location now for more than 25 years! 61968 is climbing out of Hawick with an Edinburgh-Carlisle goods and, taking no risk of slipping, the steam-operated sanding is being used.

BOILERS:
2828.
8800 *(ex1133)* 19/12/42.
8966 *(ex1890)* 10/1/47.
7207 *(ex61987)* 25/1/52.
7246 *(ex61827)* 24/12/54.
4915 *(new)* 15/11/56.
7253 *(ex61886)* 28/11/58.

SHEDS:
Doncaster.
Gorton 20/1/37.
Annesley 30/10/43.
March 27/9/53.
Staveley 27/3/60.
Langwith 18/6/61.
Sheffield 10/9/61.

RENUMBERED:
1976 22/9/46.
1976 1/5/48.

CONDEMNED:
4/1/62.
Cut up at Doncaster.

3817

Darlington.

To traffic 26/11/36.

REPAIRS:
Don. 27/11-25/12/37.**H.** *After mishap at Liverpool.*
Gor. 4-7/5/38.**L.** *Front heat.conn.*
Gor. 24-25/6/38.**L.**
Don. 19/8-23/9/39.**G.**
Don. 9/5-6/6/42.**G.**
Don. 2-30/9/44.**G.**
Don. 1-8/12/45.**L.**
Don. 17/10-13/12/46.**G.**

Don. 25/9-19/11/48.**G.**
Don. 3-26/4/49.**C/L.**
Don. 8/5-6/6/51.**G.**
Don. 18/3-8/5/53.**G.**
Don. 18/6-27/7/55.**G.**
Don. 19/7-21/8/56.**G.**
Don. 6/12/57-17/1/58.**G.**
Don. 17/6-9/7/58.**C/L.**
Don. 17/3-23/4/60.**G.**

BOILERS:
2788.
9628 *(new)* 13/12/46.
27168 *(ex61868)* 6/6/51.
27128 *(ex61817)* 27/7/55.
27282 *(ex61947)* 17/1/58.
24907 *(ex61836)* 23/4/60.

SHEDS:
Doncaster.
Trafford Park 19/1/37.

Gorton 9/9/37.
Annesley 30/10/43.
Colwick 17/2/52.
Stratford 5/10/52.
Parkeston 4/12/58.
Lincoln 4/12/60.
Colwick 11/12/60.

RENUMBERED:
1977 29/9/46.
61977 19/11/48.

CONDEMNED:
16/9/62.
Sold for scrap to Albert Looms, Spondon.

Falahill summit on the Waverley route with St Margarets shedded 61823 taking a goods from Edinburgh to Carlisle. The signalman there would have no difficulty in keeping his mind on his work - there is not a single bird, animal, or human habitation to be seen in the whole of this wide landscape, and on this line, Falahill was not by any means alone in its isolation. But it *was* a fascinating place for railway enthusiasts.

3818

Darlington.

To traffic 27/11/36.

REPAIRS:
Don. 13/5-24/6/39.**G.**
Don. 25/10-6/12/41.**G.**
Don. 3-24/1/42.**L.** *After collision.*
Don. 4/3-1/4/44.**G.**
Don. 28/9-26/10/46.**G.**
Don. 2-20/6/47.**L.**
Don. 11/8-27/9/48.**G.**
Don. 2-23/11/48.**L.**
Don. 1-27/2/51.**G.**
Don. 24/10-21/11/52.**G.**
Don. 28/10-25/11/54.**G.**
Don. 16/8-27/9/56.**G.**
Don. 24/11/58-2/1/59.**G.**

BOILERS:
 2829.
D1709 *(ex180)* 24/6/39.
 9282 *(new)* 6/12/41.
 9987 *(new)* 27/9/48.
27145 *(ex61948)* 27/2/51.

27253 *(ex61844)* 21/11/52.
27231 *(ex61856)* 25/11/54.
27169 *(ex61889)* 27/9/56.
24915 *(ex61976)* 2/1/59.

SHEDS:
Doncaster.
Mexborough 21/1/37.
Doncaster 25/8/46.
March 27/9/53.
New England 4/11/56.

RENUMBERED:
 1978 24/7/46.
 61978 25/9/48.

CONDEMNED:
17/8/61.
Cut up at Doncaster.

3819

Darlington.

To traffic 2/12/36.

REPAIRS:
Gor. 21-26/2/38.**L.** *Front heater conn.*
Gor. 5-9/7/38.**L.**
Don. 17/12/38-28/1/39.**G.**
Don. 6/4-11/5/40.**G.**
Don. 14/11-19/12/42.**G.**
Don. 16/12/41-27/1/45.**G.**
Don. 12/10-16/11/46.**G.**
Don. 9/12/48-14/1/49.**G.**
Don. 8/7-8/8/51.**G.**
Don. 25/7-25/8/52.**C/L.**
Don. 7/6-16/7/54.**G.**
Don. 27/7-12/8/55.**C/L.**
Don. 29/5-12/7/56.**G.**
Don. 4-17/4/58.**C/L.**
Don. 20/1-28/2/59.**G.**

BOILERS:
 2796.
 2801 *(ex3821)* 19/12/42.
 9625 *(new)* 16/11/46.
27181 *(ex61801)* 8/8/51.
27237 *(ex61967)* 16/7/54.
27103 *(ex61800)* 12/7/56.
27272 *(ex61971)* 28/2/59.

SHEDS:
Doncaster.
Colwick 22/1/37.
Gorton 3/3/37.
Annesley 30/10/43.
March 20/9/53.
New England 4/11/56.

RENUMBERED:
 1979 29/9/46.
 61979 14/1/49.

CONDEMNED:
16/10/61.
Cut up at Doncaster.

3820

Darlington.

To traffic 8/12/36.

REPAIRS:
Gor. 12-16/7/38.**L.** *Front heater conn.*
Don. 17/9-8/10/38.**G.**

)on. 17/8-21/9/40.**G.**
)on. 25/4-23/5/42.**G.**
)on. 27/2-6/3/43.**L.**
)on. 17/6-22/7/44.**G.**
)on. 20/10-14/12/46.**G.**
)on. 28/1-3/3/49.**G.**
)on. 6/10-10/11/50.**G.**
)on. 30/10-20/11/51.**C/L.**
)on. 24/2-25/3/52.**C/L.**
)on. 2-29/7/53.**G.**
)on. 6/4-12/5/55.**G.**
)on. 11/7-9/8/57.**G.**
)on. 1-28/7/59.**G.**
)on. 24-27/7/60.**N/C.**

OILERS:
2830.
2796 (*ex3819*) 22/7/44.
8970 (*ex2471*) 14/12/46.
7118 (*ex61921*) 10/11/50.
7156 (*ex61896*) 29/7/53.
7222 (*ex61899*) 9/8/57.
7217 (*ex61893*) 28/7/59.

HEDS:
oncaster.
orton 4/3/37.
nnesley 30/10/43.
rdsley 17/5/59.

ENUMBERED:
980 14/7/46.
980 3/3/49.

ONDEMNED:
7/12/62.
ut up at Doncaster.

321

arlington.

traffic 14/12/36.

EPAIRS:
or. 28/3-2/4/38.**L.** *Front heater*
nn.
or. 29/6-2/7/38.**L.**
on. 4/2-4/3/39.**G.**
on. 15/2-15/3/41.**G.**
on. 7/11-5/12/42.**G.**
on. 10/2-24/3/45.**G.**
on. 22/7-6/9/47.**G.**
on. 30/10-2/12/49.**G.**
on. 4/12/51-9/1/52.**G.**
on. 30/12/53-28/1/54.**G.**
on. 2/7-4/8/54.**C/L.**
on. 15/1-24/2/56.**G.**
on. 6/3-10/4/58.**G.**
on. 22/3-29/4/60.**G.**

OILERS:
2801.
)687 (*ex1125*) 5/12/42.
)687 (*ex2934*) 24/3/45.
968 (*ex1982*) 2/12/49.
7203 (*ex61863*) 9/1/52.

27264 (*ex61959*) 28/1/54.
27184 (*ex61987*) 10/4/58.
27282 (*ex61977*) 29/4/60.

SHEDS:
Doncaster.
Gorton 3/3/37.
Annesley 30/10/43.
New England 18/11/45.
March 16/6/46.
New England 21/10/46.
March 16/2/47.
Lowestoft 15/10/47.
Norwich 19/1/49.
March 13/3/51.
Lowestoft 7/10/51.
Norwich 2/12/51.
Lowestoft 5/10/52.
Norwich 25/1/53.
Lowestoft 15/2/53.
Norwich 5/4/53.
Staveley 13/3/60.
Mexborough 18/6/61.
Colwick 3/6/62.
Lincoln 17/6/62.
Doncaster 16/9/62.

RENUMBERED:
1981 1/11/46.
61981 2/12/49.

CONDEMNED:
4/11/62.
Sold for scrap to Cox & Danks, Wadsley Bridge.

3822

Darlington.

To traffic 21/12/36.

REPAIRS:
Dar. 7/9-28/10/38.**G.**
Dar. 11-29/12/39.**L.**
Dar. 26/9-1/11/40.**G.**
Dar. 4-9/11/40.**N/C.**
Dar. 23/5-8/7/43.**G.**
Don. 4/4-31/5/45.**G.**
Don. 13/6-26/7/47.**G.**
Don. 16/10-25/11/49.**G.**
Don. 12/7-11/8/50.**C/L.**
Don. 16/8-2/10/51.**G.**
Don. 30/6-6/8/52.**C/L.**
Don. 7/4-19/5/54.**G.**
Don. 3/2-9/3/56.**G.**
Don. 11/3-25/4/58.**G.**
Don. 3-12/2/60.**N/C.**
Don. 25/5-7/7/60.**G.**

BOILERS:
2808.
8969 (*ex2465*) 1/11/40.
2799 (*ex3814*) 8/7/43.
8968 (*ex1884*) 26/7/47.
9375 (*ex1915*) 25/11/49.
27192 (*ex61866*) 2/10/51.

27232 (*ex61957*) 19/5/54.
27183 (*ex61959*) 9/3/56.
27117 (*ex61831*) 25/4/58.
27170 (*ex61875*) 7/7/60.

SHEDS:
York.
Colwick 23/11/40.
Annesley 28/11/40.
Gorton 3/5/43.
Annesley 30/10/43.
Lincoln 17/6/46.
Colwick 15/10/50.
Stratford 5/10/52.
March 27/9/53.
Colwick 16/9/56.

RENUMBERED:
1982 24/11/46.
61982 25/11/49.

CONDEMNED:
16/9/62.
Sold for scrap to Albert Looms, Spondon.

3823

Darlington.

To traffic 23/12/36.

REPAIRS:
Don. 25/8-28/9/38.**G.**
Cow. 4/11/39.**G.**
Cow. 8/12/39.**L.**
Cow. 21/12/40.**G.**
Cow. 30/1/43.**G.**
Cow. 3/6/44.**G.**
Cow. 14/2-23/3/46.**G.**
Cow. 14/12/46-18/1/47.**L.**
Cow. 5/7-18/8/47.**L.**
Cow. 3/5-5/6/48.**G.**
Cow. 24/3-29/4/50.**G.**
Cow. 12/8/50.**L.**
Cow. 28/10/50.**C/H.**
Cow. 8/4-17/5/52.**H/I.**
Cow. 8/7-15/8/53.**H/I.**
Cow. 1/3-9/4/55.**G.**
Cow. 13-14/4/55.**N/C.**
Cow. 29/4-7/5/55.**N/C.**
Cow. 2/7-25/8/56.**H/I.**
Cow. 16/4-24/5/58.**H/I.**
Cow. 2-3/6/58.**N/C.**
Cow. 22/9-4/10/58.**C/L.**

BOILERS:
2836.
8130 (*ex1992*) 5/6/48.
2865 (*ex1898*) 28/10/50.
Renumbered 27324 17/5/52.
27323 (*ex61882*) 9/4/55.

SHEDS:
Heaton.
Tweedmouth 25/1/37.
St Margarets 19/3/39.

RENUMBERED:
1983 17/11/46.
61983 5/6/48.

CONDEMNED:
10/7/59.
Sold for scrap to J.McWilliam, Shettleston.

3824

Darlington.

To traffic 30/12/36.

REPAIRS:
Dar. 7/10-26/11/38.**G.**
Dar. 24/6-2/8/40.**G.**
Dar. 1/6-3/7/42.**G.**
Don. 8/5-10/6/44.**G.**
Don. 16/2-23/3/46.**G.**
Dar. 1/5-2/6/47.**L.**
Don. 18/5-19/6/48.**G.**
Don. 19/1-18/3/50.**G.**
Don. 4/1-1/2/52.**G.**
Don. 8/12/53-8/1/54.**G.**
Don. 12/12/55-20/1/56.**G.**
Dar. 16/1-14/3/58.**G.**
Don. 4/11-11/12/59.**G.**

BOILERS:
2838.
8129 (*ex1308*) 26/11/38.
8968 (*ex2458*) 2/8/40.
8118 (*ex1100*) 3/7/42.
2909 (*ex2429*) 10/6/44.
10501 (*new*) 19/6/48.
10801 (*new*) 18/3/50.
27210 (*ex61929*) 1/2/52.
27281 (*new*) 8/1/54.
27168 (*ex61934*) 14/3/58.
27274 (*ex61892*) 11/12/59.

SHEDS:
York.
Heaton 1/6/40.
Twwedmouth 11/9/60.
Ardsley 10/9/61.

RENUMBERED:
1984 25/8/46.
61984 18/6/48.

CONDEMNED:
2/11/62.
Cut up at Doncaster.

3825

Darlington.

To traffic 7/1/37.

REPAIRS:
Dar. 14/12/38-27/1/39.**G.**
Dar. 12/3-7/6/40.**L.**

WORKS CODES:- Cow - Cowlairs. Dar - Darlington. Don - Doncaster. Ghd - Gateshead. Gor - Gorton. Inv - Inverurie. Str - Stratford.
REPAIR CODES:- **C/H** - Casual Heavy. **C/L** - Casual Light. **G** - General. **H** - Heavy. **H/I** - Heavy Intermediate. **L** - Light. **L/I** - Light Intermediate. **N/C** - Non-Classified.

After the special mention which 61893 got in the text, it pleases me to be able to include a photograph of it, especially as it is at work in the Hull area. Here in its final days (with BR crest duly corrected) it has a very mixed goods at Ferriby.

27267 *(new)* 1/1/52.
27184 *(ex61951)* 27/11/53.
27299 *(ex61820)* 30/10/57.
27261 *(ex61906)* 27/10/59.

SHEDS:
York.
Gateshead 4/12/41.
Heaton 21/3/42.
March 30/5/48.
Heaton 31/10/48.
Tyne Dock 4/12/60.
Hull Dairycoates 30/7/61.

RENUMBERED:
1987 17/11/46.
61987 17/12/48.

CONDEMNED:
19/3/62.
Cut up at Doncaster.

Dar. 7/3-12/4/41.**G.**
Dar. 16/10-20/11/43.**G.**
Don. 15/12/45-26/1/46.**G.**
Don. 8-22/3/47.**L.**
Don. 19/6-19/7/47.**L.**
Don. 31/3-15/5/48.**G.**
Don. 8/2-15/4/50.**G.**
Don. 10-23/8/50.**L.**
Don. 7/6-13/7/51.**G.**
Don. 30/7-8/8/51.**L.**
Don. 25/3-28/4/53.**G.**
Don. 20/12/54-21/1/55.**G.**
Don. 1/1-2/2/57.**G.**
Don. 2/2-12/3/59.**G.**
Don. 19/5-30/6/61.**G.**

BOILERS:
2840.
2845 *(ex3826)* 27/1/39.
8137A *(ex1325)* 12/4/41.
8122 *(ex1117)* 20/11/43.
2840 *(ex28)* 15/4/50.
27176 *(ex61886)* 13/7/51.
27222 *(ex61956)* 28/4/53.
27294 *(new)* 21/1/55.
27288 *(ex61970)* 2/2/57.
24909 *(ex61850)* 12/3/59.
24918 *(ex61971)* 30/6/61.

SHEDS:
Gateshead.
Blaydon 28/3/43.
Heaton 19/6/43.
Gateshead 8/7/43.
Heaton 6/2/49.
Tweedmouth 6/1/52.
Hull Dairycoates 20/11/60.

RENUMBERED:
1985 17/11/46.
61985 20/4/48.

CONDEMNED:
21/12/62.
Cut up at Doncaster.

3826

Darlington.

To traffic 15/1/37.

REPAIRS:
Dar. 29/10-15/12/38.**G.**
Dar. 9-27/2/40.**N/C.**
Dar. 30/12/40-1/2/41.**G.**
Dar. 4/3-19/4/43.**G.**
Dar. 24/7-17/8/44.**L.**
Don. 19/1-23/2/46.**G.**
Don. 1/12/47-24/1/48.**G.**
Don. 14-26/2/49.**C/L.**
Don. 2/11-10/12/49.**G.**
Don. 11/12/50-24/1/51.**G.**
Don. 29/5-11/7/52.**G.**
Don. 16/3-9/4/54.**G.**
Don. 8/8-16/9/55.**G.**
Don. 20/6-1/8/57.**G.**
Don. 9/6-16/7/59.**G.**
Don. 21/5/62.*Not repaired.*

BOILERS:
2845.
8133 *(ex1102)* 1/2/41.
D1652 *(ex36)* 19/4/43.
8924 *(ex1959)* 24/1/48.
9800 *(ex1810)* 10/12/49.
Renumbered 27137 24/1/51.
27103 *(ex61800)* 11/7/52.
27265 *(ex61942)* 9/4/54.
27190 *(ex61939)* 1/8/57.
27338 *(exCow and 61937)* 16/7/59.

SHEDS:
Gateshead.
Stockton 16/10/39.
Darlington 16/7/40.
Blaydon 13/6/41.
Gateshead 26/6/43.
Heaton 6/2/49.

Tyne Dock 4/12/60.
Thornaby 18/12/60.
Hull Dairycoates 11/6/61.

RENUMBERED:
1986 1/12/46.
E1986 24/1/48.
61986 2/1/49.

CONDEMNED:
28/5/62.
Cut up at Doncaster.

3827

Darlington.

To traffic 21/1/37.

REPAIRS:
Dar. 27/1-10/3/39.**G.**
Dar. 21/7-4/8/39.**N/C.**
Dar. 15/2-7/4/40.**L.**
Dar. 17/7-23/8/41.**G.**
Dar. 17-31/10/42.**L.**
Dar. 17/7-18/9/43.**G.**
Don. 28/5-13/7/45.**G.**
Don. 10/10-26/11/47.**G.**
Don. 20/9-4/11/49.**G.**
Don. 5/12/51-1/1/52.**G.**
Don. 2-27/11/53.**G.**
Don. 30/11-4/12/53.**C/L.**
Don. 6-23/7/54.**C/L.**
Don. 19/8-30/9/55.**G.**
Don. 1-30/10/57.**G.**
Don. 30/9-27/10/59.**G.**
Don. 6/3/62.*Not repaired.*

BOILERS:
2848.
2840 *(ex3825)* 10/3/39.
D1645 *(ex1392)* 23/8/41.
RS4075 *(ex2458)* 18/9/43.
8140A *(ex1927)* 26/11/47.

3828

Darlington.

To traffic 27/1/37.

REPAIRS:
Dar. 19/10-6/12/38.**G.**
Cow. 15/6/40.**G.**
Cow. 4/3/42.**G.**
Dar. 19/5-22/6/42.**L.**
Cow. 7/8/43.**G.**
Cow. 14/8/43.**N/C.**
Cow. 10/10-22/11/45.**C/H.**
Cow. 10/6-10/7/47.**L.**
Cow. 21/9-5/11/48.**G.**
Cow. 10/8-10/9/49.**L.**
Cow. 29/5-7/7/51.**G.**
Cow. 13/11-5/12/52.**H/I.**
Cow. 11-26/5/54.**H/I.**
Cow. 23/11-25/12/54.**N/C.**
Cow. 28/6-1/9/56.**G.**
Cow. 23/5-15/6/57.**C/L.**
Cow. 16/5-21/6/58.**H/I.**
Cow. 11/4-12/5/59.**C/L.**

BOILERS:
2852.
2838 *(ex3824)* 6/12/38.
7992 *(ex195)* 15/6/40.
D1655 *(ex1368)* 22/11/45.
C1823 *(ex1937)* 10/7/47.
27325 *(ex1924)* 7/7/51.
27344 *(new)* 1/9/56.

SHEDS:
Tweedmouth.
St Margarets 19/3/39.

RENUMBERED:
1988 17/11/46.
61988 5/11/48.

CONDEMNED:
16/11/59.
Cut up at Cowlairs.
Not in use 225 days in 1944.

All good things come to an end, and that has been reached for 61921 at Doncaster as seen on 20th August 1961. By 29th December 1962, the last of the 193 had been taken out of running stock, and none was ever ear-marked for possible preservation.

Carlisle 15/3/39.
Haymarket 1/12/41.
Carlisle 17/4/43.
St Margarets 21/4/47.

RENUMBERED:
1991 20/10/46.
61991 26/6/48.

CONDEMNED:
7/5/59.
Cut up at Cowlairs.
Boiler 27305 sent to Doncaster 5/59.

3832

Darlington.

To traffic 26/2/37.

REPAIRS:
Don. 27/4-1/6/38.**H.**
Cow. 23/1/40.**G.**
Cow. 6/12/41.**G.**
Cow. 21/9/43.**G.**
Cow. 18/3-10/5/46.**G.**
Cow. 24/3-24/4/48.**G.**
Cow. 15/5-10/6/50.**H/I.**
Cow. 16-26/10/51.**L.**
Cow. 5/12/51-4/1/52.**L/I.**
Cow. 5/5-4/6/53.**G.**
Cow. 12/4-1/5/54.**C/L.**
Cow. 20/12/54-29/1/55.**H/I.**
Cow. 4-5/2/55.**N/C.** *Tender only.*
Cow. 8/1-16/2/57.**H/I.**
Cow. 22/5-8/6/57.**C/L.**
Cow. 13/6-5/7/58.**G.**
Cow. 4-7/8/58. **N./C.**

BOILERS:
2867.
8130 *(ex1900)* 10/5/46.
8911 *(ex1958)* 24/4/48.
Renumbered 27317 4/1/52.
27331 *(ex61881)* 4/6/53.
27335 *(ex61854)* 5/7/58.

SHEDS:
St Margarets.
Carlisle 15/3/39.
St Margarets 9/44.

RENUMBERED:
1992 8/9/46.
61992 24/4/48.

CONDEMNED:
6/6/60.
Cut up at Cowlairs.
Not in use 227 days in 1944.

829

arlington.

o traffic 3/2/37.

EPAIRS:
ar. 6/12/37-14/2/38.**G.**
ar. 31/10-1/12/39.**G.**
ar. 15/4-14/5/42.**G.**
ar. 8/9-20/10/43.**L.**
on. 16/11-22/12/44.**G.**
on. 10-20/1/45.**L.**
on. 20/3-16/5/47.**G.**
on. 23/4-30/5/49.**G.**
on. 18/3-18/4/51.**G.**
on. 23/12/52-23/1/53.**G.**
on. 15/11-15/12/54.**G.**
on. 3/12/56-19/1/57.**G.**
on. 5/11-17/12/58.**G.**

OILERS:
2859.
1650 *(ex1322)* 1/12/39.
2859 *(ex1398)* 14/5/42.
796 *(new)* 16/5/47.
995 *(new)* 30/5/49.
157 *(ex61945)* 18/4/51.
291 *(new)* 15/12/54.
918 *(new)* 19/1/57.
914 *(ex61942)* 17/12/58.

EDS:
veedmouth.
arch 22/5/42.
orwich 15/10/47.
westoft 6/10/48.
orwich 12/12/48.
westoft 11/10/53.
orwich 10/1/54.
westoft 18/7/54.
orwich 7/11/54.
armouth 22/12/57.
orwich 16/2/58.
aveley 20/3/60.
exborough 18/6/61.
illhouses 16/7/61.

Staveley 10/9/61.

RENUMBERED:
1989 13/10/46.
61989 28/5/49.

CONDEMNED:
19/6/62.
Cut up at Doncaster.

3830

Darlington.

To traffic 11/2/37.

REPAIRS:
Cow. 7/10/37.**L.**
Cow. 25/6-11/7/38.**G.**
Cow. 9/3/40.**G.**
Cow. 13/12/41-31/1/42.**G.**
Cow. 27/2/43.**G.**
Cow. 9/10/43.**L.**
Cow. 22/3/44.**L.**
Cow. 13/5-7/6/45.**G.**
Cow. 6/1-10/4/47.**G.**
Cow. 10/5-4/6/48.**L.**
Cow. 1/12/48-2/2/49.**G.**
Cow. 27/6-25/8/51.**G.**
Cow. 21/4-22/5/53.**L/I.**
Cow. 17/3-10/4/54.**N/C.**
Cow. 1/9-28/10/54.**C/L.**
Cow. 22/3-7/5/55.**G.**
Cow. 16/10-17/11/56.**H/I.**
Cow. 27/6-14/8/58.**L/I.**

BOILERS:
2861.
8138 *(ex1399)* 10/4/47.
27319 *(ex1988)* 25/8/51.
27332 *(ex61909)* 7/5/55.

SHEDS:
St Margarets.
Carlisle 15/3/39.
St Margarets 21/4/47.

RENUMBERED:
1990 3/11/46.
61990 5/6/48.

CONDEMNED:
13/10/60.
Cut up at Inverurie.

3831

Darlington.

To traffic 18/2/37.

REPAIRS:
Cow. 15/10/37.**L.**
Don. 20/1-12/2/38.**H.** *Soot blower removed.*
Cow. 26/8/39.**G.**
Cow. 2/8/41.**G.**
Cow. 23/4/43.**G.**
Cow. 12/5/43.**L.**
Cow. 16/7-8/9/45.**G.**
Cow. 15/5-21/6/47.**G.**
Cow. 23-25/6/48.**L.**
Cow. 9/11-18/12/48.**G.**
Cow. 5/8-16/9/50.**G.**
Cow. 9-23/12/50.**C/L.**
Cow. 14/3-1/5/52.**L/I.**
Cow. 23/2-11/4/53.**L/I.**
Cow. 20/10-6/11/53.**C/L.**
Cow. 21/1-25/2/54.**C/L.**
Cow. 13/5-2/7/55.**G.**
Cow. 21/6-17/8/57.**H/I.**
Cow. 21/7-22/8/58.**C/L.**
Cow. 19/12/58-30/1/59.**C/L.**

BOILERS:
2865.
C1743 (ex2768) 8/9/45.
8115 *(ex1931)* 16/9/50.
Renumbered 27303 1/5/52.
27305 *(ex61858)* 2/7/55.

SHEDS:
St Margarets.

"The Man That Never Was", or at least never spelled his name like Darlington works did. 3442 otherwise without a spot or blemish on it poses outside Darlington paint shop for an official photograph. One is inclined to think that they proudly took this picture for presentation to somebody of importance, because for almost all their official photography, they specially painted them grey, lined in black, and with white figures and letters, for maximum clarity, as they had done when 3441 was new. If correct, little did they know what a fall their pride was very shortly to suffer. *National Railway Museum.*

The prototype No.3441 took the place of a K3 (which would have become 3833 on the 1936 building programme) and was specifically designed for working on the West Highland line. Completed in January 1937, Darlington painted it works grey for this official photograph, but put it into black with red lining to go into service as a mixed traffic engine. 3441 had cylinders similar to those on K3 class which had the elbow joint of the steam pipe between where it left the smokebox, and where it passed through the running plate (see opposite). *L.N.E.R.*

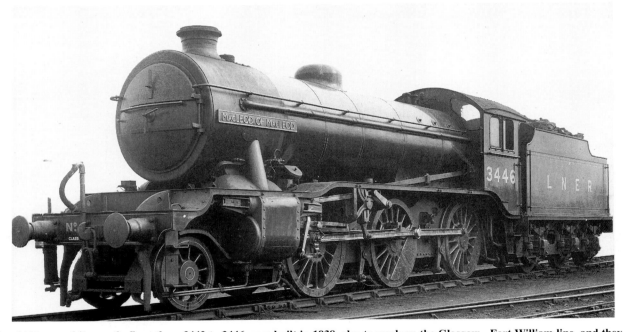

After 3441 proved its worth, five others 3442 to 3446 were built in 1938, also to work on the Glasgow - Fort William line, and they were accorded the passenger green painting. 3446 was the second of the five (3442 was the other) to have its original name changed. For its first three months it ran as LORD OF DUNVEGAN, but the male line of that clan had died out in 1935, and the current Clan Chieftain was a Lady, not a Lord, so Dame Flora negotiated the change on 30th March 1939 to MacLEOD OF MacLEOD.

(left) The steam passages had been altered to eliminate the elbow joint on nos.3442 to 3446 to facilitate easier flow. Their steam pipe casing was nearer to vertical, because the flange on the cylinder was 5" closer to the frame.

CLASS K4

This was always a special favourite of mine, not only because of the attractions of the area in which all its work was done, but 3442 provided me with a tremendous photographic scoop, despite my only camera being a box Brownie which formed part of my wife's dowry. In July 1938 I broke into a family holiday at Scarborough to make a brief visit to LNER sheds in Edinburgh and Glasgow, some of them for the first time. So far as I was then aware, class K4 consisted of only black painted 3441, which had been named LOCH LONG as an extension of the named engines of K2 class, which K4 was intended to replace on the heavier trains due to the increasing tourist traffic on the West Highland line. Taking advantage of my permit, I made a thorough investigation of what was on Eastfield shed where, tucked away in the back of the shed building, I made the pleasantly surprised discovery of a green painted K4 class no.3442. On a day when the shed was pushed to the limit for power to deal with Glasgow Fair holiday excursion traffic, I could not understand why such a godsend was so obviously discarded, and not being used at all. Very tactful enquiry elicited that Darlington Works had offended Gaelic susceptibilities by using wrong spelling on the nameplates, and that the engine had to be hidden until substitution could be made, replacement plates from Darlington being awaited.

Where 3442 was standing the light was abysmal, and I had no tripod to facilitate a time exposure, nor had I possessed, or used a light meter. By sheer chance, the running plate of a "NOT TO BE MOVED" goods engine was in the only place from which an acceptable photograph of 3442 could be attempted, and it also provided a firmer camera position then any tripod. The remaining problem was - what time exposure to give? Firmly dismissing extravagant use of film from my thoughts, I took 15 seconds, 30 seconds, and a full minute shot, and to my subsequent great relief, one of them (I have never recalled which) gave a tolerable result.

About 30 years later I was on an enthusiasts special hauled by 3442 (then owned by Viscount Garnock), when he came down the train and I took the opportunity of telling him about taking that picture. He was unaware that ANY photograph had been taken of his engine other than as named THE GREAT MARQUESS, so I duly sent him a print. One of my greatest railway treasures is the charming letter of thanks which I received from him. Some ten years later I discovered - with very mixed feelings - that before releasing newly built 3442, Darlington had taken a superb official photograph of it, blissfully unaware of the Scottish wrath about to descend on them, and of their affront to the Chief of the Campbell clan. So that photograph was judiciously hidden away, and only surfaced when the National Railway Museum acquired Darlington's negatives. Both my effort, and their admittedly better one, are in this Volume.

The prototype, no.3441 worked to King's Cross on January 29th 1937 for official inspection, otherwise you had to travel to Eastfield shed and the West Highland line to see a K4. From new until April 1940, no.3441 was in the black, red lined mixed traffic painting, but the other five were all accorded green passenger livery, which 3441 had also gained when it came out of Cowlairs on April 20th 1940. Wartime repainting sadly put all six into unlined black, and with only N E on tender. No.3445 changed to K1/1 class through a Thompson rebuilding and of the remaining five (renumbered 1993 to 1996 and 1998 during 1946), only 1996 in July, and 1995 in November 1947 managed to have green and L N E R restored. Curiously, no.61998 was put into green painting but with BRITISH RAILWAYS on its tender. All five duly acquired B.R. fully lined black painting, also the 1949-56 variety of their emblem. They also survived long enough to have the emblem replaced by the crest, but on the right hand side it was the one with the lion facing the wrong way, and that was not corrected before they were withdrawn.

Coupled to all six was the Group Standard 3500 gallon flush sided tender, although 3441 had the low front plate, whereas by the time the others were built, change to high front plate had taken place. Then in September and November 1959, when they left the West Highland line to work goods trains from Thornton shed, nos 61993-96 were changed to 4200 gallon Group Standard tender, rendered surplus from K3 class engines which had been withdrawn, but no.61998 retained a 3500 gallon type. During its restoration, no.3442 reverted to the smaller capacity tender, but it is one of the Group Standard ones with low front plate, which would have been correct for 3441 but not for 3442.

I saw all six working on the West Highland line to and from Fort William, and both on passenger and goods trains by August 1943, but to my lasting regret, never managed to be hauled by one, my likeliest opportunity producing a pair of K2 class instead of the expected K4 from Fort William to Glasgow. After withdrawal, and subsequent restoration to running order, 3442 did give me some memorable hours on a railtour between Northallerton and Newcastle, and over some lines rarely traversed, in an area where it must have felt at home, as it had been built at Darlington Works.

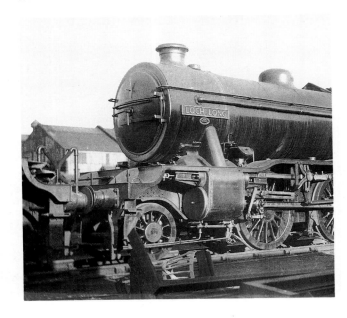

(right) **The front end of 3441 LOCH LONG showing that the casing over the steam pipe came almost to the edge of the running plate.** *J.W.Armstrong.*

All six had an inheritance from K3 class in that they were fitted with two pairs of guard irons at the front end, although it had long ago been admitted that those on the frame ends were not needed. They were removed from 61993 LOCH LONG when ex-works in April 1949, but it was into the early 1950's before some of the others lost them. 1998 had them taken off in May 1946, and 3445 was so denuded by Doncaster when they rebuilt it.

3441

Darlington.

To traffic 28/1/37.

REPAIRS:
Cow. 19/6/37.**N/C.** *Press.put to 200lb.*
Cow. 6/7/37.**N/C.** *Speed recorder fitted.*
Cow. 21/5/38.**H.**
Cow. 25/1/39.**L.**
Cow. 3/3/39.**L.**
Cow. 12/5/39.**L.**
Cow. 1/6/39.**L.**
Cow. 30/3-20/4/40.**H.**
Cow. 23/8/40.**L.**
Cow. 17/5/41.**H.**
Cow. 11/9/41.**L.**
Cow. 23/1/42.**L.**
Cow. 14/3/42.**L.**
Cow. 6/6/42.**L.**
Cow. 3/7-14/8/43.**H.**
Cow. 4/12/43.**L.**
Cow. 8/8/44.**L.**
Cow. 20/9/44.**L.**

Cow. 28/11/44.**L.**
Cow. 6/3/45.**L.**
Cow. 27/4-1/6/45.**G.**
Cow. 1-8/9/45.**C/L.**
Cow. 30/11-1/12/45.**N/C.**
Cow. 14-16/2/46.**C/L.**
Cow. 25/2-22/3/47.**G.**
Cow. 11/10-1/11/47.**L.**
Cow. 15/4-11/5/48.**L.**
Cow. 10/2-1/4/49.**G.**
Cow. 11/11-22/12/50.**G.**
Cow. 27/2-5/4/52.**G.**
Cow. 14-22/5/53.**C/L.**
Cow. 26/10-14/11/53.**C/L.**
Cow. 29/3-24/4/54.**H/I.**
Cow. 23/2-24/3/56.**G.**
Cow. 26/11-21/12/57.**H/I.**
Cow. 15-16/1/58.**N/C.**
Cow. 18/12/58-17/1/59.**L/I.**
Cow. 3/9/59.**N/C.**
Cow. 1/10-5/11/59.**C/H.**

BOILERS:
  2851.
  2979 *(ex3443)* 22/3/47.
29555 *(ex1998)* 5/4/52.
29551 *(ex spare and 61998)* 24/3/56.

SHEDS:
Eastfield.
Thornton Junction 24/4/59.

RENUMBERED:
  1993 14/9/46.
61993 11/5/48.

CONDEMNED:
2/10/61.
Cut up at Townhill (Dunfermline).

3442

Darlington.

To traffic 6/7/38.

REPAIRS:
Cow. 26/11/38.**N/C.** *Snow plough fitted.*
Cow. 28/12/38.**N/C.** *Flaman recorder fitted.*
Cow. 19/5/39.**L.**
Cow. 9/3/40.**L.**
Cow. 7/9/40.**L.**

Cow. 5/7/41.**H.**
Cow. 6/5/42.**L.**
Cow. 26/9/42.**L.**
Cow. 27/3-24/4/43.**H.**
Cow. 23/6/43.**L.**
Cow. 18/11/43.**L.**
Cow. 26/5/44.**L.**
Cow. 1/10-4/11/44.**H.**
Cow. 26-28/4/45.**C/L.**
Cow. 30/6/45..**L.**
Cow. 20/8/45.**L.**
Cow. 10/8-11/9/46.**G.**
Cow. 8/1/47.**L.**
Cow. 1-29/11/47.**G.**
Cow. 13/9-22/10/48.**G.**
Cow. 10-13/10/49.**N/C.**
Cow. 5-9/12/49.**C/L.**
Cow. 8/9-12/10/50.**H/I.**
Cow. 17/1/52.**N/C.**
Cow. 12/11-10/12/52.**G.**
Cow. 13/8/53.**N/C.**
Cow. 28/9-23/10/54.**L/I.**
Cow. 8-12/11/54.**N/C.**
Cow. 23/3-16/4/55.**N/C.**
Cow. 18/4-26/5/56.**H/I.**
Cow. 24-27/6/57.**N/C.**
Cow. 1-26/10/57.**G.**
Cow. 6-9/11/57.**N/C.**
Cow. 14-23/11/47.**C/L.**
Cow. 16-24/9/59.**N/C.**
Cow. 2-9/10/59.**N/C.**
Cow. 12/12/59-9/1/60.**L/I.**
Cow. 4-12/2/60.**C/L.**
Cow. 14-15/2/61.**N/C.**
Cow. 22-24/2/61.**N/C.**
Cow. 23-26/5/61.**C/L.**
Cow. 7-8/6/61.**N/C.**

In 1942, 3443 (1995 from 1946) was fitted with the left-hand cylinder from 3441; that had an elbow joint steam pipe so the casing had to be altered. For it, Cowlairs made one similar, but not identical, to those used on the V1 class 2-6-2 tank engines.

When new, all had the current Group Standard top lamp bracket, but Cowlairs were adept at exchanging smokebox doors. Here at Fort William shed on April 15th 1952, the top bracket is the original Great Northern type with clover-leaf, three-bolt fixing. Note 61996 is correctly rendered on smokebox plate, but not on cab, also that tender still has the green paint and L N E R which it got at its July 1947 repair. *D.A.Dant.*

BOILERS:
2943.
2983 *(ex1995)* 29/11/47.
29550 *(ex61996)* 10/12/52.
29552 *(ex61995)* 26/10/57.

SHEDS:
Eastfield.
Thornton Junction 4/12/59.

RENUMBERED:
1994 22/9/46.
61994 15/10/48.

CONDEMNED:
18/12/61.
Sold to Viscount Garnock
for preservation in working order.

3443

Darlington.

To traffic 20/12/38.

REPAIRS:
Cow. 30/12/38.**L.**
Cow. 7/6/39.**L.**
Cow. 1/2/40.**H.** *Flaman repaired &*
recorder re-fitted.
Cow. 13/12/41.**L.**
Cow. 6/2/42.**L.**
Cow. 23/5/42.**L.**
Cow. 19/9-10/10/42.**H.**
Cow. 22/10/42.**N/C.**
Cow. 19/2/44.**H.**
Cow. 12/10/44.**L.** .
Cow. 4/11/44.**L**
Cow. 14/4-12/5/45.**L.**
Cow. 8/6/45.**L.**

Cow. 1/2-16/3/46.**G.**
Cow. 24-25/4/47.**N/C.**
Cow. 10-30/5/47.**N/C.**
Cow. 8/9-30/10/47.**G.**
Cow. 15/6-3/7/48.**L.**
Cow. 14/12/49-28/1/50.**G.**
Cow. 7/5-7/6/52.**G.**
Cow. 9-28/2/53.**C/L.**
Cow. 19/2-20/3/54.**H/I.**
Cow. 12/7-20/8/55.**H/I.** *W.P.U.gear*
removed.
Cow. 31/8-10/9/55.**N/C.**
Cow. 22/11-3/12/55.**N/C.**
Efd. 9-29/5/56.**C/L.**
Cow. 18/3-13/4/57.**G.**
Cow. 1-20/12/58.**L/I.**
Cow. 12-14/9/59.**N/C.**
Cow. 12-13/10/59.**N/C.**
Cow. 22/5-3/6/60.**C/L.**
Cow. 28/7-3/9/60.**C/L.**

BOILERS:
2979.
2983 *(ex3445)* 16/3/46.
2982 *(ex1996)* 30/10/47.
29552 *(ex61993)* 7/6/52.
29555 *(ex61993)* 13/4/57.

SHEDS:
Eastfield.
Fort William 3/10/39.
Eastfield 24/5/54.
Thornton Junction 9/12/59.

RENUMBERED:
1995 8/9/46.
61995 3/7/48.

CONDEMNED:
2/10/61.
Cut up at Townhill (Dunfermline).

3444

Darlington.

To traffic 21/12/38.

REPAIRS:
Cow. 7/4/39.**L.**

Cow. 8/5/39.**L.**
Cow. 25/5/39.**L.**
Cow. 7/10/39.**H.** *A.R.P.*
Cow. 17/1/40.**L.**
Cow. 19/4/41.**H.** *Fall plate moved to*
engine.
Cow. 5/9/41.**L.**
Cow. 8/11/41.**L.**
Cow. 12/2/42.**L.**
Cow. 18/6/42.**H.**
Cow. 6/2/43.**H.**
Cow. 7/5/43.**L.**
Cow. 26/2-25/3/44.**H.**
Cow. 12/12/44.**L.**
Cow. 19-26/5/45.**C/L.**
Cow. 1/10/45.**N/C.**
Cow. 8/10/45.**N/C.**
Cow. 11/12/45-21/1/46.**G.**
Cow. 5-9/3/46.**N/C.**
Cow. 4-11/1/47.**N/C.**
Cow. 1/6-18/7/47.**G.**
Cow. 18/10-25/11/48.**L.**
Cow. 14/2-11/3/50.**G.**
Cow. 24/6-15/7/52.**G.**
Cow. 18/1-20/2/54.**L/I.**
Cow. 3/5-2/6/56.**H/I.** *W.P.U.gear*
removed.
Cow. 8-10/8/57.**N/C.**
Cow. 30/4-24/5/58.**G.**
Cow. 27-31/5/58.**N/C.**
Cow. 7-8/1/59.**N/C.**
Cow. 25-26/11/59.**C/L.**

BOILERS:
2982.
2851 *(ex1993)* 18/7/47.
29553 *(ex61995)* 15/7/52.
29554 *(ex61998)* 24/5/58.

(below) **That definitely odd casing remained a 'one-off' and gave the singularly unusual view from the front end seen here on 61995 at Eastfield shed on 16th January 1949, which continued through to that engine's withdrawal in October 1961.**

As seen on 3441, until during the war, the outside cylinder drain pipes were clipped together and they extended as far as the front footstep, to which they were attached. Probably the carrying of a snow plough interfered with dispersal of steam from them, so they were cut back simply to right-angle bends. All the class were accorded the standard livery for BR mixed traffic engines with red, cream, and grey lining, with 28" size emblem on tender. 61996 LORD OF THE ISLES is at Eastfield 27th August 1957. *P.H.Groom.*

SHEDS:
Eastfield.
Fort William 23/10/39.
Eastfield 24/5/54.
Thornton Junction 24/4/59.

RENUMBERED:
1996 1/12/46.
61996 27/11/48.

CONDEMNED:
2/10/61.
Cut up at Inverurie.

3445

Darlington.

To traffic 30/12/38.

REPAIRS:
Cow. 22/4/39.**N/C.** *A.R.P.screens.*
Cow. 30/8/39.**L.**
Cow. 27/1/40.**L.**
Cow. 30/5/40.**H.**
Cow. 6/7/40.**L.**
Cow. 9/8-6/9/41.**H.**
Cow. 19/6/42.**L.**
Cow. 5/12/42.**H.**

Cow. 28/8/43.**L.**
Cow. 13-27/5/44.**H.**
Cow. 21/2/45.**L.**
Cow. 14/7/45.**L.**
Don. 18/8/45. *for rebuilding to Class K1.*

BOILER:
2983.

SHED:
Eastfield.

3446

Darlington.

To traffic 30/12/38.

REPAIRS:
Dar. 3-10/1/39.**N/C.**
Cow. 29-30/3/39.**N/C.** *Nameplates changed.*
Cow. 17/6/39.**L.**
Cow. 21/10/39.**L.**
Cow. 29/6/40.**H.**
Cow. 3/5/41.**H.** *Fallplate moved to engine.*
Cow. 11-25/7/42.**H.**
Cow. 31/10/42.**L.**

Cow. 28/11/42.**L.**
Cow. 21/5/43.**L.**
Cow. 17/6/43.**L.**
Cow. 27/7/43.**L.**
Cow. 8/4-6/5/44.**H.**
Cow. 20/1-3/2/45.**L.**
Cow. 28/4-5/5/45.**L.**
Cow. 10/8/45.**L.**
Cow. 12/11/45.**L.**
Cow. 2/4-4/5/46.**G.**
Cow. 25/4/47.**N/C.**
Cow. 18/3-20/4/48.**G.**
Cow. 26/5-18/6/49.**L/I.**
Cow. 12-13/7/49.**N/C.**
Cow. 20/2-11/3/50.**C/H.**
Cow. 20/3-1/4/50.**C/L.**
Cow. 23/10-18/11/50.**L/I.**
Cow. 11/1-2/2/52.**H/I.**
Cow. 16-17/7/52.**C/L.**
Cow. 21/1-21/2/53.**G.**
Cow. 23/4-29/5/54.**H/I.**
Cow. 29/11-24/12/55.**L/I.**
Cow. 22/10-16/11/57.**G.**
Cow. 25/6-12/7/58.**C/L.**
Cow. 11-30/5/59.**G.**
Cow. 4-12/8/59.**C/L.**
Inv. 15/2-24/3/60.**N/C.**
Cow. 26/7-4/8/60.**C/L.**
Cow. 16-24/12/60.**N/C.**

BOILERS:
2987.
2943 *(ex1994)* 20/4/48.
Renumbered 29551 2/2/52.
29554 *(ex61994)* 21/2/53.
29550 *(ex61994)* 16/11/57.

SHEDS:
Eastfield.
Thornton Junction 9/12/59.

RENUMBERED:
1998 4/5/46.
61998 20/4/48.

CONDEMNED:
2/10/61.
Cut up at Inverurie.

At Fort William on 11th June 1950 LOCH LONG was in service with a smokebox door which did not have a knob fitted, although it did have that amenity both earlier, and later. Under the front end of the cab note the bracket for a Flaman speed recorder to be driven from the right hand trailing coupling pin, although no gear for it is fitted. From 6th July 1937 it had carried a Flaman recorder fitted for drive from the trailing coupling pin on the left hand side, but ex Cowlairs on 25th January 1939, it had been fitted with a new one with the drive changed over to the right hand side. The recording instrument and gear for it had been taken off during the war, only the bracket remaining, because paper rolls and spares could no longer be obtained from that French source; they were never reinstated, but all kept the resultant useless bracket to withdrawal. Between July 1942 (3446) and August 1943 (3441), all six lost their green paint, being changed to unlined black and with only N E on tender, due to war conditions. In 1947 nos.1996 (July) and 1995 (October) regained green lined livery with L N E R restored. Class leader LOCH LONG was not so fortunate, never acquiring either. From its May 1948 light repair it got these 10" cab figures - with wrong 6 and 9 - the smokebox plate being added at the April 1949 general repair. Despite another general repair in December 1950, at none of those three works visits was any painting attention given to the tender, so it continued to display the 1943-applied, N E until it went for repair in February 1952. *R.J.Buckley.*

(right) The valid reason for including this very sub-standard photograph of 3442 as it first arrived at Eastfield is fully explained in the Introduction. Few indeed saw that engine unacceptably named MAC CAILEIN MO'R.

Pictures of K4 class 3445 at work are rather rare when it did not start working until 30th December 1938 and the war put a stop to such photography only eight months later. Before that could legitimately be resumed, 3445 had been rebuilt from a K4 to a K1/1 class. Further the superb background scenery on the line beyond Craigendoran ensured that was where most of the pictures were taken. So the almost level stretch of the line bordering the River Clyde tended to be neglected, but I have been able to include one of 3445 at speed running through Kilpatrick in April 1939 on its way to Glasgow from Fort William.

CLASS K5

Always ready to interfere with Gresley designs, Thompson called K3 no.206 into Doncaster works in February 1945 to be rebuilt with 2 instead of 3 cylinders as part of his proposals for standard classes. When back to traffic on June 16th it had a boiler pressed to 225 lb. instead of 180 lb. to serve the two cylinders, but apart from the tender and cab, everything else even down to the buffers was new, so it was not a cheap conversion. In comparative trials against a couple of K3 class, the rebuild showed about 10% reduction in coal and in water consumption, and certainly gave improved riding, and easier maintenance at its shed. But the time out of traffic for rebuilding, and especially the cost of it, did not make further conversions an economic proposition, so Thompson's K5 remained an orphan.

The same tender was attached throughout its life as K3 and as K5 class, and was the Group Standard 4200 gallon type with stepped coping. From as late as March 1957 however the back plate of the coal space was moved forward and increased in height.

For livery, the K5 began with unlined black and only N E on tender: the 206 in shaded transfers gave place to 1863 in only 8" high stencilled figures on Sunday March 31st 1946. It did manage to have L N E R restored - only just in time - for it was ex works on December 19th 1947 still in unlined black, but with letters and figures in 12" yellow paint and without any shading. Changed to 61863 when ex works on January 4th 1950, it had acquired standard British Railways lined black, with emblem on tender and cast number plate on smokebox door. It did not change from emblem to crest, because its final repair and repaint saw it back to traffic on March 22nd 1957, the month before the crest began to be used.

Due to its being a 'one-off', K5 class was not readily recorded, but on June 7th 1946 I did manage to see it working a down goods through Biggleswade on the East Coast main line.

206

Rebuilt from K3 .

To traffic 16/6/45. Altered to Class K5 on 13/10/45.

REPAIRS:
Don. 11-25/8/45.**L.**
Don. 24/11-19/12/47.**G.**
Don. 27/11-49-4/1/50.**G.**
Don. 26/3-6/4/50.**C/L.**
Don. 28/4-24/5/51.**C/L.**
Don. 15/6-5/7/51.**C/L.**
Don. 24/3-28/4/52.**G.**
Don. 22/7-25/8/54.**G.**
Don. 31/8-3/9/54.**N/C.**
Don. 18/2-22/3/57.**G.**
Don. 24-26/3/57.**N/C.**
Don. 19-27/9/58.**N/C.**
Don. 9/2-6/3/59.**C/L.**
Don. 6/5/60.*Not repaired.*

BOILERS:
9547.
10540 *(new)* 4/1/50.
Renumbered 27226 28/4/52.
27132 *(ex61943)* 22/3/57.

SHEDS:
Doncaster 25/6/45.
New England 13/9/45.
Hull Dairycoates 27/10/46.
St Margarets 15/1/47.
New England 28/2/47.
March 8/4/47.
Stratford 4/5/47.
March 17/5/47.
New England 23/11/47.
Stratford 12/10/52.

RENUMBERED:
1863 31/3/46.
61863 4/1/50.

CONDEMNED:
6/6/60.
Cut up at Doncaster.

(top) **No.206 illustrates Thompson's intention to rebuild the K3 class into one of his planned standard classes, but of the one hundred and ninety three, it remained the only one so treated. Only the cab and the tender were retained from the K3, all else being new, so it was an expensive change. Before the value of the change could be assessed properly, Thompson had reached his retirement age and had departed from Doncaster.** *(bottom)* **Renumbered to 1863 and to 61863 by BR, the loco spent much of its early life working from New England shed. On 12th October 1952, New England were able to hive it off to Stratford shed, from where it did its remaining work, here being used as station pilot at Liverpool Street.**